PUTTING SOCIOLOGY
TO WORK

PUTTING SOCIOLOGY TO WORK

CASE STUDIES
IN THE APPLICATION OF SOCIOLOGY
TO MODERN SOCIAL PROBLEMS

EDITED BY ARTHUR B. SHOSTAK
DREXEL UNIVERSITY

DAVID McKAY COMPANY, INC., NEW YORK

Illustrated with photographs by James Foote

Putting Sociology to Work:
Case Studies in the Application of Sociology
to Modern Social Problems
Copyright © 1974 by David McKay Company, Inc.

International Standard Book Number: 0–679–30247–6
Library of Congress Catalog Card Number: 73–92760
Manufactured in the United States of America
Designed by Angela Foote

For my father, Milton L. Shostak, whose
love for community and service to
others long ago helped me better
understand what we can do
together. . . .

*As life is action and passion, it is
required of a man that he should share
the passion and action of his time, at
peril of being judged not to have lived.*

—Oliver Wendell Holmes, Jr.

*We cannot stand still in the world.
Only by moving out into the world do
we keep it real. If we do not grow into it,
it closes in on us, and turns, as it does
for so many, into a haze of fantasies,
delusions, nightmares.*

—John Holt

ACKNOWLEDGMENTS

Over the two-year period entailed in completing this project I was assisted by several friends without whose help and encouragement I might not have persevered: Michelle Pruyn and Ed Artinian believed in the project. Typists Veronica McLean and Susan R. Gershuni were patient, swift, and supportive, as was my student research assistant, Gail Katz. Meredith Burke helped check copy, as did Carl Gause. Once again, as in the case of the other two books I have prepared at Drexel, I am indebted to the staff of the library, under the directorship of Mr. Richard L. Snyder, for their considerable cooperation and many courtesies. Finally, the friendly prodding of my young sons, Scott Elliot and Mark Judah, helped make the difference when the going got rough. Needless to say, none of the above are responsible for what goes hereafter.

The editor wishes to thank the following for their permission to reprint:

For "When a Sociologist Gets into the Act," by C. M. Deasy, reprinted with permission from *AIA Journal* 49 (January 1968): 72–76. Copyright © 1968 The American Institute of Architects.

For "Strategy for Change: Bristol Township Schools," by Thomas J. Cottle, reprinted with permission from *Saturday Review*, September 20, 1969, pp. 70–71, 79–82. Copyright © 1969 *Saturday Review, Inc.*

For "The Flawed Consultant (A Fantasy)," by Meyer M. Cahn, reprinted with permission from *Journal of Humanistic Psychology* (Spring 1971): 76–84. Copyright © Association of Humanistic Psychology.

PREFACE

Helping America to make substantial headway against its social problems in the 1970s is a fast-growing, if hard-pressed, minority of academic sociologists who "give a damn" and try to "make a difference" with their professional skills in the off-campus world. Their particular way of making sense of our social universe, of "seeing" such abstractions as class, norms, values, and statuses within a continuous field of movement, sets them apart from other professional social scientists and brings them to the fore in the analysis, resolution, and prevention of social problems *in the field.*

In this volume a representative sample of these men and women offer first-person accounts of their attempts to help others better help themselves. The twenty-four essays (twenty-one written for this volume) range far and wide—from accounts of tension-fraught efforts to "cool-out" powder-keg racial confrontations to much cooler studies of the design preferences of college students concerning a projected student center. Many contributors frankly share their disappointments and regrets, always searching for constructive insights and lessons of wide general applicability (see especially essays concerning an ill-fated community self-help program in an urban ghetto, and a sorely tried project to control lead poisoning of children). Several authors make a special effort to earn our support for novel aids in the applied-sociology campaign, aids that include simulation and gaming, applied mathematics, and computer-based multi-city "conferences."

Over and again a series of critical assumptions are apparent in the essays:

—that it is possible to rely heavily on sociology to meet real-world emergencies even while believing sociology underdeveloped and much in need of improvement;

—that it is possible to be an action sociologist and yet remain keenly involved in theory construction, research frontiers, and other "armchair" pursuits sometimes little valued by applied types;

xi

—that it is possible to work intimately with people far removed from one's own style of life (and perhaps even earn a living thereby) without patronizing or exploiting them;

—that it is possible to pursue action projects knowing that key public officials and relevant professionals do not regard your efforts very seriously (although this predicament may be resolved successfully before the decade's end).

These assumptions are drawn from seasoned reflection (action sociology goes back more than sixty years, to the profession's founding in America), and are held with as much good humor and as little stridency as possible. If somewhat disquieting, they are nonetheless inescapable.

Taken together, then, the essays offer more candid and timely insight into the frustrating problems and enormous potential of applied sociology than is available anywhere else in this format. I have learned much in the arduous process of assembling this volume. Long active in applied projects in industrial race relations, Job Corps designs, antipoverty efforts, and, most recently, in New Towns social planning, I have completed this volume with renewed confidence that sociology itself is becoming more constructively involved in problem prevention and resolution than at any previous time. Should *you* leave our book with a keener curiosity about the possible applications of sociology to real-life problems, one that might possibly draw you someday into action sociology itself, the efforts of all of us will have been amply rewarded.

Arthur B. Shostak
January 1974.

Philadelphia, Pa.

CONTENTS

part four SOCIAL CONFLICT 105

part five CLIENT PARTICIPATION IN ARCHITECTURAL DESIGN 147

part six NEW TOOLS FOR RESEARCH 165

part seven APPLIED RESEARCH 193

part eight SELF-KNOWLEDGE 221

part nine SELF-IMPROVEMENT 249

PUTTING SOCIOLOGY
TO WORK

The real illness of the American city today, and especially of the deprived groups within it, is voicelessness.

—Harvey Cox, *The Secular City*

part one

URBAN AND RURAL DEVELOPMENT

From the origins of the profession in the early 1900s American sociologists have been occupied with a search for answers to increasingly complex and costly problems of urban and rural development. Prime among these have been such issues as keeping government responsive to the needs of citizens, helping people to lead better lives by teaching them to help themselves, aiding the public to counter bureaucratic obstacles, and enlarging the vision of smaller-town residents now required to think and plan on a larger scale.

Each of these challenges is addressed in one of the four personal-action reports that follow: J. David Colfax relates the considerable human hazards that undermine efforts to eliminate a serious lead-poisoning threat to youngsters; Henry Etzkowitz analyzes the failure of a ghetto self-help business project to fulfill the original intentions of its sociologist sponsors; Edward E. Cahill assesses how a university planning project can help community activists prepare for "the intricate machinations of policy makers and implementers that work at cross purposes to the social value of self-determination"; and Otto G. Hoiberg continues to unfold a tale begun in another work as he recounts his successful effort to help small-towners accept a new "expanded community," or area-wide basis, for critical planning purposes.

One is encouraged in these essays by the examples of personal resiliency, perseverance, and creativity. We *are* capable of making substantial headway against our urban and rural challenges, and these reports of action sociology help show the way.

one

SOCIOLOGY AND THE POLITICS OF POISON
J. David Colfax

Progress against the epidemic level of lead-poisoning cases in youngsters comes at an inhumanly slow and uneven pace: you will no longer wonder why, after you have read the eye-opening account below. Frank in its full account of setbacks and disappointments, the essay is equally illuminating where unexpected gains are concerned; for example, the unique insights into urban realities secured by undergraduate activists linked to the People's Coalition Against Lead Poisoning. Throughout the essay one senses the urgency that drives the sociologist-reformer and the citizen pressure groups here; few accounts convey as sharply the life-and-death stakes entailed in certain reform efforts dependent on critical sociological inputs. This particular campaign has far to go before leaded paint no longer kills children; thus the essay addresses—and possibly recruits—each one of us.

I

Lead paint kills children. So do bombs, automobiles, sickle-cell anemia, and pneumonia. There is a crucial difference. Lead-paint poisoning can be eliminated through the enforcement of minimum housing codes and ordinances which many city councils have recently adopted in order to qualify for federal "renewal" funds. Lead poisoning, which results from the ingestion of pieces of leaded paint and plaster, annually kills 200 children and inflicts permanent brain damage upon another 6,000. But because it primarily affects black inner-city children, the problem is generally regarded as not very important.[1]

---

1. For a discussion of some of the medical implications of lead-poisoning organizing, see Tom Bodenheimer and J. David Colfax, "Introduction to Lead Poisoning Supplement,"

Leaded paint is found in housing units built prior to 1945—its use in interiors was virtually discontinued after World War II—and thus lead poisoning is directly related to the quality of housing in the inner city. In this era of federally funded "renewal" programs, substandard housing provides ample opportunities for real-estate speculation and profiteering by real-estate corporations and slumlords. Real-estate speculators—who own up to 80 percent of residential property in some ghetto areas—permit and even encourage the wholesale deterioration of their properties, since they are able, in the face of acute low-income-housing shortages, to obtain rents from dwellings regardless of their condition, and, more significantly, they are often able to obtain high prices for their land when a neighborhood that they have helped to blight is consequently designated as a "renewal" area.

Lead poisoning was recognized as a problem affecting inner-city children in the early 1960s. The response has varied from city to city, and federal action has been negligible. In New York, landlords who own property in which a child has been poisoned are given two weeks to detoxify the unit; failing this, the city does the job and bills the landlord. The response is curative rather than preventive—the work is done only after the child has been poisoned. In California, in contrast, statutory authority permits tenants who live in toxic units to withhold their rents and use the money to make repairs. Philadelphia's program is relatively straightforward: violators are quickly brought to court and heavily fined. In general, however, programs have been of a stopgap nature rather than preventive, and patterns of enforcement are tied closely to the quality of housing and the character of the housing market. A clear indicator of the lack of concern for the victims of the "silent epidemic" was recently demonstrated at the federal level: a sum of $7.5 million in lead-poison-abatement funds slated for local use was held up for over a year by the Bureau of the Budget; with its release now imminent, there is little reason to believe that the money will have an appreciable impact on the problem, as twenty cities are contesting for what is, considering the magnitude of the problem, a relatively small allocation of funds.[2]

The city of Saint Louis, where we have been conducting a continuous

---

Health Rights News 3 (November–December 1971): 1–3; and Robert Knickmeyer and J. David Colfax, "Lead, Laws, Landlords—and Health," ibid. Bodenheimer and Colfax point out that phenylketonuria, which affects a very small percentage of *all children*, is subject to an elaborate screening and control program, whereas lead poisoning, which affects a large percentage of *black children*, is virtually ignored. A bibliographic report on the medical, economic, and political aspects of lead poisoning is available for $1.00 from the People's Coalition Against Lead Poisoning, 14th and Park Streets, Saint Louis, Missouri.

2. The amount allocated for lead poisoning might be compared with a routine military expenditure; a single air force bomber is armed with missiles costing $20 million.

and intensive anti-lead-poisoning campaign for nearly two years, provides an interesting case study of the politics of lead poisoning. Despite the fact that the inner city has some of the worst slum housing in the United States, interest in lead poisoning was virtually nonexistent until the spring of 1970, when a black community organizer charged that the lead-poisoning problem had reached epidemic proportions. Shortly afterward, a child died of lead poisoning, and the local health and medical community began to stir. By midsummer, personnel in the federally funded, ghetto-situated Yeatman Health Center, with the assistance of medical students, began a systematic screening of children in the area. Their data showed that approximately 60 percent of the children tested had 40 micrograms or more of lead per 100 milliliters of blood, a level which is considered dangerous. Projections based on this and subsequent screenings indicated that approximately 10,000 inner-city children were suffering from similarly elevated lead levels.

At this point a number of concerned social workers, medical personnel, parents, and local community leaders formed the People's Coalition Against Lead Poisoning. Their aim was to call public attention to the magnitude of the problem, the paucity of resources that were being employed toward its elimination, and the role of local-real estate interests and city officials in its perpetuation.[3]

Faced with increasing black-community awareness of the problem, local institutions responded predictably. City hospital spokesmen began to acknowledge a problem they had all but ignored for years, but claimed that they did not have the bed space to accommodate children in need of treatment.[4] Local politicians, seeing little immediate political capital in the issue, eventually allocated $60,000 to the Health Department to develop a program to deal with the problem. Health officials, in turn, hired additional administrative personnel and launched a poster campaign instructing mothers living in dilapidated housing to "Teach Your Children Not to Eat Paint." Here and in events to follow, the mayor and his staff made it clear that the 1970 city ordinance which made landlords responsible for providing tenants with a "lead-free environment" would not be enforced. The response of some of the more progressive elements of the local medical community was a "federalized" one. They characterized the lead-poisoning epidemic as a "medical" problem, and formulated proposals to bring federal aid into the city, but avoided the politically sensitive issues relating to medical care for the poor and politics of housing.

3. Groups represented in the Coalition included the Medical Committee for Human Rights, Saint Stephen's Parish, National Welfare Rights Organization, the Black Panther Party, RAP, the Association for Human Rights, and Parents Against Lead Poisoning.
4. This later proved to be false: a regional health committee report later showed that Saint Louis hospitals had a surplus of bed space.

Two Saint Louis newspapers, the liberal *Post-Dispatch* and the conservative *Globe-Democrat*, increasingly took editorial notice of the problem. Both, however, were careful to avoid direct references to the landlords' responsibility for these conditions and City Hall's failure to enforce the lead ordinance. Their moralizing editorials seemed calculated not to offend the real-estate interests, which provided a large proportion of their advertising.[5]

In the months that followed the initial screening by the Yeatman Center, the Coalition engaged in a number of activities intended to raise public consciousness about lead poisoning and the fact that the city was doing virtually nothing about it. These included (1) demonstrations at the suburban homes of slumlords who owned properties in which children had been poisoned; (2) meetings—and, eventually, in the face of apathy, confrontations—with the deans of the medical schools and officers of the local medical societies; (3) the establishment of free screening clinics in the ghetto; (4) the filing of a mandamus suit against city officials in an effort to compel enforcement of the lead ordinance; and (5) the detoxification of a home in which a three-year-old had been poisoned for the third time because the real-estate company that owned it refused to comply with the code. Each of these tactics had limited success:

Demonstrations at the homes of slumlords were intended to embarrass them in front of their suburban neighbors, but there was no evidence that people in these areas were particularly concerned about the slumlords' activities or the plight of inner-city residents.

Under considerable pressure from community groups, the medical establishment hired an out-of-town "lead coordinator" on a Danforth Foundation Grant of $15,000 (Danforth was dean of the Washington University Medical School and a leader in the conservative local medical establishment). This action was taken without consultation with community organizations actively concerned with lead poisoning, however, and it was not surprising that the coordinator experienced considerable difficulty in relating to such groups. Upon his sudden death shortly after taking the position, he was not replaced, and the medical community temporarily retired from the field.

The establishment of the free screening clinic by the Coalition was intended to compensate in part for the failure of the medical community to respond to the problem as well as call public attention to the city's negligence in this area. But with the filing of the mandamus suit against

5. One need only check the Sunday newspapers to get an idea of the amount of advertising placed by large real-estate companies. In return for this advertising, these newspapers devote a number of editorial pages to "news of real estate."

city officials, the screening operation was terminated. The City Health Department withdrew the required medical technician from the project and threatened action if the Coalition further attempted to operate the Center without authorization.

The courts' interpretation of Missouri common law predictably protected landlords' interests. The courts ruled that city officials could not be compelled to enforce the lead ordinance, as the mandamus suit had requested. The decision made it virtually certain that tenants who withheld their rent to pay for detoxification would be evicted.[6]

Finally, the detoxification of a house in which a child had been poisoned was done on an ad hoc, emergency basis (the grandmother was a member of the Coalition). Accordingly, little time was spent developing community support for the action, and the effort did not mobilize wider interest in the issue.

Nevertheless, the Coalition's campaign against lead poisoning, focusing as it did on city officials, the medical community, and real-estate interests, was having some impact. In April 1971 members of the Coalition confronted physicians at the annual banquet of the American Academy of Pediatrics, which was holding its national convention in Saint Louis, and demanded that the organization immediately investigate the failure of the local medical establishment to take significant action in dealing with the lead-poisoning epidemic. In subsequent discussions, the Coalition convinced officers of the Academy to discontinue plans for their "don't eat the paint" campaign against lead poisoning, since it placed blame on the victims rather than the victimizers, and created the impression that the medical community was significantly involved in the fight against lead poisoning when, in fact, their efforts were minimal. In a later press conference held by the Academy, Saint Louis representatives of the medical community acknowledged their failure to become significantly involved in the campaign against lead poisoning and listed planned programs to deal with the problem. As it turned out, these programs did not materialize, but the Academy's support of the Coalition's position against the local medical establishment helped to substantiate its charges of "genocide by neglect."

And in July 1971, in an effort to deal both with teen-age unemployment and pressure to do something about the lead-poisoning epidemic, the mayor created the "Spare One" corps of two hundred inner-city youths who, under the direction of City Hall and "community relations special-

6. Eviction in such instances is not necessarily punitive; rather, a landlord can get higher rents from the detoxified, improved units. Most tenants in these areas had month-to-month leases.

ists" from Saint Louis University's Community Medicine Program, were to be trained to detoxify inner-city homes over the summer. Financed with over $200,000 in federal funds, the program was, as the Coalition had predicted, a failure. City officials who were unwilling to antagonize real-estate speculators by enforcing the lead ordinance were similarly unwilling to violate "property rights" by providing detoxification crews with access to units which landlords had refused to detoxify. After six weeks funds for the "Spare One" program ran out, and a disgruntled youth corps was disbanded. They had not detoxified a single unit.

II

If one assumes that sociology is essentially a value-neutral discipline, that it should not interact with the social environment within which it is practiced, or that sociologists should merely place their work in the marketplace of ideas without assuming any responsibility for its use, then the Coalition Against Lead Poisoning is of interest merely as an object of study, a source of raw materials from which academic commodities might be fabricated to fill the storehouse of "scientific" sociological knowledge. But if one believes, as I do, that the primary objective of sociological research—or any serious intellectual effort—is to advance human well-being, that the sociologist has a responsibility to formulate and carry out his work with that goal in mind,[7] and that those who have constructed theories removed from practice have "only *interpreted* the world differently,"[8] then the Coalition provides an ongoing opportunity for the implementation of those values.

The sociologist who engages in indigenous, unfunded, nonbureaucratic, and radically oriented community-action programs has a number of personal and professional assets that are of value in his work. Modest as they are, they include *technical skill, authority, time,* and *access to manpower.*

The *technical skills* consist of a trained capacity to deal with social issues in holistic, structural terms, competence in assembling and evaluating large bodies of data, and an ability to grasp the significance of relationships among personal, organizational, and institutional needs and imperatives. Second, his *authority* is associated with his professional status in a

7. I have developed this idea in my "Knowledge for Whom?" *Sociological Inquiry* 80 (Winter 1970): 78–83, and in "Prospects and Varieties of 'Radical Scholarship' in Sociology," in *Radical Sociology*, ed. J. David Colfax and Jack L. Roach (New York: Basic Books, 1971), pp. 81–92.

8. This is, of course, the eleventh of Marx's "Theses on Feuerbach": "The philosophers have only interpreted the world differently, the point is to *change* it."

credentials-oriented society. Protected by class and collegial norms, he frequently has access to individuals and data that uncredentialized community people often do not have. Third, like the attorney who can take time away from his practice to run for political office, the sociologist, like most academics, has a relatively flexible work schedule and large amounts of *time* at his disposal. Teaching consumes relatively few hours per week, and if one's research and writing is, as I believe it should be, an integral part of one's political and community activities, the academic has considerably more time available than do most other volunteer or part-time activists.[9] Finally, the academic sociologist has *access to* manpower—students whose interests and training dispose them toward involvement in research and organizing activities.

These assets are, in some respects, also liabilities. The skills of the sociologist, unlike those of the storefront attorney or free-clinic physician, are often of little apparent value to nonacademic activists. Rather, the skills of the sociologist, particularly in his relationships with nascent nonbureaucratic organizations, are primarily those of the intellectual, and as such can be handicaps. To avoid the celebrated isolation of the intellectual, he must become directly and immediately involved in the ongoing activities of insurgent groups. Under such circumstances his skills, limited and arcane as they might appear at first, can be put at the service of the collectivities with which he is involved.[10]

The authority of the academic is perhaps his most easily eroded asset. As

9. It is perhaps important in this context not to perpetuate a pseudo issue. *All* academics, I contend, are engaged in *political* activity, even in the routine conduct of their work. The sociologist who writes reports for the Carnegie Foundation is engaged in activity as manifestly political as the sociologist who organizes a tenant strike; the critical difference is not merely that different clients are involved, as some would have it (see, e.g., Alvin W. Gouldner's cynical "The Sociologist as Partisan," *American Sociologist* 3 [May 1968]: 103–16), but that different *goals* are involved, and these can, of course, be ranked in terms of a hierarchy of values. Less obvious, perhaps, but no less political, is the case of the specialist who prepares a monograph on, say, *Moby Dick*. The political nature of his seemingly apolitical exercise is, first, that his selection of this, rather than other forms of activity, is in itself an expression of a political preference. Second is the fact that the university which provides him an opportunity to write his monograph is built upon wealth (or value) created by the larger community. This value can be "consumed" in a politically responsive or irresponsible manner. Since it is labor—and not the elite which runs the university—which creates this value, we would argue that the responsible academic should understand his obligation to those classes which have, often inadvertently or unwillingly, created the wealth which allows for the "philanthropic" creation and maintenance of the university. To engage in activities that challenge the authority and infringe upon the interests of those in power is to incur the wrath of the "philanthropists" who run the universities, for their interests are seldom, if ever, philanthropic.

10. For a relevant and provocative discussion of the radical intellectual and social movements, see John Fraser, "Marxists and the Intellectuals," *Science and Society* 35 (Fall 1971): 257–85.

he becomes identified with too many unpopular causes or becomes intensively involved in a particular issue, his opponents or those in positions of authority will attempt to dismiss him as one undeserving of serious attention, and to the extent that his behavior does not conform with the popular image of the "responsible" academic, this tactic can prove relatively effective.

And despite the apparent fact that the academically based sociologist has time to devote to community organizing, his formal, if not personal, commitment is to his profession and the university, which define his role and have purchased his labor power, respectively.[11] Obvious identification with community groups, rather than with the self-styled "community of scholars" of the university, can provoke conflict with professionally oriented associates or public-relations-conscious administrators, who can often impede his work in the local community.

Finally, the question of manpower—of student involvement—is a rather complex matter, as I hope to indicate in section 5.

III

Theory, it has been said, comes out of practice. And so it was during the first year of the existence of the People's Coalition Against Lead Poisoning. As a community organizer I found myself engaged in confrontations with city and health officials, writing leaflets, photographing violations, knocking on doors to locate children for screening, and supervising the detoxification of homes. As a sociologist I conducted research into patterns of slum ownership, researched lead-poisoning activities throughout the country, wrote background papers, and helped to evaluate past and formulate future strategies.

Mistakes were committed. Lacking a fully developed plan to deal with detoxification, emergency medical care, and the quality of inner-city housing, members of the Coalition spread themselves thin, functionally and geographically. For example, because more whites than blacks were members of the Coalition, an effort was made to begin lead screening in the predominantly white low-income Soulard area of the city. Almost immediately, city housing inspectors followed the organizers into the neighborhood and began issuing citations for building-code violations. And because most of the buildings in this area were owner-occupied duplexes or single-unit dwellings, small property owners—themselves often elderly and impoverished—rather than real-estate companies were being made

11. This is a point that is often lost on academics who consider themselves "professionals," free of the constraints of the commodity marketplace of capitalism.

the targets of City Hall's selective "law and order" campaign. When the organizers realized what was happening and moved out of the area in order to take the pressure off small property owners, the city housing inspectors also left.

One thing was becoming increasingly clear: city and health officials, although now coming to recognize the magnitude of the lead-poisoning epidemic, had no comprehensive program for its elimination. The reason for this was obvious: there was money to be made in speculation in deterioration housing in blighted areas, but there was little or no money to be made in the construction of low-income housing—nor was tax money available for the latter. Given these political and economic constraints, it was apparent that the Coalition's efforts to eliminate lead poisoning required a protracted struggle centering upon the root cause of the epidemic: the political economy of *housing*. The campaign would have to center upon the idea that a profit-oriented housing industry could not provide adequate low-income housing: it simply didn't pay.[12]

IV

From its inception, the Coalition repeatedly experienced two difficulties: pressures on its members to withdraw from its activities, and a scarcity of resources. During its first year, two black workers most directly involved in the Coalition's activities were dismissed from agencies ostensibly concerned with the problems of low-income communities. In the first instance, community organizer Lawrence Black was dismissed from the federally funded Community Medicine Program of Saint Louis University. He had become actively involved with the Coalition and continued to work with it after being warned that his activities did not conform to his "job description." When asked why an organizer who had been hired to organize people around the lead issue was now prevented from working with the organization that had the broadest base of community support, administrators of the Community Medicine Program said they simply "disagreed with the Coalition's orientation"; Black would either have to conform to their ad hoc standards or be dismissed.

Directors of the Community Medicine Program, ever cognizant of the federal funding situation, were concerned with obtaining funds for new programs and seemed to fear that the kind of community organizing being done by Black was undermining their definition of the situation as a

---

12. Here the Coalition is in agreement with slumlords who claim that the ownership of slum properties doesn't pay: the only way slum properties can be made to pay is to eliminate maintenance costs—which is precisely what most slumlords do.

"medical problem"—i.e., one "best" dealt with by welfare professionals and medical personnel, rather than one requiring a community, or political, solution. Black was dismissed from his position in July 1971, but continued to work full-time without pay with the Coalition through the fall of 1971, when the Coalition was able to hire him as its first full-time community organizer.

But in the fall of 1971 another black social worker, William Preston, who as director of the Red Cross's only low-income project in the city had organized his community around the lead poisoning issue, found his project terminated and himself without a job. Red Cross officials claimed that funds were not available to continue the year-old demonstration project, but in light of the fact that the local chapter received nearly $1.75 million annually from the Saint Louis United Fund and the project cost less than $30,000, the claim was not very convincing. More plausible was the view that officials of the conservative Red Cross were embarrassed by and resented an earlier request by members of the Coalition that the agency mobilize its resources to conduct mass screening and provide emergency treatment in order to deal with the lead-poisoning "disaster." In refusing to take such action, officials of the Red Cross asserted that such activities were alien to its central tasks of dealing with "natural disasters," running the blood-donor program, providing aid to military families, and conducting their "groovy grooming program" for inner-city youth.[13] And so William Preston was fired and the Red Cross's only poverty-area program was allowed to die.

Less dramatic were those problems caused by the limited resources of the Coalition. Financed almost entirely by contributions from its members, the Coalition was able to initiate a number of programs—screening, detoxification, and education—but these could not compete with city and federally funded programs which continued to insist that lead poisoning was a medical problem and could be solved by "teaching the children not to eat the paint," rather than one which required a reordering of urban priorities and the massive reallocation of resources. In the face of this propaganda, a number of parents and community workers who had joined the Coalition in the hope that it would somehow provide an immediate solution to the problems of poor housing and lead poisoning withdrew when they came to perceive the Coalition's analysis as being insufficiently "realistic," or its programs as inadequate. Some were drawn off by programs such as "Spare One," which promised much but delivered little.

13. Some of the Red Cross's most sacred programs are not above criticism: see, e.g., Richard Titmuss, *The Gift Relationship* (New York: Pantheon, 1971), for a discussion of the class biases in blood donorship and use.

Others became apathetic or cynical as repeatedly unproductive meetings with city officials dimmed their hopes that something could be accomplished by petitioning authorities.

Nevertheless, the Coalition possessed a number of qualities lacking in other organizations which had now begun to relate to the lead epidemic. Unlike the federally funded medical community, the Coalition had no vested interest in maintaining close ties with the city's corrupt and ineffectual poverty agency. It had no need to compromise in order to gain support for funding proposals that required political clearance. And unlike the city health and housing departments, it was not bureaucratically limited by the usual budgetary considerations that are so often invoked to justify agency ineffectuality and neglect. Further, none of the Coalition members stood to gain much from their activities. Since the Coalition was generally regarded as a radical insurgent group more concerned with forcing the city to move on housing than in developing "realistic"—i.e., stopgap—programs, it did not provide the status and prestige payoffs that "responsible" social-service activities often do. Accordingly, Coalition members came to be viewed by members of the low-income communities as being primarily concerned about people rather than programs. The Coalition, in the year and a half of its existence, had established high creditability in poverty areas, but had become an anathema to the political and health establishment.

Nevertheless, by September 1971, the city's lead ordinance was not being enforced. Hospital officials, claiming that they were overburdened with the few cases the Coalition had brought to them for treatment, raised the level at which children would be hospitalized from 40 to 80 micrograms of lead in 100 milliliters of whole blood.[14] The courts had upheld property rights over the right of people to have nonlethal housing. And many people who had heard about lead poisoning for the past year and saw nothing being done about it had become disillusioned.

V

The termination of the Red Cross project had served to reorient and

14. In an effort to justify the increase in the toxicity level, hospital officials claimed that "nothing could be done" until the levels reached the 80-microgram level—the level at which many children go into convulsions or suffer permanent damage. They admitted that children at the 40-microgram level *should* be removed from the leaded environment and hospitalized, but since this would overburden hospital facilities and homes were not being detoxified, it was an impossible demand. Consistent with the profit motive of the American health-care system, however, hospitals were providing care for children whose parents could pay for treatment, regardless of the toxicity levels. Only poor children were "healthy" at 40 micrograms.

revitalize the Coalition. With the firing of William Preston, the Coalition publicly challenged the role of the Red Cross in the community: although the recipient of the largest single share of United Fund money, the Red Cross obviously felt little obligation to maintain even its current level of involvement in the low-income community. Fortunately, several members of the Coalition had earlier researched the local United Fund as a part of a nationwide effort to expose the restrictive policies of United Fund campaigns, and their booklet was standard reading in the local schools of social work.[15] Consequently, large numbers of students were drawn to the Preston case. They began to pressure social-work school administrators to withdraw their field-placement students from the Red Cross, and student interest in the lead-poisoning issue began to grow.

When Preston was fired, the Coalition, though badly hurt by the loss of a key organizer, recognized the potential of student mobilization around the issue of lead poisoning. Accordingly, I decided that it would be worthwhile for me to challenge an earlier decision of the Washington University administration and sociology faculty to deny me tenure and dismiss me at the end of the academic year. When being considered for tenure, I had been formally examined by the senior faculty and was asked to defend my relationship with the Black Panthers, my work with welfare recipients, and my "objectivity" as an activist social scientist, and it was patently clear that the decision to deny me tenure had been in large part motivated by political considerations. I had originally decided not to challenge the decision: I could only appeal it before a powerless "Dean's Committee" which had already concurred in the decision to deny me tenure, and felt that there were more important political tasks than taking on the university in a futile battle for tenure. With the firings of Black and Preston, it became obvious that the Coalition could not survive if its key members were forced out of jobs, and in the hope that interest in my case would generate student interest in the efforts of the Coalition, I hired an attorney, publicly challenged the tenure decision, flew several professional colleagues to Saint Louis to testify in my behalf, and focused considerable attention on the reasons for my dismissal. The immediate result—the tenure matter is still the subject of committee deliberations in which we are unable to participate, since Washington University does not abide by AAUP guidelines—was that a large number of students previously oblivious to the epidemic now wanted to know what they could do to assist us in the fight against lead poisoning. The Coalition had anticipated this, and, as the initial furor surrounding my tenure appeal subsided, it held a series of meetings with concerned students.

15. RAP, *Center of Power in St. Louis: Interlocking Directorates and the United Fund*, Saint Louis, 1970; and "United Fund Round-Up," *Hotchpot* (December–January 1970–71): 1.

The initial plan was to ask students to assist in the raising of funds—finances were the Coalition's most immediate problem. The student response was somewhat different than had been expected, however. They expressed a desire to become directly involved in the activities of the Coalition, and to do something immediate and concrete for the victims of lead poisoning. While many recognized the need for support efforts and protracted struggles, considerable sentiment existed for more direct involvement in the issue, for concrete experience. They suggested that they detoxify a house with funds raised on campus.

For the Coalition this idea posed some problems. All but a very few of the students were white, and a white "do-gooder" project might well be counterproductive in neighborhoods where we had been organizing tenants to put pressure on landlords to detoxify homes and bring buildings up to code standards. Furthermore, the detoxification of a single unit—at a cost of about $300—in a city of more than 50,000 such units might serve to allay white guilt, but in and of itself hardly began to address the overall problem. Indeed, it would be counterproductive if it led students to believe that the lead-poisoning epidemic could be solved if only everyone worked for a weekend, like themselves, to detoxify a home.

Accordingly, the background of the problem and the Coalition's views were discussed at length in an effort to provide a clear understanding of the implications of a program which had detoxification as its *primary* focus. Eventually a plan which coincided with and extended the Coalition's strategy was developed. While not articulated in such terms at the time, it was based on the following set of propositions: First, the position of the Coalition was that the lead epidemic could not be solved until people became organized at the local level; forced slumlords out of the ghetto; established community control of the area and the buildings; and compelled city officials to reorder priorities, develop a progressive taxation system, and provide adequate low-income housing in the city. Second, code enforcement was clearly impossible, since profits could be made in low-income housing only as long as the building code was not enforced. Accordingly, the people forced to live in such housing could build pressure by organizing rent strikes and resisting evictions, while the Coalition provided emergency services and raised public awareness of the "genocide by neglect" that was taking place in the inner city. To move in this direction the Coalition's primary need was for money to support its full-time community organizer. It also needed resources to undertake projects in the ghetto that gave residents a sense that community organizing made *some* immediate change possible; otherwise the Coalition's organizers could talk only about long-range solutions or, worse, talk in terms of the same kinds of stopgap measures that the liberal bureaucrats had been advancing for the past two years. Moreover, the Coalition needed broad-based community support in order to weather attacks on it by various city agencies and institutions.

Student participation in a detoxification effort was to provide experience that could be used in the development of programs to educate others and generate financial support for the activities of the Coalition. Ideally, students who took part in the detoxification program would become suburban community organizers of similar activities, and help to build an ever-widening base of involvement and support. The efforts of other groups to raise funds for detoxification would create community awareness of the issue, and the experience of detoxification would create commitment.

Within a week the newly formed Student Committee raised over $500, and three apartments selected by the community organizers were scheduled for detoxification. In one sixteen-unit building managed by one of the more notorious of the real-estate corporations, two apartments were to be detoxified as "demonstration" projects and to provide tenants with a focus for a rent strike. The other was a single-family unit in which a lead-poisoned child who had been treated was in immediate need of a detoxified environment. In terms of the Coalition's program, the first two units were regarded as "strategic" detoxifications since they were designed to help build community support toward a rent strike; the third unit was an "emergency" detoxification, since the building was in a difficult-to-organize area of deteriorated private homes and single-unit residences.

In mid-October over one hundred students turned out to detoxify the three units. The work consisted of paneling over lead-infested walls, tearing down and replacing crumbling ceilings, patching roofs, scraping and reframing windowsills and doorways, plastering, and painting.

For many, the task, which took place over three weekends, was an exhilarating experience—the sense of doing something concrete and meaningful was highly rewarding. For others, it was profoundly depressing—after hundreds of hours of work it was clear that little really had been accomplished. The people living in these units were impoverished and crowded in substandard quarters, and their children undernourished and poorly clothed. Only three of the fifty thousand units were no longer lethal, and perhaps a bit cheerier. Some found that the experience confirmed stereotypes—reality was harsher and more complex than they had been prepared for by liberal sociology courses. Why were the apartments so dirty? Why wouldn't a mother take an obviously sick child to the clinic? Why don't tenants try to maintain the buildings? These were the questions that experienced members of the Coalition found themselves trying to answer, in an effort to make students understand that the problems of the urban poor were a consequence of capitalist social structure rather than something for which the people themselves were responsible. Many students seemed to acquire a fuller understanding of themselves and their society; others probably did not.

Following the detoxification, black organizers for the Coalition, who had been warned by the slumlords to "keep those people out of the building," continued to organize toward an area-wide rent strike. Buttons and bumper stickers with the slogans "Get the Slumlords out of the Ghetto" and "Slumlords Kill Kids" were distributed throughout the city.

The Student Committee, with the experience of detoxification behind them, moved into the next phase of their activities: the mobilization of church and school groups to engage in fund-raising and detoxification efforts in support of the Coalition's program. Two committees were formed and several research projects begun. The school committee had the task of contacting suburban schools and colleges and arranging for opportunities to present a program on lead poisoning. A churches and synagogues committee had a similar task. These activities required students to develop a program for presentation, and this, in turn, required self-education. A film, a slide program, and a photography exhibit illustrating the magnitude and intensity of the problem were prepared. A junior-high-school class organized a door-to-door fund-raising campaign. Other students, now interested in documenting the relationships among real-estate interests, tax policies, city officials, local corporations, and the housing situation in Saint Louis, planned a long-term research project that would deal with these issues, and hopefully, would provide a base for further organizing, as did the United Fund research project. An interdisciplinary group of faculty initiated plans for a general-studies course on the social, political, economic, and medical aspects of lead poisoning, in order to provide activist students with a technically comprehensive base for their organizing efforts. The student newspaper carried a series of articles dealing with the local epidemic and what was being done about it. Students who had been mobilized by the detoxification program registered for independent study in the various aspects of low-income housing, and others took advantage of the urban-semester program of the university to work closely with the Coalition on a full-time basis.

With the publicity that accompanied the students' efforts, awareness that the Coalition was expanding its base of operations prompted the city health and housing officials to claim that they were obtaining landlord "compliance" in 75 percent of the cases in which violations were found. When pressed on this claim, they admitted they had no clear criterion against which to measure "compliance," and were backed into the position of having lamely to reiterate that it was financially impossible for slumlords to provide the "lead-free" environment called for in the city ordinance. What this meant, of course, was that city agencies were continuing to operate within a framework in which landlords who failed to maintain their properties could continue to extract profits from slum housing. The poor continued to have the choice of raising their children in lethal environments or going without housing altogether. The Coalition, with the support of a growing segment of the suburban community and financial resources which enabled it to subsidize a community organizer who could not be fired because of "overidentification with tenants," prepared to continue the struggle.

VI

What were the unique contributions of sociology to this effort? They are not, in their totality, particularly impressive; they constitute a style, an approach, rather than a collection of techniques and methods. For example, the initial orientation of most students was politically liberal rather than radical; at the same time they were capable of identifying elements of social structure and committed to uncovering hidden connections among social phenomena. Exposed to the concrete realities of trying to bring about change in the city, many of these students were capable of going beyond the liberal rhetoric of change and developed a fuller understanding of the social and political forces which perpetuated the oppression they had seen.

A second contribution of sociology was its emphasis upon the importance of the empirical, of contact with concrete phenomena, and its repudiation of "armchair philosophizing." In practice, of course, the ideal is seldom realized: hip texts, term papers, and field trips provide the typical sociology undergraduate with his closest contact with the oppression that characterizes much of urban America. But given an opportunity to become involved in a complex and long-term problem such as lead poisoning, the student can learn that the sociologist who is serious about his trade is not afraid of getting his hands dirty, and many adapt to this role quite readily.

A third attribute of sociology is its belief in and commitment to change. For the most part, such notions are of a liberal cast, of course, but the commitment provides a base for the development of broader conceptions of how change can be achieved. Student sociologists working with the Coalition did not have to be convinced that change was possible: the task was merely one of developing awareness of the magnitude of changes that would be required before an epidemic such as lead poisoning could be eliminated.

Finally, most sociology students possess some understanding of, if not experience in, carrying out sociological research. Given adequate guidance and a significant topic—one that is tied to an ongoing program for change—most students can learn to do the kinds of work useful to community-organizing efforts, and even learn to endure, in the name of the effort, the tedium often involved in such undertakings.

My own role as sociologist-organizer has been threefold. As "detached" sociologist-organizer I initially devoted most of my time to projects that drew upon my personal and professional abilities, but made little use of my institutional affiliations to elicit student participation in these activities. Only when it became clear that members of the Coalition were being systematically dismissed from their jobs did it become apparent that my situation at the university could be used to dramatize the needs of the Coalition and to mobilize student support. Second, as teacher-organizer I served as liaison between the newly formed Student Committee and the inner-city organizers. And, finally, as teacher-researcher I committed myself to the supervision of lead-poisoning and housing research.

In this brief discussion of the activities of the People's Coalition Against Lead Poisoning I have attempted to illustrate some of the uses of sociology in action. Yet in this era of increasing repression, both within the university and outside, there is good reason to question whether or not sociologists will be able to continue effectively to participate in insurgent movements and remain in the university. The dead hand of Weberian self-censorship hovers above the academy. At this juncture, however, after a number of years of work as a radical activist and a member of two sociology departments, I would not say that it is impossible to be an effective organizer of community groups of the kind described here and still remain in the university. Obviously it is not *impossible;* it is merely *difficult.* Measured against the problems of the dispossessed, the poor, and the hopeless, the difficulties of the activist sociologist fade into insignificance. *Angst* incapacitates academics, but leaded paint kills children.

two

REFORM AS REVOLUTION: THE BEDFORD-STUYVESANT COMMUNITY COOPERATIVE CENTER IN PERSPECTIVE
Henry Etzkowitz

How can the sociologist help an urban community in fresh and vital ways? What kind of obstacles may he encounter within the sociological profession? Most important, how should we assess a short-lived community project seven years after it was completed; what can we learn from our setbacks? These strategic matters are treated in the essay that follows. The author reassures us that new variations of action sociology useful to the community at large will continue to have a place in the utopian task we share.

As a Peace Corps volunteer in Nigeria in the early 1960s I participated in carrying out the work of a local secondary school but was enjoined from participating in local politics. These instructions made sense: I was not a citizen of Nigeria but a guest in that country. At the time I accepted my inability to influence Nigeria's political future as proper. Of course, as I later came to realize, my presence as a teacher and that of hundreds of my fellow volunteers was in part an instrument to maintain a policy of excluding qualified Nigerians (from other parts of the country) from teaching. They supported the regional policy in an area which did not at that time have sufficient university graduates of its own. Thus, the Peace Corps volunteers were to "hold" the teaching positions for members of the specific ethnic groups of the designated area in which they would teach. Whatever the merits of this policy, my fellow volunteers and I were carrying out a political design, whether we realized it or not.

On returning to the United States I became a graduate student in sociology at the New School for Social Research. There again I learned that to be an objective sociologist one did not participate. The role of an observer was the only legitimated one in studying events. And it was then that it occurred to me that the regulations on participation at the New School were even stricter than those of the Peace Corps. For while the Peace Corps disallowed political activities in a foreign country, New

School sociology disallowed all involvement of an activist nature. We were being trained to be theorists of society—observers but not activists.

About this time I read Alvin W. Gouldner's essay "Anti-Minotaur: The Myth of a Value-Free Sociology," [1] which demonstrated that sociologists who adopted the strictures of the "objective" role were nevertheless subject to bias. Now the question plagued me, Was I to give up my rights of citizenship in my own country when they were not even exchangeable for objectivity? I then asked myself, How did the New School commitment to noninvolvement come about?

At the New School there was a belief in scientific objectivity for its own sake. Part of this desire of the graduate faculty to remain apart from American society was motivated by the belief held by those who had lived through the Nazi period in Germany that, if the university involved itself in anything which might be defined as political, the university might be invaded and destroyed by outside forces. This fear was a reaction to historical reality. Nationalistic German scholars in the 1930s had involved the university in politics. At the New School the faculty believed that the German faculty's involvement had cost the university its neutrality and had opened it to invasion and destruction by Hitler. These fears were reinforced by the McCarthy period in the United States. This period of academic harassment again called forth to many émigré scholars the prospect of a repetition of the process that had forced them out of Nazi Germany.

By the 1960s, liberal-radical American scholars, by involvement in open political activities, had broken the university's neutral silence. Students who came back to their campuses from summers in the civil-rights movement in the mid-'60s worked with local civil-rights groups to organize against facilities that discriminated in their hiring practices.[2] Students were now organizing people on campuses to carry out political activities off-campus. Berkeley students first raised the issue by using the campus as a base from which to recruit adherents to carry out civil-rights actions in the community.

These early attempts to facilitate social change from a campus base did much to call attention to existing inequities and effected some change, but seemed to lack a permanent institutionalized base to carry on social-change activities. It was my belief that for large-scale and long-range change to be effected, a self-perpetuating, financially viable, and independent movement would have to be created.

1. *Social Problems* 3, no. 9 (Winter 1962): 199–213.
2. See Jack Newfield, *A Prophetic Minority* (2nd ed.; New York: New American Library, 1970).

Much as we have learned in the past two or three years that government grants could run out and not be renewed, it was already evident in the mid-'60s that the interests of philanthropists and student activists could change. There is no guarantee of continuity in a movement unless a means exists to maintain consistent and concerted effort.

The argument against overdependence on temporary volunteers and philanthropists is simply that they lose interest or shift their priorities of interest to other problems, especially when change does not occur rapidly.[3] For example, it is not unreasonable to assume that a student, while on a voter registration drive in the South, can become concerned with the plight of blacks and work with great intensity to alleviate it. But the following summer this same student may go on a fishing vacation and return home far more concerned with the hazards of polluted streams.

Only the individual who must remain in the situation and has little chance for escape will be motivated, if he is not completely overwhelmed by apathy, to maintain the continuity of activity to work for relief of the plight with which he is himself afflicted. To forestall apathy and promote hope, a permanent institutional mechanism through which people can work for change is needed.

In the summer of 1966, while teaching at Brooklyn College, a fellow sociologist and I discussed the possibility of organizing an action-research social-change project to form an economic base that would provide social services and serve as a political base for the Bedford-Stuyvesant ghetto in central Brooklyn, New York, the largest concentrated black population in the United States. The project, which would serve as a model, would also provide a base from which to do research on the ghetto, and the community researched would receive benefits from the project in return.

I then proposed to the sociology faculty of the New School that the Bedford-Stuyvesant project should be organized under the aegis of the New School for Social Research, where I was a graduate student. My theoretical framework was that if the New School, and more especially the sociology department, could be persuaded to sponsor such a project, the direction of the university could be reoriented from an isolated "ivory tower" atmosphere to one that participated in the attempt to bring about change in American society.

At a meeting with us in August 1966, the chairman of the New School sociology department appeared intrigued by the idea for the project. He signed a cover letter, which we drafted at his request, to accompany a

---

3. Or significantly, when change occurs rapidly, they often become frightened and want to stop it. See Henry and Shari Etzkowitz, "The Trotsky Effect: A Study of Why Change Stops in Ongoing Social Movements" (forthcoming).

proposal to a foundation for financing the Center. I also proposed, and obtained approval from the department chairman, to do a study of the project for my doctoral dissertation.

In our draft proposal for the Bedford-Stuyvesant Community Cooperative Center and for an Institution Formation sociology, we hypothesized that sociologists could organize new institutions and simultaneously study the institutions being created. We believed that these new institutions should be organized to help meet social needs in areas of society where no similar institutions existed. We further believed that after organizing such a new institution, the sociologists might later withdraw from it and reflect back insightfully. At this point the sociologists might use as data not only their observations of other people within the institution but of themselves as major participants within the situation. Thus Institution Formation sociologists would not have to rely solely on interviewing and the goodwill of informants to research an institution. Rather, as they participated in the institution's creation they had license to tape record and film any and all natural interaction as it occurred.[4]

Our hypothesis was that Institution Formation would connect the researcher to individuals and groups which would support the project, or oppose it. Through this interaction generated by the working of the institution, a study of the community could be derived.[5] Our proposal for the Co-op Center was now stamped with the imprimatur of the New School sociology department. With this legitimation we sent off to the liberal-radical foundations that had financed much of the civil-rights movement, to seek funding. Before we received any replies from the foundations, we discovered that we were in serious trouble at the New School. The departmental chairman, who had signed a glowing cover letter to our proposal, was now backing down. Contacted by the foundations from whom we sought support, he denied that his letter intended sponsorship by the department, but was merely an expression of his own personal interest in the idea.

The chairman, Arthur Vidich, in a book he co-edited,[6] took the position that the sociologist should make a value commitment: that this was a legitimate act and indeed one which could not be avoided. This background may well explain his initial sympathy and interest in the proposal for the Bedford-Stuyvesant project. His later disinterest can

4. See Henry Etzkowitz, "Institution Formation Sociology," *American Sociologist* (May 1970): 120–24.

5. See Henry Etzkowitz and Gerald Schaflander, *Ghetto Crisis: Progress vs. Bureaucracy in Bedford-Stuyvesant* (Boston: Little, Brown, 1972).

6. Maurice Stein and Arthur Vidich, *Sociology on Trial* (Englewood Cliffs, N.J.: Prentice-Hall, 1963).

perhaps be explained by the fact that a value-committed stance, for him, existed solely on the theoretical level. In my opinion he did not relate a movement from a value-committed standpoint on the theoretical level to a value-committed approach on the activist level.

He now wished to dissociate himself and the commitment he gave on behalf of his department from our embryo project. We then realized that it was naive of us to have ever expected him to sponsor us, for if such a project ever came to fruition, it would poke a hole in his ideology which, like Marcuse's, professed the impossibility of social change.[7] Thus we had to give up on the possibility of using a connection to the university to help bring the institution into being. With the help of an attorney, we hammered out a charter for a nonprofit research-and-development corporation and resubmitted our proposal to the foundations—this time on an independent basis.

By now we had so motivated ourselves that without severing our relationship to the New School as students, we went into Bedford-Stuyvesant to begin the project without waiting for full financing. Indeed, we funded the beginnings of the project with our teaching salaries. We began holding organizing meetings in churches and meeting halls in Bedford-Stuyvesant in the Fall of 1966, in order to gain community commitment to the project.

The following is a tape transcript of how we addressed ourselves to the people and of how we perceived our role as sociologists in the community.

[Etzkowitz:] Usually a sociologist goes in and asks people some questions and then disappears and goes away and you never see him again. But we're a different kind of sociologist than that. Not only are we going to stay in one place and find out what's going on—but we're going to do something more than this. We're going to set up a new institution or, more exactly, take an old institution which has worked well in another part of society, make some fundamental changes in it, and then set it up so it can hopefully work in the ghetto in this new place. By making these changes we hope to build a new institution which can begin to meet the problems of Bedford-Stuyvesant.

And while we're doing this—while we're taking this new institution and setting it up with you—we're going to study and see what happens. We'll talk to the people who come to the cooperative—who are buying things there—see what they think about it. And we'll see what difference it makes to their lives in building this institution in Bedford-Stuyvesant. This is what is meant by action sociology or "involved observer" research. Getting out there and doing something and seeing how it works. Not just looking at it, but doing it!

7. See Herbert Marcuse, *One-Dimensional Man* (Boston: Beacon Press, 1964).

The Community Cooperative Center was established in the winter of 1967. Our plan was to develop enterprises such as supermarkets, gas stations, and drugstores; the profits from these would be rechanneled into social services. We hoped that as our businesses grew and we extended these enterprises throughout the Bedford-Stuyvesant community, eventually profits could be used not only for social services but also to facilitate social change through developing and supporting movements to build a political power base within the community. Thus we hypothesized that the Co-op would be a model to demonstrate the possibility that revolutionary effects could be accomplished by ghetto residents when they attained control of the resources of their community by establishing an independent economic base. For the Co-op's profits would be kept within the community and not flow out to the suburbs, and the people of the community could benefit from the labor and profits of their community.

A further hypothesis was that the residents of the community who became members of the Community Cooperative Center would have their consciousness raised and see capitalism not solely in terms of individual financial gain; rather, they would gain commitment to the ideal of using the Community Cooperative Center profits to benefit the community at large.

Nevertheless, the project did not follow the originally intended course of development. Instead, it moved into the second phase, that of social services, before the completion of the first phase of successful businesses. At the time, this collapsing of the stages and attempting to organize both phases at once seemed a viable course of action, given the obstacles encountered in organizing the first projected business, a supermarket. The need of the organizers to maintain the momentum of the group by proceeding to Phase 2 in advance of Phase 1 and organizing a social service, i.e., an infant- and child-care center, meant the destruction of the revolutionary model we had created.

From the vantage point of five years after the event, I must now say that we would have been better Institution Formation sociologists had we been more conservative businessmen. Our inability to establish and sustain profit-making businesses before we attempted to introduce social services into the community frustrated an important goal of our project in that we did not show that a community could support its own social welfare through viable paying businesses. Perhaps it was the desperate need of the community for the services we did offer; perhaps it was the temptations of our excellent ethnographic vantage point and our doubts about preserving the project's momentum if we did not do something; but we made the mistake of encouraging the Bedford-Stuyvesant community to establish yet another dependent institution rather than holding to the original goals of establishing an independent economic base.

A misfortune of the Co-op was that there was no hard businessman in the project who would say: "Not one cent will be spent on social welfare until profits are realized." By allowing social services to precede the establishment of the unique profit-making aspect of the project the CCC failed to clarify its position in the community as quite separate and distinct from the OEO model, i.e., social services paid for and controlled from the outside. In retrospect, our project did not make clear enough that if sufficient profits were not realized, it would die. Everyone in the CCC became dependent on the belief that still another "check" would be forthcoming to save the institution.

Certainly, as long as we allowed the institution to be dependent on philanthropic support and not able to achieve total economic independence through owning the means of consumer distribution and the profits that went with it, we had frustrated any hope of the institution's achieving its eventual goal of having independent resources and eventually the ability to gain political control within the community.

Similar to the conservative position that accepting federal funds inevitably means an extension of federal control, we found that by accepting private philanthropic funds to maintain social services instead of using them first to begin profit-making institutions, we left our flanks open for control by our benefactors. This became apparent when we were finally ready to open a supermarket and were placed in the double bind of having our major contributor refuse to provide funds for the day-care center if we did not acquiesce to his viewpoint: that a supermarket was not a viable choice for a profit-making enterprise.[8]

Once the project deviated from the original plan, it contained the seeds of its own destruction. It could never become a model for an independent socio-economic institution.

In one respect the original intentions of the sociologists were at least partially fulfilled. We hoped the project would be a training ground for the youth of the community. We envisioned that with the project's growth the sociologists would depart, leaving viable businesses and social services to the ghetto residents. Because the social scientists involved in the project were much more facile in dealing with bureaucracies than they were in conducting business operations, it is not surprising that the members of the project picked up bureaucratic but not business skills from the sociologists.

Yet, even though the social scientists often did not display business acumen, members of the ghetto community appeared to gain business

8. For a short time, later in the project, a gas station and a drugstore were opened. However, by that time these two small enterprises were incapable of making a sufficient profit to support the staff of a day-care center that housed 150 children.

skills in spite of or perhaps because of the sociologists' business ineptitude, and were able to use the experience gained in the Community Cooperative Center for furthering their own pursuits. For example, the chairman of the board learned how to secure loans, make deals, and manage creditors with more skill and finesse than he previously had. When interviewed recently, he said that "someday, when I make it bigger and get all these other deals squared away, I'm going to open up that day-care center again and run it like you people didn't know how."

In summation, the Co-op was a large-scale social laboratory which brought together diverse elements of a fragmented population and tested the proposition that these divergent elements could work together to form a new and revolutionary institution. Thus, during the time of the project, black groups that were normally apart interacted, worked together, often argued with each other, but also provided data both about themselves and about how transactions and common working relationships could be established between highly differentiated elements within the same community. By bringing groups together that did not normally interact, the social scientists were instrumental in creating a social reality that would not have existed otherwise. Once this was done, we could test the theory that such coalitions could be created not only to reach social goals but also to provide data about coalition formation.

Many radicals argue that attempts at building new institutions such as the Community Cooperative Center are inherently self-defeating. They argue that if reforms are attained and the conditions of people's lives are improved, they will be less willing to work for social change; indeed, they might actively work against it, for they will be coopted and become a part of a system they have an interest in maintaining.

Proponents of this perspective on social change say that what is needed to create the potential for change is for conditions to become worse rather than better. The proponents of the "worse the better" theory, wishing to attain large-scale social change, tend to oppose small-scale attempts at creating models for change in the here and now. The "worse the better" advocates will work for reform only as a tactic to raise consciousness in the belief that the failure to gain the reform will activate people to work for the revolution. They will oppose reform that shows signs of succeeding because they believe it ultimately inhibits the possibility of the revolution taking place.

Some theorists do not agree. Philip Slater, in his work *The Pursuit of Loneliness*,[9] argues that the worse conditions get, the less possibility there will be for people to see a need to change conditions. He argues that

9. Boston: Beacon Press, 1970.

without reforms to set new goals for them, people will passively accept the status quo, and it is only when people are involved in working toward and successfully achieving small-scale reforms that they will attempt to see both the necessity and possibility for achieving change on a larger scale.

I believe that the way to permanent, long-range social change is through the building of new institutions and the obtaining of successive reforms in old institutions. Through this "long march through the institutions," and around them and into new ones, a larger and larger free space within the old society can be created. Eventually, if this process continues and gathers momentum, reform has the possibility to attain the goals of the revolution.

Social scientists who hold these values can combine their role as social scientist with their rights as citizens. They can act to further these goals while they derive new theories about what these goals should be. Social scientists in this position must combine a concern both for the ethics of means as well as ends. For they are not merely observing their own society but are participants in it. And their participant role is not a hidden or separate one from their role as social scientist, but a complementary and even a symbiotic one with it. As ethically committed activists as well as social scientists straining toward the achievement of objectivity, we must take up the utopian task while maintaining our critique of it.

three

SOCIOLOGISTS AS PLANNERS
Edward E. Cahill

What does the sociologist have to offer to the urban planner or to the community that wants to participate in planning its future? Why have planners and community leaders made so little use of the insights of sociology? And what are the prospects for stronger ties between sociologists and urban planners that will be mutually rewarding? The essay that follows offers succinct and revealing answers to these questions, grounding them in the author's personal experience with an institute for environmental studies at a major eastern university. The critical review of the frustrations encountered in an action role is an indictment of the conventional way in which we teach sociology. Yet the account of limited success with a dynamic brand of applied sociology is encouraging; such successes point the way for reforming both the sociological profession and urban planning.

Plan or Be Planned for. This motto of the Mantua Community Planners, a grass-roots organization in the heart of a West Philadelphia ghetto area, characterizes the challenge and dilemma facing communities and public agencies throughout America today. It also epitomizes some of the problems that face academicians in all disciplines, as well as college and university administrators, regarding the relevance of academic curricula to societal problems.

The question today is not whether or not there is going to be a planned society but rather who is going to do the planning, what values will prevail, and at whose cost the plans will be implemented.[1]

More than thirty years ago Mannheim saw that as a result of vast technological changes, planning was a sine qua non for maintaining man's freedom. After describing three stages in social evolution, he states:

---

1. See Amitai and Eva Etzioni, eds., *Social Change Sources, Patterns and Consequences* (New York: Basic Books, 1964); and Warren G. Bennis, Kenneth D. Benne, and Robert Chin, eds., *The Planning of Change* (2nd ed.; New York: Holt, Rinehart & Winston, 1969).

Technique, while forcing us from tyranny of nature, gives rise . . . to new forms of dependence. All progress in technique is bound up with social organization. . . .

At the third stage, that of planning, freedom cannot consist in the mutual control of individual institutions, for this can never lead to planned cooperation. At the highest stage, freedom can only exist when it is secured by planning. It cannot consist in restricting the powers of the planner, but in a conception of planning which guarantees the essential forms of freedom through the plan itself . . . at the stage of planning, freedom can only be guaranteed if the planning authority incorporates it into the plan itself.[2]

Change in the Planning Profession

In searching for a definition of planning in various texts and journals, I was reminded of Furfey's working definition of sociology:

. . . that which is taught under that name in colleges and universities, that which is contained in periodicals, books, monographs and dissertations which profess to treat of sociology, and that which is presented before the meetings of sociological societies, in so far as such material can be classified as science.[3]

One need only substitute "planning" for "sociology" and "sociological" to have a definition of planning. Although descriptive, it is imprecise and borders on the tautological "Planning is what planners do" concept.

Petersen, after examining several definitions of planning, concludes, "So long as 'planning' can mean almost anything planners can both use the approbation the concept brings and avoid the limitations imposed by any single designation of function." [4] Perhaps no better definition may be found than that contained in Webster which defines "plan" as a "method or scheme of action, procedure or arrangement; project, program, outline or schedule."

Recent attempts to scientify ("make a science of") planning notwithstanding,[5] it remains essentially an action-oriented profession concerned

2. Karl Mannheim, *Man and Society in an Age of Reconstruction*, trans. Edward Shils (New York: Harcourt, Brace, 1935), pp. 373, 378.

3. Paul H. Furfey, *The Scope and Method of Sociology: A Metasociological Treatise* (New York: Harper & Brothers, 1953), p. 2.

4. William Petersen, "On Some Meanings of Planning," *Journal of the American Institute of Planners* 32, no. 3 (May 1966): 131.

5. See, for example, Alfred Kuhn, "Science, Models and Systems," in *The Study of Society—A Unified Approach* (Homewood, Ill.: Irwin and Donsey, 1963), pp. 27–54; Charles E. Lindbloom, "The Science of Muddling Through," *Public Administration Review* (Spring 1968): 79–88; Herbert A. Simon, *The Sciences of the Artificial* (Cambridge, Mass.: MIT Press, 1969); Martin Genberger, ed., *Computers and the World of the Future* (Cambridge, Mass.:

with making positive changes in society, especially in cities and urbanized regions. Originally oriented toward spatial location and "aesthetics of physical facilities and features," it is today, conceptually at least, "becoming much more comprehensive—incorporating economic, political, social, legal, environmental, communicative, and scientific-technological considerations far more than it has in the past." [6]

Because of a shift from the purely physical design, space-allocation orientation to a recognition of the social, economic, political, legal, communicative, etc., aspects of planning, there is an increasing need and expanding role for the sociologist in the field of planning. This need and elements of the role were pointed out by Gans in 1962 and again in his article on "Urban Poverty and Social Planning" in 1967.[7]

Historically, the groundwork for sociologists' participation in the planning process has been well established from the work of the early urbanologists,[8] through the thoughtful considerations of Mannheim,[9] to the work today of Gans,[10] Gutman,[11] Thomlinson,[12] Keller,[13] Eldredge,[14] and a host of demographers[15] who developed from sociological backgrounds.

MIT Press, 1962); and Highway Research Board, *Urban Development Models Special Report 97*, Publication 1628 (Washington, D.C.). See also, John W. Dyckman, "The Scientific World of the City Planners," *American Behavioral Scientist* 6, no. 6 (February 1963): 46–50; Britton Harris, ed., "Urban Development Models: New Tools for Planning" *Journal of the American Institute of Planners*, 31, no. 2 (May 1965).

6. Melville C. Branch, *Comprehensive Urban Planning* (Beverly Hills, Calif.: Sage Publications, 1970), p. 11. See also Mel Scott, *American City Planning Since 1890* (Berkeley and Los Angeles: University of California Press, 1969), esp. chap. 8, "Search for a New Comprehensiveness," pp. 554–653.

7. Herbert Gans, "Urban Poverty and Social Planning," in *Uses of Sociology*, ed. Paul Lazarsfeld, William Sewell, and Harold Wilensky (New York: Basic Books, 1967), pp. 437–76.

8. I refer especially to the work of Robert E. Park, E. W. Burgess, R. D. McKenzie, and the many fine students who examined and developed their work, including F. Thrasher, L. Wirth, Clifford Shaw, H. Zorbaugh, and others.

9. Esp. the previously mentioned *Man and Society in an Age of Reconstruction*; and Hans Gerth and Ernest K. Bramstedt, eds., *Freedom, Power and Democratic Planning* (London: Routledge & Kegan Paul, reprinted 1965).

10. Gans, "Urban Poverty"; idem, *The Urban Villagers* (New York: Free Press of Glencoe, 1962); idem, *People and Plans* (New York: Basic Books, 1968).

11. For example, Robert Gutman, "Site Planning and Social Behavior," *Journal of Social Issues* 22, no. 4 (October 1966): 103–15; idem, "A Sociologist Looks at Housing," in *Toward a National Urban Policy*, ed. Daniel P. Moynihan (New York: Basic Books, 1969), pp. 119–31; idem, "What Schools of Architecture Expect from Sociology," *Journal of Architectural Education* (March 1968): 69–83.

12. Esp. Ralph Thomlinson, *Urban Structure: The Social and Spatial Character of Cities* (New York: Random House, 1969).

13. Suzanne Keller, *The Urban Neighborhood: A Sociological Perspective* (New York: Random House, 1968).

14. H. Wentworth Eldredge, ed., *Taming Megalopolis*, 2 vols. (New York: Doubleday & Co., 1967).

15. Demographers are frequent consultants to planners because of the specificity of their knowledge and the belief in their ability to predict accurately population growth in given

Despite these pioneering efforts, I am continually amazed when I encounter students, professors, and planners in the field who are woefully ignorant of these works both regarding methodology and results.

Part of this ignorance is due to the admission procedures of Departments of City and Regional Planning which have not been overly balanced in favor of students or faculty with a sociological preparation (economics, political science, engineering, and architecture backgrounds predominate), but part is also due to the myopic view that many sociologists have taken toward planning both as an academic discipline and as a profession (probably because of its action orientation). This view is yet another replay of the pure vs. applied sociology conflicts, of the value-free, value-recognition dilemmas that have occupied so much of sociologists' time in the past.

Role of Sociologist in Planning

Planning, like sociology, is not value free.[16] Values, value conflict, and their resolution are an integral part of the planning process. While some planners have striven and will continue to strive for the primacy of the logos over the ethos, as with sociologists it will remain a state of "striving for" rather than "attaining" that goal. For indeed if the goal of rationality in the ordering of the universe is achieved, then, as Petersen points out, "planners will be unemployed" [17] (as will sociologists) for there will be no need for them.

One of the principal roles of sociologists' participation in planning is engagement in the process of identifying value differences and the opportunity to speak to the broader social implications of particular plans developed from them. Who is going to be affected by this or that plan? How are they going to be affected? Will a given plan improve the living conditions of the people thus affected, or will it force their removal and displacement to improve the physical appearance or infrastructure of an area while increasing the inequalities between income groups? These and

---

areas. Their results have tended to be incorporated in planning reports often without critical cross-examination. Unfortunately the techniques of demography are more effective in large-scale analysis than in small area prediction. The works of many demographers have been used by planners including those of Philip Hauser, Donald Bogue, Judith Blake and Kingsley Davis, Everett Lee, Otis Duncan, Amos Hawley, Dorothy Thomas, and many others too numerous to mention here.

16. Cf. Alvin W. Gouldner, "Anti Minotaur: The Myth of a Value-Free Sociology," *Social Problems* 9, no. 3 (Winter 1962): 199–213; Furfey, *Scope and Method of Sociology*, chap. 1, "The Nature of Metasociology," pp. 1–19, and chap. 4, "Metasociological Value Judgments," pp. 87–107. See also Paul H. Furfey, "Sociological Science and the Problem of Values," in *Symposium on Sociological Theory*, ed. Llewellyn Gross (Evanston, Ill.: Row, Peterson, 1959), pp. 509–30.

17. Petersen, "Some Meanings of Planning," p. 146.

many other similar questions reflect the value judgments which must be made in effectuating the work of the planners. They also reflect the type of questions the sociologist should try to answer with scientific objectivity.

Sociologists, by virtue of their methodological training and knowledge, have much to offer planners in their approach to these and similar social problems. Gans has outlined areas with regard to poverty programs,[18] but there are many other areas in which planners are "directly" involved that are virtually unaffected by sociologists even though the social implications of such planning are overwhelming. For example, decisions are made constantly about land use favoring one type of development as opposed to another—commercial vs. educational, revenue producing vs. revenue absorption, housing needs for selected groups (elderly, poor, minorities) vs. investment of financial resources in transportation systems or commercial developments, and so on ad infinitum, each representing value judgments and priorities of many powerful voices. The formulas used for making such decisions often are based almost completely on economic cost-benefit theories and/or political considerations devoid of sociologic or humanistic considerations. This may be due either to the failure to include such insights in the education of planners or of the "pure" sociologists' disdain for action and decision making in policy formation. Yet the definition of such situations still remains real in their consequences. What I suggest is that sociology bring a perspective to defining situations, a perspective that would be very valuable to the society as a whole if not to the particular interest groups that formulate plans. This perspective consists essentially in maintaining the objectivity of insight for which sociologists are trained.

Even as sociologists have developed specialized roles in the professional fields of education, crime and correction, law, medicine, social work, and industry, so, too is there a role for sociologists in planning and public administration. Legislative acts, following the trend established in the 1960s,[19] will probably enhance that role. It is inconceivable that major social legislation can be passed today without built-in protections for some element of community self-determination or control to reduce existing inequities. Following such legislation there will be increased intergroup relations and small community participation in planning. This will demand effective communication between community groups and public agencies, between professionals and laymen, between the "haves" and the "have-nots." Therein lies yet another role of the sociologist—or at least those with sociological training—viz., bridging the gaps, resolving value con-

18. Gans, "Urban Poverty," note 10, pp. 450 ff.
19. Esp. the Economic Opportunity Act of 1964, the Demonstration Cities and Metropolitan Development Act of 1966, and the pending Community Self-Determination Act.

flicts, comprehending and instructing (but not dominating or dictating), in a word, enhancing the democratization of planning because of an understanding of social processes and structures, functions and frustrations, behavior and rationale. Moreover, sociologists generally may offer critical appraisal of social facts and figures, of manifest and latent consequences of policies and critical examination of proposed programs of action. Finally, one of the greatest assets the sociologist may bring to planning is the systematic evaluation of programs and plans in terms of their goals, means, and effects. The objective analysis of successes and failures with feedback to planners and communities alike should be beneficial to both, as well as to the sponsoring agency.

University in Action Research

The position of action research by social scientists has been discussed at some length by Fairweather,[20] Sanford,[21] and others.[22] The marginal status of action researchers presents some difficulties in placing them in more traditional academic molds. Yet some place must be found for them in universities if objective, unrestricted action research is to be done.

One such attempt has been made at the University of Pennsylvania. In 1964, the Human Resources Program was established by the University to

> provide an administrative mechanism whereby the University could respond more effectively to the social and economic changes occurring in the urban community . . . supported by private and public funds, these activities shared a twofold objective: While serving an immediate and practical need, each was designed as a pilot project to provide increased knowledge about the complex human problems and interactions of our urban environment.[23]

When it became clear that the activities of the program had broad implications for teaching and research, the decision was made to bring the program into the Institute for Environmental Studies, the research unit of the Graduate School of Fine Arts. Simultaneously, Howard E. Mitchell, Ph.D., Director of the Human Resources Program, was appointed the

20. George W. Fairweather, *Methods for Experimental Innovation* (New York: John Wiley, corrected printing, 1968).

21. Nevitt Sanford, "Whatever Happened to Action Research?" *Journal of Social Issues,* 26, no. 4 (1970).

22. See Arthur B. Shostak, ed., *Sociology in Action* (Homewood, Ill.: Dorsey Press, 1966), esp. the essays by Otto G. Hoiberg, "Self-Help Planning in Small Communities"; Ritchie P. Lowrie, "Influencing Leadership in Community Studies: Moral and Political Roles of the Political Scientist"; and Carla Eugster, "Equipping Deprived Community to Help Itself."

23. Human Resources Center, Graduate School of Fine Arts, University of Pennsylvania. Printed leaflet, 1968.

university's first Professor of Human Resources in the Department of City and Regional Planning. Subsequently in 1968 the program was formally enlarged into the Human Resources Center. I was engaged as Coordinator of Field Services for the Center and appointed to the faculty in the Department of City and Regional Planning.

In the words of its director,

> the underlying thrust of the Human Resources Center projects has been toward developing notions about planned change which would indicate how public and private services might better serve a wider array of citizens. We have been particularly concerned with the role of the urban university as a factor in promoting social change and helping citizens to achieve their potential.[24]

In the three years since the Human Resources Center has been a part of the Graduate School of Fine Arts, our activities have revolved around relatively small area action-research projects, involving faculty, students, alumni, neighborhood and community groups, and some administrative offices of the university.

Included in these projects[25] have been:

—a research-coordination program studying the employment of minorities in the building and construction trades in Philadelphia, with a view toward developing a model plan for increasing the utilization of minorities in university and college building programs;

—an evaluative study of the Job Loan and Urban Venture Corporation of Philadelphia to determine the effectiveness of loans to minority entrepreneurs and a plan for improving the success of such entrepreneurs;

—a pilot research program to assist indigenous community leaders in strengthening their leadership capabilities and to learn from them ways in which professional training at the university may be made more effective in dealing with social problems at the community level;

—a training program in urban problems for suburban women to help them understand problems of growth and social change that they may become effective interpreters of constructive social change in their respective communities;

—the development of the Urban Workshop in the Graduate School of Fine

24. Annual Report 1969–70, Human Resources Center of the Institute for Environmental Studies.
25. Mimeograph reports on each of these projects are available through the Human Resources Center of the University of Pennsylvania. A brief description of each project is contained in the aforementioned Annual Report, 1969–70.

Arts of the University to provide a practical application of acquired knowledge to community problems.

In these programs we have been called upon to work cooperatively with architectural, planning, law, and social-work students, as well as neighborhood groups in developing plans for community enhancement in the Philadelphia area.

Personal Reactions

This interdisciplinary effort with persons ranging in degrees of sociological knowledge from scarce to fairly sophisticated has been both frustrating and fulfilling. Frustrating, because the generalities developed and acquired through years of studying sociological techniques and empirical studies have had, as often as not, little application to the concrete problems presented by community groups; frustrating, because many of the questions asked of sociologists by these groups have not been researched in any depth by professionals in the field and the paucity of knowledge has necessitated ad hoc research from individual groups; frustrating, too, because the desire and expectation for constructive social change among most community groups are constantly thwarted by the inability of institutions to respond to the needs of communities on either a small or large scale, be it in housing, education, gang control, job training, health care, or day care for children.

(The "power of the people" seems to lie less in its ability toward self-determination than in its ability to obstruct institutional controls, thus allowing institutional processes and bureaucracies to consume large sums of money without producing desired effects in impoverished communities.)

While the methodological training of sociology develops an ability to name and categorize problem areas of human involvement in social institutions, it does little to prepare for the frustrations involved in seeing communities unable to find the funding resources necessary to ameliorate prevailing conditions after problems have been categorized.

Academic sociology, while hinting at causal explanations for social problems in its quest for scientific objectivity, does not prepare the individual for the intricate machinations of policy makers and implementers that work at cross purposes to the social value of self-determination.

The complexities of corporate domination, legislation, litigation, and exploitation are easily avoided by sociologists too timid to investigate those areas where major decisions are made affecting the social fabric of our cities—the board or meeting rooms of planning commissions, financial institutions, large corporations, public utilities, and even existing governmental agencies. Thus, while attention is focused on maintaining scientific objectivity through the use of a great variety of sophisticated statistical techniques and methodologies, many key issues and decisions on a day-to-day basis escape our attention.

I do not suggest eliminating the tools of objective analysis that we have developed, but rather that sociologists need to ask and study questions much more relevant to impolite societal needs, however controversial they may be. It is much easier, if not more scientific, to discuss social questions at a very high level of generalization with limited data than to discuss those same questions as they may relate to a proposed policy decision in smaller areas such as a neighborhood, a community, a city, or a region, where much social data and many social groups are ignored.

Today, large segments of the planning profession are looking more for sociological analysis that is both rigorous and relevant—rigorous in the sense of maintaining methodological sophistication and objectivity, yet relevant to the particular problems being analyzed in small areas and regions.

It is in this latter aspect that elements of fulfillment and satisfaction have been achieved, for we have seen decisions favorably affected by presentation of facts derived from sociological analysis. We have seen communities drawn closer together as a result of objective presentation of data, and we have witnessed a new zest for self-determination in groups which had seemed defeated through the techniques of recounting the success of similarly thwarted groups which would not be defeated on specific issues. While elements of gratification are achieved from these small victories, a sense of estrangement from more academic sociology colleagues still remains for having participated in this action-oriented profession of teaching sociological analysis to planners.

four

ESSENTIALS OF AREA DEVELOPMENT
Otto G. Hoiberg

Nowadays the rural town struggles to hold on to a positive role for itself in a city-oriented society. This plight of rural America has been both grimly portrayed in the movie drama, "The Last Picture Show," and caricatured in the movie comedy, "Cold Turkey." The small town has been prematurely disregarded by unknowing urbanologists, whose neglect is both short-sighted and counter-productive. At present few are planning to coordinate answers to the needs common to cities and their surrounding towns. Immediate long-range planning for an "expanded community"—planning on an area-wide basis—is urgently called for. This essay provides such a model capable of wider application; for example, similar efforts would be appropriate in current attempts to democratize planning in areas where black ghettoes and white ethnic enclaves come together. The social-psychological obstacles to sound area planning are especially provocative because they are surely found outside the Great Plains centers discussed here.

It is said that nothing is quite so powerful as an idea whose time has come. The truth of this is undeniable, but it does not follow that a transformation of such an idea into actual practice is either automatic or assured.

For years we have been watching area economies developing, gradually but irreversibly, in the state of Nebraska. The state contains 30 municipalities of more than 5,000 inhabitants, about 508 incorporated cities and villages of not more than 5,000 population, and probably well over 300 small unincorporated places. Generally speaking, the places below 5,000 population have become more and more closely integrated with the larger trade centers in their respective areas, thanks to our age of increasing mobility and better communication. Some writers have referred to the resulting expanded complexes as "satellite systems," the larger trade centers constituting "growth centers," with many of the surrounding smaller towns (often declining) transferring function after function (high-school education, medical care, commercial recreation, and merchandising of many kinds) to the central cities. With every such transfer of function, the smaller towns in a given system inevitably have become more dependent upon the central city. What is happening is that new, enlarged "area communities" are taking shape.

Many small-town residents are vaguely aware of this long-term, slowly developing sociological phenomenon. They know full well that they must now go to the central city to buy a pair of shoes, see a doctor, get a prescription filled, or attend a movie, while in an earlier day these goods and services could largely be obtained at home. Nevertheless, they fail to realize that their growing dependence upon the larger trade center in actual fact makes them informal members of a much larger community. Similarly, they fail to sense that they have any responsibility for community planning as it relates to the larger area. Conversely, the central city, while enjoying increasingly closer economic and social ties with the surrounding communities, has a difficult time recognizing that its planning activities should therefore include active participation by its satellites.

In short, community planning tends to be restricted to traditional community boundaries, as these exist in the minds of people, and has not yet matured to the point where it really operates on an "expanded community" or area-wide basis. This is becoming a "cultural lag" of considerable proportions; and it seems that the community development specialist (change agent) would have a genuine contribution to make in helping people overcome it. If properly approached, the practice of area-wide planning will benefit both the central city and the surrounding smaller towns.

This lag of area-wide *planning* behind actual area-wide socioeconomic *development* is a cause for concern because it leads to less-than-optimum future development for an area, to say nothing of causing extra expense and difficulty in rectifying mistakes that could have been avoided by advance planning.

The Change Agent's Role

What can a community-development specialist do to encourage and facilitate sound community planning on an area basis, whether the area concerned encompasses (1) a "satellite" system centered about a relatively large trade center or (2) a group of communities or counties that constitute a logical entity for action on a specific problem? Experience to date indicates that a change agent must be conscious of the following essential responsibilities toward the communities with which he or she works in an advisory capacity:

1. *Endeavor to make them fully aware of the socioeconomic trends* that

are gradually merging them into larger, multicommunity social systems, and *help them to understand that area-wide planning must supplement local planning* if full potentials are to be realized. This is an adult-education task at the community level which entails careful study and discussion of such subjects as population trends, including migration; business and industrial development; consumer purchasing habits (goods and services); and the pattern of social interaction as a whole.

If the communities of an area are looking forward to engaging in a comprehensive planning program with the help of a professional planning consultant, the community-development specialist can perform a vital function by working with the planning commission(s) concerned in making some type of preliminary reconnaissance study of the area to point up socioeconomic trends, resources, needs, and problems that ought to be uppermost in their minds as they approach their planning program. Such reconnaissance study, in effect, constitutes a warmup exercise for the planning commission prior to the active appearance of the planning consultant. It gives the planning commission a "running start" and tends to assure that the plan developed by the consultant will be as nearly "tailor made" for the local area as possible.

2. *Help them to distinguish between the phases of community life for which planning and development should be considered on an area-wide basis and those which can be handled satisfactorily at the traditional local level.* At the poles of this continuum, the distinction is quite clear. It is obvious, for example, that one-room rural school systems can ordinarily not afford to provide special education for handicapped children. Hence multicounty Educational Service Units have been established throughout Nebraska, each of which has a sufficient number of school districts involved to hire specialized teaching personnel by pooling financial resources. It is equally obvious, on the other hand, that laying plans for and conducting a clean-up, paint-up, fix-up campaign in a village or city is largely a local matter. In between such extremes, however, are numerous facets of community development that are not readily analyzed in the local vs. area context. Will a cluster of communities gain more in tourist promotion, for example, by attacking the problem on a joint, cooperative basis or by going at it on their own, each competing against and trying to outdo the others? In such situations a social scientist, who recognizes both the objective and the emotional factors involved, can be of service. His help can take the form of analytical discussion, with or without related research activity, but leading to the adoption of realistic short-term and long-range goals.

The various units of an area-wide social system need help in understanding that sound area-planning is not a strategy whereby the central trade center is enabled more readily to develop itself, at the expense of the surrounding small towns. This misconception is widespread and needs to be corrected. The actual truth is that the small surrounding towns are in far greater danger of strangulation if the area develops in an unplanned manner (as has largely been the case hitherto) than if an effort is made by all communities, large and small, to study the evolving social system together and to work out an overall plan wherein the respective viable municipalities and/or counties have constructive and reasonably stable roles to fulfill.

It is not in the best interest of the central city to have its satellite communities wither into nothingness. An economically viable small town provides local purchasing power that influences favorably the business and professional life of the central city. However, it does not make sense for a village to continue to provide a business or professional service which it is not prepared to handle adequately. The ideal, though ever-evolving, arrangement is an integrated social system where each unit at any given time carries on the programs and provides the services for which it is best adapted and in which it has competitive strength. To encourage the development of this integrated whole is the purpose of area-wide planning.

3. *Conduct research,* both "pure" and "applied," which will strengthen the scientific foundation upon which area planning rests. Area-wide programs are growing rapidly in number throughout the nation, and a concerted effort must be made to study, analyze, and learn from them, both in terms of theory and practice.

In addition to conducting research programs on his own, a social scientist may cooperate with community leaders in structuring self-surveys that are to be carried out by local citizens under his guidance. This approach, where it can be employed, has the advantage of greater community involvement and normally leads to a more active local interest in the findings.

4. A logical and essential sequel to research activity is the *production of educational materials* based upon research findings. The community-development specialist has an obligation to translate findings from technical jargon into language that is comprehensible to the layman. Without such scientifically derived information in layman's language at hand, local community leaders are left with only a trial-and-error approach at their disposal. The latter is certainly an old and reliable standby, but it is often costly and discouraging; and the need for it recedes as dependable research data become available.

The principal media for transmitting "translated" research findings to community laymen include books, pamphlets, articles; films, filmstrips, color slides; tapes; the mass media; and personal consultation. To illustrate, the University of Nebraska Extension Division has recently issued a bulletin[1] intended to direct the attention of logical groupings of rural communities to the possibilities inherent in area-wide cooperation for recreation leadership. It describes, by word and diagram, a program in which public and voluntary agencies of five small communities pooled their financial resources to obtain professional leadership for their summer recreation programs in the whole area—leadership which had never been feasible under the former "each community for itself" approach. The bulletin will presumably serve a purpose in opening the eyes of villages and small cities to the possibilities of area-wide cooperation.

Similarly, the Nebraska State Office of Planning and Programming[2] and the University of Nebraska Extension Division[3] have each issued a small, attractive brochure on the COG (Council of Governments) concept, its rationale and basic structure. As a sequel to these, a more extensive bulletin has been published, describing ongoing COG programs in area-wide comprehensive planning, joint purchasing, code enforcement, law enforcement, economic development, and in a variety of other program areas which lend themselves to the area-wide approach.[4]

5. Since any type of area-wide program entails a new pattern of intercommunity relationships, there is a need to *tap the resources of group dynamics/sensitivity training*. If communities that have tried to work independently of each other in the past are now to engage in joint endeavor toward certain common ends, they need to become more sensitive not only to their own individual situations but also to the aspirations, problems, and special features of others. A change agent who is well versed in this subject area can be of immeasurable help to the communities involved by providing, formally or informally, a training experience that will enable them to work together more effectively.

6. Another respect in which a change agent—particularly a community-organization specialist—can be of assistance relates to the effort of a cluster of communities to *create a viable framework for joint action*. A professional who is conversant with the structures and procedures that characterize the different types of area-wide planning and/or action is invaluable to any group that is trying to organize along these lines. The types are many and diverse: councils of governments; area health planning

1. Robert M. Dula, "School District No. 145 Recreation Program," University Extension Division, University of Nebraska, Lincoln, Neb., October 1970.
2. "A COG Is Yesterday's Neighborliness Meeting Today's Challenge," State Office Planning and Programming, P.O. Box 946601, State Capitol, Lincoln, Neb.
3. Larry M. Hammer, "Councils of Governments—COG—Local Governments Working Together," University Extension Division, University of Nebraska, Lincoln Neb., 1971.
4. Larry M. Hammer, "COG—What It Can Do for You," University Extension Division, University of Nebraska, Lincoln, Neb., 1972.

councils; multicounty comprehensive planning commissions; educational service units; rural community-action programs (CAPS); metropolitan-area planning bodies; intercommunity recreation groups; and many others. There is a common core in all of these endeavors; but in any new program being established, it is important that the principal alternatives for organization and procedure be carefully scrutinized and evaluated before a final decision is made as to the specific approach to be used.

7. As society becomes more complex, the difficulty encountered by communities in *identifying relevant resources* grows apace. With a two-inch-thick catalog of federal financial aids and a host of agencies (in federal, state, local governments; institutions of higher learning; voluntary associations; and private enterprise) providing assistance in community development, where does a community or incipient group of communities start in its search for help? In many instances, particularly the smaller communities are overwhelmed at the very thought of trying to pinpoint the proper agency for guidance or financial aid; and so they struggle along without the helping hand that could have been theirs.

In view of this situation, a central clearinghouse of some type is essential—an agency to which communities can turn for information concerning the most appropriate channels for obtaining the kind of help that they desire. Any such clearinghouse should be as nearly unbiased and devoid of vested interests as possible and should not harbor the thought that referral to a more relevant agency will necessarily undermine its own position or prestige. Interagency competition often complicates the situation, but there are normally within governmental, university, or voluntary organizations certain offices of sufficiently low-key orientation to do the job.

8. Another type of educational assistance that can be performed by a community-development specialist is to maintain a continuing *"follow-up" relationship with the communities* which he has assisted. When a new council of governments (COG) has been organized, for example, the most critical period really lies immediately ahead. The real proof of the pudding lies not in the craftsmanship of its structural framework/constitution/ bylaws, important as this certainly is, but rather in the effectiveness with which the organization operates, once it becomes a going concern. In a new, serious-minded intercommunity organization, the honeymoon period is ordinarily very short indeed, as the various elements get down to the actual joint planning and action. Here again, a change agent who knows what it is all about can help the fledgling group gain its sea legs by maintaining close liaison with it until such time as it attains maturity.

9. A final input of the community "change agent" relates to *motivation*. Many smaller communities are running scared because of adverse trends to which they are subjected. They need reassurance to try anything new, such

as an area-wide approach to problems they traditionally have tackled independently.

There is much debate in community-development circles today as to the proper role of the outside professional change agent in regard to "motivation." At one extreme, the view is expressed that such an outsider should be purely a resource person who has no interest whatever in what the community decides about any proposal under consideration and who makes no effort to influence the decision in any way. At the other, one finds an activist approach which holds that the outside professional knows far better than the community leaders what action should be taken and that he has a right, if not an obligation, to try to sell them on his proposal even if this necessitates manipulation and maneuvering on his part.

The golden mean probably points the way to the most rational approach here. Certainly the professional has an obligation to share his knowledge concerning both the favorable and unfavorable features of any proposal under consideration. If the community wants a recommendation from him, there is ordinarily no reason why such recommendation should not be made; but in expressing his personal view, he should make it clear that it *is* his personal opinion and that, as an outside observer, he may not have the whole story. The important thing to remember is that it is not his function to sell them a bill of goods, using any sales strategy at his disposal. The ultimate decision must be made by the community itself, with all facts and viewpoints fully considered. A community will be motivated to creative action in a genuine sort of way when this situation comes to prevail.

Obstacles in the Community

The path to sound area development is beset with many obstacles. The problems undoubtedly differ in various parts of the United States, but the following have come to light in work with Nebraska communities and are probably rather prevalent in the Great Plains region.

1. *Rugged individualism.* The historic requirements of the western frontier, coupled with the Protestant ethic, have built into the very souls of the people in this region a belief that hard work is a virtue and that each man must stand on his own two feet. To be sure, this orientation has not precluded mutual aid for the common good, but the prevailing sentiment since earliest frontier days has nevertheless been one of individualism. This admirable spirit still exists, but it is being tempered by the logic of the social system that is evolving. Certain obvious benefits, not available today through independent effort, can now be gained through joint action. Comprehension of this fact is growing at a slow rate, however, and represents a psychological obstacle to area planning and action.

2. *Fear of statism.* Closely related to the foregoing is a rather widespread

belief that area planning may be primarily the brainchild of bureaucrats in Washington, D.C. This fear is quite understandable, in view of the prominent place currently afforded the area approach in funding federally supported projects. Many people at the grass-roots level realize, of course, that area-wide planning per se makes good sense; but much of the impetus for it has nevertheless hitherto come from the federal level. The latter fact alone, to say nothing of historic attitudes, is a cause for suspicion in the minds of many persons. Further, where federal funding is concerned, there is also the realization that a change of administration may pull the rug out from under any ongoing program.

3. *"Their gain is our loss."* Many years ago, at a meeting in a small Nebraska village, a little time was given to two representatives of the dominant trade center of the area to solicit help for a new hospital project, the proposed hospital to be located in their centrally located city. After the representatives had left, one of the local stalwarts voiced his opinion of the proposal as follows: "I'll give the very shirt off my back for anything that goes up in our own little town, but I won't donate a (censored!) penny to support a hospital or anything else for that town!" Similarly, it is often felt that a town has "lost out" to a neighboring community when a new industry decides to locate in the latter in preference to the former. People do not always seem to realize that hospitals, industries, etc., are usually regional in character and that they provide medical care, employment, and added economic strength for communities in the entire region concerned, regardless of the specific location of the facility.

4. *Difficulty in understanding the concept of a "community of communities."* "Ever since I can remember, the term 'community' has meant our own little village and surrounding trade area. It's hard now to begin thinking of ourselves also as a part of a larger 'community' including a whole cluster of towns in this area." The person who made this comment is at least on his way toward realizing that a certain duality is becoming necessary when he thinks about his "community." Others of his friends and neighbors cannot, or will not, begin to think in these terms.

5. *Identification of services and merchandise lines in which the small town can hold its own.* Ordinarily a good garage and service station in a small town will maintain a competitive advantage locally over a similar firm at some distance in a larger trade center, while the opposite will be true of a millinery shop; but if the small-town mechanic is a poor craftsman and charisma graces the milliner, exactly the reverse may be true. Generally speaking, however, certain types of business places have survival value in municipalities of different sizes. In a well-integrated "area community," this optimum distribution of business types has been successfully resolved; and the balance attained remains sensitive to the facts of economic life as they further evolve.

The typical small town, when invited to participate in a planning and action program involving a larger trade center, is often apprehensive and fearful that such participation may hasten the transfer of additional business and/or professional functions to the larger town. There is a feeling that area-wide planning may actually be a case of cooperating toward its own demise.

6. *Traditional rivalries, antagonisms, jealousies, and lack of confidence.* Some communities in a logical development area at times have emotional barriers that make cooperative effort toward common goals virtually impossible. It may be the memory of an historic battle over the location of the county courthouse that still sticks in the craw of the loser; or perhaps the athletic rivalry between towns is of such intensity that it spills over into intercommunity relationships in general.

7. *The misconception of planning as a "one shot" proposition.* Enthusiasm for area cooperation may initially run high among the communities of a given region. When the task of creating the organizational structure has been completed, however, there is a tendency to feel that "now the job is done." A multicounty planning commission, for example, may even go so far as to complete an attractively bound comprehensive plan with the help of a consultant before the satisfying, "mission accomplished" feeling makes its appearance.

It is really quite difficult for a group of communities to grasp the concept of planning as a *continuous process,* particularly if community planning has not been a part of their respective individual community traditions. Long-range, area-wide action is not feasible without area-wide planning.

8. *Lack of leaders trained for area work.* Years ago Robert Merton drew a helpful distinction between *local* and *cosmopolitan* influentials in the community. Effective as a "localite" may be in relation to issues concerning primarily his own community, it takes a leader with a bit of the cosmopolitan orientation to exercise leadership in area development. Contemporary trends in mobility and communications are undoubtedly increasing the number of cosmopolitan leaders in communities, large and small; but the supply, particularly in the smaller communities, is still somewhat less than adequate.

The following brief message, published by the Community Development office of the University of Nebraska Extension Division in the February 1970 edition of *Newsletter,* Nebraska Planning and Zoning Association, represents an effort to help local communities overcome some of the foregoing obstacles to area-wide planning and action.

AREA . . . OR AREA NOT?

The reader will please forgive the slight play on words in this title. It was perpetrated as an attention-getting device, to bring an increasingly urgent problem into brief focus.

During recent years, growing numbers of regional or area programs have appeared on the Nebraska scene: Vision-17; the Southeast Nebraska Joint Planning Commission; our twenty-six . . . designated Planning and Development Areas; the Blue Valley Community Action Program; the Metropolitan Area Planning Agency; and many others in fields such as health, recreation, agriculture, education, cultural activities, and so on.

This development is important because it holds significant potential for both urban and rural communities. In metropolitan settings, it provides a coordinated, orderly alternative to urban sprawl. In nonmetropolitan regions, it promotes constructive, functional relationships between small towns and pertinent larger growth centers, with each viable trade center regardless of size playing a role in an integrated whole.

It is by no means a foregone conclusion, however, that the area approach will work. Even though the organizational framework be perfect and the "paper" program flawless, the whole thing may still come to naught unless certain subtle, yet fundamental, ingredients are present. Some of these ingredients are reflected in the following questions, all of which should be of genuine concern to any cluster of communities tooling up to operate on an area basis. Let us paraphrase the foregoing title and ask: As a community, ARE YOU . . . OR ARE YOU NOT ready, willing, and able to:

1. Identify psychologically with the larger area community of which your own traditional community is becoming a part?

2. Sacrifice a bit of your sovereignty as a community, in the interest of decision-making regarding common goals established for the area as a whole?

3. Understand that a favorable development (e.g., a new industry or recreation facility) in one community may benefit all other communities in the area?

4. Bury the hatchet (personally and as a community) concerning destructive rivalries and antagonisms that may be a part of your tradition?

5. Distinguish between the goals of your community that should continue to be implemented locally and those which can be most effectively handled through an area-wide approach?

6. Work diligently and cooperatively at the challenging task of area development, assuming your full share of the responsibilities as well as enjoying your rightful share of the benefits?

7. Accept long-range community planning as a way of life?

If the communities of your area are negatively oriented on matters such as these, then they need further education (which the reader can help to provide) for successful joint pursuit of common goals. If, on the other hand, their reactions are positive, clearly the situation is conducive to progress.

The Future

As we evaluate prospects for the future in Nebraska, it is gratifying to observe that planning and action on an area basis are already underway on several fronts. These are occurring principally where the shoe pinches and/or where the benefits of area-wide cooperation seem rather obvious.

State-enabling legislation for intergovernmental cooperation of many types has been enacted during the past few years, and so there is no problem on the legal-authorization side. The job that now lies before our many towns, counties, and other public bodies is to catch a vision of the potentials for development that beckon through area-wide planning and action. The piecemeal experimentation that has been undertaken to date can and should become part of a broader, more highly integrated whole.

"I have a dream that my four little children will one day live in a nation where they will not be judged by the color of their skin but by the content of their character."

—Martin Luther King, Jr.

part two

RACE RELATIONS

Three high-tension matters preoccupy us in this section: What innovations can we offer to defuse explosive situations of racial and ethnic prejudice within many crucial public institutions such as school systems, planning programs, or police systems? How should we estimate the potential long-term effects of our handiwork? And what should be our next step?

Many sociologists believe that racial and ethnic tensions will increase during the 1970s. Some contributory factors will be the anger of the hard-core black unemployed, the status anxiety of the white laboring class, the defensiveness of white middle-class suburbanites, the inflammatory political rhetoric of white supremacists and black separatists, the apparent impotence of liberal integrationists, and the ineffectiveness of political accommodations. Added to these persistent sources of tension will be the present federal executive administration's opposition to busing schoolchildren to achieve racial integration or balance and the potentially reactionary judgments of the Supreme Court.

Nevertheless, one can find hopeful signs in the sharp decline in property riots in recent years, the sharp rise in black political effectiveness (including officeholding in the South), in Representative Shirley Chisholm's 1972 presidential primary campaigns, in perceptive media coverage of increasingly rare instances of racist crime (e.g., police brutality, wanton murder of law-enforcement officers), and in the new soberness in white-black relations generally (the white ethnic revival has "Archie Bunker" join in black advocacy of cultural pluralism).

It is all too clear that the situation in 1974 is ripe for new turbulence. Will the planners of our economy ignore the special needs of minorities? Will the political strategy of the administration devalue minority support? Will new charismatic leaders arise? Will the 1976 bicentennial celebration of the American Revolution help to bring the citizenry together? Racial and ethnic tensions will make new demands on the applied sociologist. They will bring new opportunities for sociologists to help remedy the legitimate grievances of the Archie Bunkers, to develop new plans for the regional integration of vital social services, and in dozens of other ways to contribute to resolving our fundamental American dilemma.

five

STRATEGY FOR CHANGE: BRISTOL TOWNSHIP SCHOOLS
Thomas J. Cottle

How do you help keep the lid on a racially tense situation and at the same time promote planned change in the direction of more humanistic race relations? Significantly helpful in such an endeavor is the human-relations training laboratory, a variation of sensitivity training that focuses on improving work efficiency among colleagues, for example, among a school staff, a city-hall staff, or a police force, in a racially strained setting. This study of one such laboratory examines at length the strategy of concentrating on breaking down the major resistance to change in the organization's personnel. It gives particular attention to techniques that can help the change agent combat defensiveness, fear of exposure, and feelings of guilt on the part of the lab members. Using role modeling, group interviewing, and other such techniques, participants in the lab increase their self-awareness; their problems are displayed openly so that they can be assessed and corrected. Controversial and demanding, the human-relations training laboratory has been steadily gaining support across the nation.

The civil-rights movement, in recent years, has sparked many efforts to improve school programs and to change the learning environment for both white and black students. Most of these attempts have failed, or have succeeded only marginally. It has become increasingly clear that promoting change in the schools, as in other social institutions, is a far more difficult task than anticipated. The enormous inertia of "the system" seems to defeat all but the most determined and ingenious efforts. A strong commitment to change by a few teachers or administrators in a school system is rarely enough. Rather, it appears that before fundamental reform can take place, all school personnel must be involved in a concentrated effort to remove both personal and institutional resistance to change. One such program that holds high promise for success is taking place in Pennsylvania, just north of Philadelphia.

For the majority of travelers, Bristol Township is merely the inevitable town adjoining the toll booth on the Pennsylvania Turnpike just before entering or immediately after leaving New Jersey. But to the people who live there it is much more.

This sprawling bedroom community contains most of Levittown's 17,000 homes and a population of more than 67,000. Many of the community's husbands and fathers commute to Philadelphia, twenty-one miles to the south, or to Trenton, roughly the same distance to the north. Of the township's 21,000 children, 14,000 attend the public schools, and, therefore, come under the watchful eye of Superintendent Knute Larson and his associates in the Harry S. Truman School Administration Building. About 7 percent of these students are black, but more significantly, enough of the township's families live at a level of poverty to entitle the district to aid under Title I of the Elementary and Secondary Education Act, which provides federal funds for the education of the disadvantaged.

Bristol Township—not to be confused with the town of Bristol—remains essentially a working-class community. Its racial and ethnic tensions are heightened by its proximity to Philadelphia and Trenton with their larger and more militant groups. It is a community that many people point to as "backlash prone"—the kind where racial problems can explode at any moment. The township made nationwide headlines in 1957 when families bitterly swarmed around the first Levittown home to be occupied by a black family while other neighbors stationed themselves on the front lawn pledging protection to the family inside. But the township is fortunate that its educational leaders are aware of the need for social and educational change if the tensions of contemporary society are to be lessened. Superintendent Larson, a large, raw-boned, pragmatic man, is skeptical of fashionable panaceas in education, but he is also sensitively aware of the community's problems. As a result, a number of fundamental actions have been taken to make the schools more responsive to all elements in the community.

First, the township built fifteen public schools (as well as four parochial schools) during a seven-year period. It also established an "opportunity class" for students who were disciplinary problems in an effort to return them to their regular classes, and launched a community-school program offering a wide variety of activities for both children and adults in a school that remained open from 8:00 A.M. to 10:00 P.M., six days a week, twelve months a year.

Second, it reassigned students in some schools when it became obvious that the overcrowding of black students in two schools was intolerable to both parents and teachers because of increasing disciplinary problems and generalized hostility. Black students were bused, without significant opposition, to less crowded, predominantly white schools. Indeed, the board of education was unwilling to perpetuate institutions where the disadvantaged grew nowhere together.

Third, the school district formed an Intergroup Education Committee that worked on curriculum changes, and then turned to an examination of the racial conflict in the community that gradually had grown to dangerous proportions. These tensions weren't omnipresent, but they were persistent and troubling. There was talk, for example, of militant community organizing going on in one black neighborhood, night fights between police and students, and an invasion of activists from Philadelphia and Trenton "stirring up unrest" in the three areas where Negro concentration is highest. Then came the action.

The story at Franklin Delano Roosevelt Junior High School began on a date few whites could remember. Blacks, however, recall the day as the anniversary of Malcolm X's death. On that day thirteen students refused to attend their homerooms. They proclaimed it a holiday and insisted that their parents wanted them home. Phone calls revealed that some mothers were confused, but all wanted their children at school. The students persevered, the principal gave them a choice, and they left, their strength and support growing. Temporary suspensions were issued immediately, but within a few days the students had returned, and the social temperature of Bristol Township climbed.

The second eruption came some months later in the second week of May 1968, soon after Martin Luther King's assassination. A black girl "bucked the line" in the cafeteria. A white teacher ordered her to go back, and—wham! She hit the teacher. Two other girls rushed to the student's defense. The three were suspended, one for the entire year. The black community was aroused. "To hear the black leaders, you'd think the teacher hit the girl with her chin," someone recalled. A group of Hell's Black Cobras, young adults, eighteen to twenty-five, snarled about the school grounds. Eventually the police entered the school grounds, and black leaders, too, intervened. Everyone was tense.

In the main, the police seemed unhappy with their charge of admitting only "proper personnel" to the schools, the teachers ambivalent about the presence of outsiders, the black community upset over the perceived Uncle Tomness of their leaders who seemed to be selling them out. The black students were exploding with demands for reinstatement of their sisters, more black teachers and counselors, and changes in the dress code.

The situation was bad, but it could have been far worse. What helped was the sensitivity and understanding shown by administrators and teachers in their negotiating with students, parents, and community leaders. Somehow, punishment seemed far less important to them than communication, and somehow, too, these administrators and teachers seemed humanly prepared for the situation.

Behind their preparation was a valuable experience with a human-relations training program from which the Intergroup Education Committee was an offshoot. The education leaders of Bristol Township had discovered the efficacy of this kind of training and during the winter of 1967–68 had asked Professor Max Birnbaum of the Boston University Human Relations Laboratory in New York City to develop a human-relations training program for the school district.

Public attention has focused increasingly, in recent months, on various approaches to "sensitivity training," and as public interest has grown, so has the confusion over just what such training is all about. There are, in fact, a number of different brands of sensitivity training, each with its own objectives, techniques, and outcomes in personal and institutional change. Professors Robert Chin and Kenneth D. Benne in their study, *The Planning of Change*, identify three different approaches. The first, based on the now traditional T-group (Training-group) experience, is designed to produce personal growth, understanding, and development. The second, aimed primarily at developing better intergroup relations, seeks understanding through radical confrontations in which members of hostile groups express their feelings, often in violent fashion, in an effort to encourage mutual understanding.

In contrast to an emphasis on personal growth and development, the third approach stresses interpersonal understanding aimed at improving work efficiency among employees or colleagues. It is this latter approach that Professor Birnbaum and his staff at the Boston University Lab employ.

The training program Birnbaum and his colleagues developed for Bristol Township's schools was based on several clearly defined assumptions about the nature of change and the ways in which resistance to change—both personal and institutional—can be overcome. First, the training program must be strongly and consistently supported by the district's educational leaders—the superintendent and his top staff. Second, the program must include the entire school community. The superintendent, his staff, and the entire teaching force must participate; ideally the program should include important lay members of the community as well. Piecemeal efforts at reform addressed to small groups within the educational system—a limited number of teachers, for instance—cannot be effective. As Birnbaum has written, "no institutional change will occur until all, or nearly all, of the individuals who must implement change have accepted the need for innovation." Third, training must be focused on personal growth *for organizational adaptation to change*, rather than on personal growth alone. This is a program of applied human-relations training that seeks simultaneously to remove both institutional and personal resistance to change. It is focused, therefore, on actual problems faced by individuals in their respective schools rather than on a therapeutic approach to individual development. In this way, participants not only become more conscious of the sources of their own attitudes and actions on the job but also come to appreciate more fully the pressures—both personal and institutional—that influence the actions of their colleagues.

Unlike some sensitivity training, the questions and problems to be explored become highly specific. The group experiences emphasizing interpersonal sensitivity and personal growth do not pretend to deal with educational change in socially charged areas. The currently fashionable "touching and feeling groups," for example, or the more traditional T-groups in which issues of authority and intimacy are "explored" and "worked through," are not necessarily dysfunctional, but seem less suitable for the needs of most school systems requiring change. It is Birnbaum's belief, moreover, that, at this point in our history, "confrontation sessions" where angry blacks intimidate whites are no longer as functional as they may have been two or three years ago. The growing resistance of whites to the black challenge today tends to reinforce the natural defensiveness induced by such sessions, and makes participants even less willing to accept change or to see the confrontation in the context of daily school relationships.

It is for these reasons that a complete-school-system approach is stressed, and emphasis is placed on specific professional problems. The overarching strategy is to work on major resistances to change in all school personnel. Where prejudices reinforce the status quo, they must be gently exposed, and then examined as part of the normal human condition to reduce the defensiveness, the fear of exposure, and the feeling of guilt. They can then be dealt with in terms that will make some change possible. The major goal of the laboratory sessions, therefore, is to help administrators and teachers reduce their fears of (and resistance to) "appropriate" and "needed" changes in teacher-administrator, teacher-student, and administrator-student relationships.

The plan for Bristol Township called for each of approximately 800 people (700 staff and 100 community representatives) to participate in one of two kinds of training groups. For selected school administrators, teachers, and principals, five-day workshops centered on skills in leadership and special sensitivities for handling so-called minority-group problems. According to the plan, these people would return to their schools where they would act as trained cadres working "actively to create a climate of mutual respect and good will [and also make] themselves available to staff, students, and the school community when problems arise in the human relations areas."

These cadres were to be the nucleus to which teachers subsequently going through training sessions would orient themselves. The cadre members were chosen in part because they were neither ultraconservative nor excessively liberal in their racial attitudes. Their job is a difficult one, for as one teacher suggested in laughing over the seeming impossibility of modeling himself after his instructor, "we were supposed to be miniatures of Birnbaum, 'mini-Maxes,' as it were."

Two-day workshops were designed for all other school personnel as well as selected parents and community leaders, including members of the police force. Ideally, even these quickie sessions would "heighten staff awareness of human relations problems," and increase the individual's capacity "for dealing with tensions and incidents that arise from majority-minority relations."

Here, then, lay not only a plan for dealing with unrest but a rather representative example of the majority of American schools' reaction to it and a circumscribed philosophy for treating it. Presently, the name of the game is to reduce racial incidents, avoid police intervention, keep schools open, and ameliorate as best as one can situations where "overly angry" demands result in harsh disciplining. Some argue that modern techniques such as group sessions maintain the status quo, and hence merely lessen the frequency of beatings and expulsions. Others feel that perhaps these techniques are a first step in real change, change that might mean the birth of new programs, new curriculums, new life. Still others can't see any connection between the techniques, as elaborate as they may appear, and radical community change that ultimately would render violent protestations obsolete and human-relations training laboratories comically anachronistic.

A two-day workshop last April, which I attended as an observer, was typical of the abbreviated training sessions. No one could tell for sure just what thoughts entered the minds of the thirty people who assembled that Thursday morning in the large dining room on the second floor of a Bristol motel. About nine o'clock in the morning they came, a bit nervous, to commence whatever it was they were about to commence. The group consisted of sixteen teachers, one principal, eight district education specialists such as librarians and music teachers, and five laymen from the community. It was a group with mixed background and experience. For instance, there were teachers for whom Negroes, and Jews, and the very concept of welfare were totally foreign before their arrival in Bristol not so many years earlier. Others had lived their whole lives in the community.

Slowly they chose chairs placed around tables arranged in a large rectangle with the center open. In front of them were name cards, and at one end, in casual dress, sat their two leaders, Birnbaum and his associate, Jim Small. Along one side of the room a waitress arranged coffee, tea, and sweet rolls on a small table. I sat removed from the group, but still in full view.

To describe in detail what transpired in the course of the next two days would be a violation of ethics, a disclosure of materials that are confidential. Without breaking a trust, however, some things may be reported.

Max and Jim, as they were instantly called, spent the entire first day, from nine in the morning until ten at night, interviewing all thirty people, one by one. The purpose of the interviews was twofold: to offer the participants an opportunity to introduce themselves to the group and give some idea of their background, and to start building a group agenda by identifying those problems and issues in the school and community that each felt to be important. The individual interviews within the group setting, as all the others listen, make it easier to speak of ethnic and racial differences and attitudes without some of the tensions normally felt in everyday social intercourse. They also help the participants to understand how influential their own religious and ethnic backgrounds have been in shaping their attitudes and actions—and how diverse these backgrounds are. And, finally, the interviews bring out personal information that helps to generate mutual trust among individuals, and contributes to the growing cohesiveness of the group.

Reluctant, at first, to reveal much of themselves, the participants were influenced, persuaded, and sometimes prodded into speaking more freely. Occasionally an important aspect of the interviewing technique would involve "role modeling," in which the leaders honestly admitted to their own prejudices, ambivalences, and insecurities, and thereby helped participants admit to their failings and uncertainties. Gradually, as trust developed and the leaders revealed so much of themselves, the others could not help but speak of the poverty they had experienced, their anger at being called a wop or a kraut, the brittle tensions between people of hard- and soft-coal mining regions, their ambivalence toward blacks, or toward young people generally. They spoke too, in these interviews, of trying to be fair with all students, taking and treating them one by one as they came along, and of their assurance that prejudice is learned in the home, rarely in the school.

Ideally, group interviewing brings out the singular identity of each participant, only to have these identities merge into a web of enduring trust and promise for change. A delicate technique, group interviewing requires a special skill in encouraging openness while avoiding psycho-therapeutic kinds of intervention. The personalities and temperaments of the leaders, perhaps even their charisma, may be essential energy that ignites and maintains the force of such a procedure. But the energy is clearly wasted if for even a moment the objective of change within the context of school is lost or submerged. For the goal is not sensitivity training for personal growth, but is always problem oriented.

As the participants' confidence in each other increased, others joined in the interviewing, reacting, probing, asking, seeking new understanding. Gradually the discussion turned to the inevitable tensions of black and white, rich and poor, old and young, male and female, teacher and student, parent and child, single and married, and always the leaders seeking the sources of conflict, without opening personal scars. Just enough so that by the next day one could ask about such matters as interracial dancing and dating, or could describe one's own experience with prejudice. Just enough persuasive joking and nagging, advancing and receding, to make it almost possible to imagine what it is like to be the single black person in a classroom, the boy called kike, or the girl not asked for a date. Just enough to permit people to tell why regulations mean so much, and why manners and order often overshadow human expansiveness, creativity, and adventure in the classroom.

A noticeable relief spills into the room when the leaders consent to a coffee break or lunch time or Coke time. Somehow the group, the all-of-them-together, has been born. The hours since the morning now mean history, the medium for recollection and trust. The hours in the future mean the moment when the interviewing radar will get to oneself. In the afternoon, television and newspapers are blamed for exacerbating racial tensions, which now, like a theme or irrepressible melody, dance in and out of the discussion, returning unexpectedly under topics like athletics or the meaning of manhood.

Just before dinner, members of the group turn to speak of their home towns where prejudice rarely existed, or at least was unrecognized. They also speak of a town's Jew Hill or its Italian ghetto. Then the undercurrent of blackness-whiteness returns. It comes back in terms of social mobility, ethnic groupings, patronage systems, rural-urban comparisons, and status inconsistencies, and the leaders spend a moment lecturing on the multiplicity of values endemic in a pluralistic society.

During the evening session, as the men and women in the motel bar below sip drinks and speak of themselves and perhaps the world, discussion in the group upstairs returns to racial tensions. The group is just now starting to label differences and "get these differences out on the table." The leaders move with special prudence, abiding by their own sense of where one can push and where one cannot. They hunt focal persons, all the while watching for others who listen more to one member than to another. Aware of the resistances, they work to pump the bubbles of energy and understanding out from the wells of self-consciousness. For the moment, however, the group moves slowly. People are tired, anxious to leave, forgetting momentarily that tomorrow means resuming.

Fresh the next morning, "old friends" convene, some seeking new seating arrangements almost as if their identities might somehow be strengthened in a different location. They are quickly at work, the discussions more open, more penetrating, their anger and defiance direct and exposed, their resistance melting a bit around the edges. The focus is on immediate problems, with the long and revealing experience of the previous day providing understanding and a context for specific issues. They are back at a brand of work they had never known, with an energy and drive that seems to them almost magical. Soon it is afternoon. Participants seem to be sensing the end, the pieces begin to fit together. Abruptly, a discussion of prayer in the public schools explodes. Everyone's talking. They've caught on. They've gotten it. It has taken many hours and four coffee breaks, but suddenly they are appreciating human differences and needs and the fact that while some men will kill to eliminate these differences, others might kill just to preserve them. They're listening, laughing, making sure they don't forget certain special phrases.

Then it is over. Some are glad to leave. Max and Jim have shaken hands and departed. Everyone moves out, trying to figure out just what has happened in these upstairs rooms—and whether the future will be altered by these two days.

To speak later with teachers is to learn that for some the impact of the experience doesn't diminish even months afterward. For the cadres, the effect remains uncertain and the feeling of inadequacy endures. "But still we've got to do something. At least things have been put on the table, and we can speak openly of black and white issues." Although their immediate concerns lie primarily with race, the effect of social class, religion, and ethnic differentiations are also more clearly understood.

Reactions to these groups are yet to be studied systematically. On the basis of a few conversations, it seems that some find the experience too blunt, wasteful, and irrelevant. Others find it valuable, useful, morale building, though anxiety provoking. Many teachers argue that the training groups have been instrumental in bringing some schools over a hump of racial unrest. And many, too, point to the dramatic example of Joe Ruane as one "who got a lot out of the group."

Joseph John Ruane, the principal of FDR Junior High School, did indeed get a lot out of the group. The story of the change in "Karate Joe," as he once was called, is far from typical; it almost borders on the apocryphal, and no one treasures this more than Joe. It was in his office that the suspension of the three girls took place. It was in his schoolyard that police stalked about keeping the Cobras away from an already "too tense situation."

Years ago, Joe Ruane was a tough man, a man who'd just as soon shove a kid up against a locker as speak with him. There were no discussions, no negotiations with Karate Joe in those days. The door to his office stayed tightly shut, opening only for disciplinary problems. Then a teacher would come in, complain or cry, and Joe would storm out to settle the matter. But no more. Discipline problems persist naturally, but Joe Ruane has changed. His door stays open, and when he cannot negotiate with tolerance, he's likely to turn to an assistant principal "who'll inevitably be seen by the kids as 'Mr. Nasty.' "

More often, however, Joe will turn over discipline problems to his Intergroup Advisory Council, a group of twenty-two thoughtful ninth-graders. Several times this past year, this group of black and white students has had to make serious decisions regarding school disruptions. Once it was about fighting in the halls, another time skirmishes after basketball games. In both cases, the council, given full control by Ruane and teacher Arnold Hillman, who sits as faculty representative, devised disciplinary procedures that worked.

To generate the council, Ruane, Hillman, and science teacher Albert Ulbinsky—all graduates of the five-day leadership workshop—aided several student leaders in planning a general student election, replete with area redistricting in order to achieve greater black representation. In the end, fifteen whites and eight blacks were elected. The actions of the council, their deliberations over drug taking, racial unrest, smoking, quality of teaching, and physical discipline have been their own, not their advisers'. A highly respected group, it remains eager to tackle any school problem from the Cobras to filth in the cafeteria.

"No one used to be more bullheaded than I," Joe will announce publicly. "The muscle worked. Now I see it's bad. I can deck 'em, but it isn't going to prove anything except that the kids are right about the Establishment." Apparently others agree. When flare-ups occurred at a neighborhood school last spring, the principal asked Ruane to speak with the parents. Quite a tribute from one principal to another.

The story of Karate Joe is told with relish in Bristol Township as dramatic proof of the effectiveness of the human-relations program, but Birnbaum demurs. "Obviously," he says, "such a miraculous conversion was a long time in preparation. Joe Ruane just happened to be ready for change, and his training group showed him how. There's nothing magical in human-relations training—if there were, we would have to be suspicious of it."

As dramatic as the story of Joe Ruane is, another event provides better evidence of the social efficacy of the program. During a 1969 football game between archrivals Woodrow Wilson and Bishop Egan, several black youths were arrested for stealing. Presumably they had snatched purses and then had been seen "walking mysteriously" through the parking lot. The police arrived and seven persons were arrested. Five of these, juveniles, were released in custody of their parents. Another two were given disorderly-conduct charges; in addition, one was charged with resisting arrest and threatening a police officer. Bail for him, originally set at $2,000, was reduced substantially after black leaders intervened.

The incident, however, was handled gently and compassionately by teachers and administrators. They were able to "hang loose" and let "the kids" handle their own behavioral reactions within the schools. After a fretful weekend in which adult activists tried to stir up action in the black community, it was the students, on Monday morning, who resolved the problem. They ran closed meetings to discuss the issues, inviting school and community officials as they saw fit. The situation was touch and go, but it never did erupt. A sufficient number of students had developed faith in the fairness of some administrators and teachers to resist the call for militant action.

Despite these promising results, for Knute Larson the Bristol Township experiment can never be totally successful. "The training groups," he says, "can do just so much." Many problems do remain. The cadres are constrained by their lack of experience in human-relations work and by other teachers' natural resentment at being "guided by their colleagues."

Larson doesn't fear dress styles, music fads, beads, granny glasses, underground newspapers, long hair, or even Students for a Democratic Society. He's proud of the 35 percent of Woodrow Wilson High School graduating seniors who go on to some form of higher education, and the fact that Bristol Township is willing and able to hire good teachers, black and white. The content of his apprehension is predictable: "Things are bad, let's face it. Nobody is doing anything about the cities, and if they go down, we will all go with them. At least we're trying to do something about our problems."

More generally, results of programs like the one in Bristol Township are always tentative, always in balance. As they say on almost every campus, "things could blow next week." So far the approach taken has worked, racial tensions have not erupted even in areas where hostilities and anger lurk almost everywhere, but no one can yet claim that the training groups significantly reduce individual prejudice, though they do seem to increase awareness and get the problems "out in the open" where they can be seen and discussed. Hopefully, this means that little-understood attitudes and feelings will not continue to control individual behavior and organizational decisions. One must ask whether political and social institutions will reinforce these changes, or will work to maintain that status quo the groups have sought to challenge. Social change is difficult to bring about, but it just may be occurring in Bristol Township.

six

THE SCENT OF WORDS: BRISTOL TOWNSHIP TWO YEARS LATER
Thomas J. Cottle

Do the effects of sensitivity training persist? The question whether sensitivity training exercises have any lasting effects is asked often and urgently, and with fairness. Two years after the Bristol Township laboratory discussed in the previous essay was conducted, Thomas Cottle contacted some key participants in that lab and prepared this unique follow-up report. Although the human-relations training seems to have "taken," the report raises still more questions. It considers the efficacy of our follow-up research in general—or more commonly, the lack of any follow-up research; it points to the intransigence of racism and the durability of racial tensions; and it finds in sensitivity training an unnerving "surrealistic something" that always seems to undercut success in programs for social change. Laboratory training definitely seems to be a useful tool for social change and to offer "a harvest of personal sensitivity and renewed awareness." Much more than this is asked of all of us in race and ethnic relations, however, if we are to banish oppression from our society and rehabilitate our brotherhood.

"Tell me one thing," I was once asked by a young man in a ghetto area of Boston. "Do you ever come back? I mean, when you've finished with whatever you do, will you come back?" A woman living in a community not far away had wondered the same thing: "Would you ever visit me when it gets a little easier for you? Then we could just talk. You could bring your wife maybe, and let me know what it is you do for a living. Surely you have other friends than the people here in Dorchester."

There is perhaps, a certain feeling of abandonment lurking in these sentiments. Each of us, in the manner, really, that lives are led, do our work and move on. I often think as I see a construction worker or a carpenter immersed in his trade, Does he get so attached to one job that he finds it difficult to leave it upon completion? Do psychiatrists dread the termination of a patient? And who returns to check up on a job, or to inquire about the welfare of someone we once called a client, or an acquaintance, the someone who provided the material for a research report or article?

It has been more than two years since I visited Bristol Township, Pennsylvania. Funny, while many of the recollections remain intact, I am barely able to place the year, or even the time of year of that trip. I had not the barest idea of what evolved in that community. I thought about the people there occasionally, and about the efficacy of the program, and, of course, about Max Birnbaum. Yesterday I called Bristol and asked to speak with Knute Larson, the superintendent of schools. "He no longer works here," came the response. "Would you like to speak with the present superintendent, Mr. ———?" Frank Daly, too, the principal of Woodrow Wilson High School, had left the area, apparently joining Knute in Massachusetts, but most of the others remained. Many had new positions. Many who had pledged to leave or to move up still occupied their former jobs. Still, merely to inquire about these people made me feel a bit complicated. Had I not, after all, written my story and moved on?

Programs of community social change, amelioration, whatever one calls them, are rarely undertaken by outsiders. It is the people who stay—I almost wrote, stay back—who sustain them. Often the gist of a program, its execution or ideology, dies not from a lack of interest or effort, but because what has been imposed cannot possibly be furthered by the people for whom it was initially prescribed. Elitism, self-aggrandizement, ignorance of areas, of people, of history, often combine to produce gorgeous plans which, when actualized, fit a community of human beings about as poorly as, well, a disheveled slum house fits the dignity and needs of civilized people who happen to be poor.

In Bristol Township, the human-relations training seems to have taken, almost as a skin graft might cover a gaping tear. Max Birnbaum's own work was concluded shortly after the time of my own visit. Since then the program has been expanded, or so some reported. The original cadre and its new trainees now run the groups, and all new teachers in the district, eighty-three last year, are obliged to undergo a two-day sensitivity session prior to the commencement of the school year. In-service training has also been expanded. The Intergroup Council for parents and young people continues with Arnold Hillman assuming a greater leadership role in the coordination of this work. Hillman is the new assistant principal at Woodrow Wilson.

Where the program has evidenced its most significant expansion, however, is in the realm of training for "biculturalism in the classroom." The problem, as one old friend remarked, came down to, "What do I do in this bicultural classroom in which I now am as sensitive as hell?" To aid teachers, Professor David Crabb of Princeton was engaged by the school district to work on anthropological issues of biculturalism. Frank Updike from Trenton State was brought in to teach black history to teachers. Updike is white. Where Max brought humanity into the schools, the focus now has turned to content. David Riesman too spent time in the region working with teachers on the problem of classroom content and curriculum. And Jim McGoldrick, who once headed the office of federal grants, is now totally involved with curriculum. The human-relations program, incidentally, is presently funded solely by district resources. The Title IV-B stipend was actually renewed one year, but the government had made it clear that this original money was to be used for launching the program, not for the continuous underwriting of it.

And so the work that began three or four years ago, the work of human beings that I witnessed in this one small portion of eastern America, is very much alive today, although the tension between the races is hardly to be dissipated by any T-groups or training courses in black history. As much as we might wish, social structures, national politics, and a form of racism that pervades our culture are not about to give way to earnest sentiment or even dedicated local-community work. Not yet, anyway.

Last year there was a riot at Woodrow Wilson High School. Seven people were hospitalized because of what was called "You know, the general racial business." No one, naturally, can re-create the history and the enormous number of events which, like arrows, come together to rip apart a school and those who gather there, for whatever purposes, five days a week. Some of the factors had to do with demands made by militants, as they are always called, who gained control of the local NAACP office. Principal Daly told the group that many of the demands were not in his purview. He had nothing to do, for example, with the hiring of teachers, black or white. On a Wednesday morning ten black students had entered his office to recite their demands. Daly arranged for a meeting with school board members and district officials to be held on Friday. at that time, with everyone properly introduced, one student rose and read a statement indicating that talk was useless and that the blacks were leaving. On Monday morning, police arrested forty-five black students, including the original ten. The NAACP officers demanded that the school board respond publicly to a host of demands. Accepting the challenge, the board announced that there were more black teachers in the district than in the entire county. As for black literature, the board happily reported that the State's Human Relations Commission had recently visited Bristol Township seeking suggestions for a bibliography in light of their fine collection.

Of course, during the time, the Ku Klux Klan was somewhat active too. They founded a junior group, soliciting membership from among high-school students, and drove around in black communities shooting kids with B-B guns.

Still, there are some who feel it could have been worse. Clearly, certain administrators did not perform as well as they might have, that is, given the sensitivity training and the hundreds of hours in which just such occurrences were considered and people were helped to "get in touch with their anger." In a few schools, however, top administrators either ignored the human-relations training or opposed it outright. Thus, some reactions were felt to be predictable.

James Small, who assisted Max Birnbaum during my stay in Bristol, was glad to hear from me. We had been out of touch for a long while. He knew only slightly about the township. No one from the laboratory had visited Bristol since their part of the program had concluded. Jim knew of some of the local departures, and through Arnold Hillman, who had attended a summer training laboratory in Massachusetts, he had heard a bit about Bristol's development. Hillman told Small that he felt the program was essentially well established although the schools in which principals had been converted were definitely faring better.

A follow-up study in fact was undertaken. Birnbaum and Small had requested that a team from Boston University visit Bristol and undertake a thorough evaluation. The final report was mammoth but it disappointed quite a few people both in New York and in Bristol. A bit of attitude-change data was included, but for the most part the report seemed overloaded with impressions. In the end, there was too little to go on. Taking some notes as the silence on the phone grew in length, I heard Jim Small say: "Thinking about Bristol is like thinking about history." I wrote his words. It *was* like history. Like the history I could barely recall studying in junior high school; Venezuelan history or Peruvian history where perhaps a single name or date comes back for no good reason, and one spends his energies attempting to calculate in which year one studied these countries rather than groping for the events that describe that country's invasion by colonialists, or the inevitable struggles for freedom, or the rise of heroes who die because their demands on humanity cannot be fulfilled.

I don't know what it is, but something always seems surrealistic about so many programs for social change. The problems don't mesh somehow with the diagnoses of them, and particularly with the strategies used to implement change and ultimately to bring progress. I recall hearing of a group of urban-design researchers who received a grant of well over $100,000. It was purely a planning grant, an amount of money allowing them to figure out ways to improve the housing conditions of the poor. Months later, they proposed the idea of movable walls, a tricky construction procedure that would permit people to rearrange their internal environments and from this gain, well, I'm not sure exactly what. In response to the proposal I said that my own home, with which I was utterly happy, had thick walls which reeked of strength and permanence, and that I would need dynamite to budge them. A young student sitting next to me said: "Maybe we should start giving the poor their own grants of one hundred thousand dollars." Someone next to him then muttered: "If not that, at least give them the dynamite."

The issues are never perfectly summarized even by notions of full autonomy and the control of one's destiny. "We are monitoring ourselves," Jim McGoldrick told me before we hung up. And then, reflecting on Max, he added: "At some point, everybody has to walk without the crutch." And so we all do. It is not surprising then, indeed it is expected, that Max and his colleagues would, after all this time, be immersed in projects in Miami and New York, and see Bristol as part of their history, a part of their valued history. I, too, have gone on to new projects and have crossed paths, as they say, with other people in cities and in universities that also call themselves American. Importantly, however, the struggle in Bristol Township, without romanticizing it, is a struggle perpetuated in part by precisely this natural passage of human beings from one stage or one client or one moment to the next. Very few of us are able to sustain interest in one thing long enough to allow us to speak of a continuing life work.

But there remains a group of people in this country who simply have no choice in the matter and must sustain whatever their simple passage through life calls for. For some of them, sensitivity training is a preposterous solution to their daily despair. For some of them, the chance even to make a demand seems to be an event that only God might have arranged. For some, the arrival of Max Birnbaum in a forgotten township meant that all at once living a life with dignity was possible. Max understood how rage, confusion, and bitterness got in the way of teaching. He never punished them, but rather let them experience life as adults. Even if his stay in the township was brief, he would at least achieve for these certain ones, a special feeling; a feeling of humanity, if you will, a feeling of self-discovery, a feeling for the pain of another person.

The fact remains, however, that no one, despite a harvest of personal sensitivity and renewed awareness, can ever hold his head high until the weight of an entire society is taken off his back and moved out of the way. Until that time there will be people who will necessarily make demands and stalk out of meeting rooms leaving only the scent of their words, and with it, the purpose of their dreams.

seven

THE ROLE OF THE SOCIOLOGIST IN A MASS MOVEMENT
Andrew Levinson

How much training must a sociologist have before he can qualify as an action sociologist? Once he accepts an active role, the sociologist must guard against performing routine tasks at the cost of not utilizing his sociological knowledge. This essay examines the question of just how vital a role sociologists have actually played in the civil-rights movement thus far. The conclusions are hardly commonplace; some of them are surely controversial. But they should stir constructive reexamination of many unquestioned assumptions about action sociology. The article also sheds new light on a very troublesome and impolite question concerning how best can we reconcile the action sociologists and other civil-rights activists who at present are estranged not only from one another but also from the larger effort that needs their collaboration.

One of the key problems sociologists have in defining their role in a mass movement is the dubious assumption of many that they really ought to be the chief strategists and planners. In the 1950s and early '60s this belief was quite widespread, and some sociologists were horribly shocked when movement groups began to look on them with something less than enthusiasm.

Although the condescension inherent in this belief is now widely realized, nothing has really arisen to replace it. The vision of the sociologist's particular role in a mass movement is still stated in the somewhat paternal context of "bringing a sociological perspective," "using his insight into society," or, on a more political plane, "programming strategies for social change."

This is, at best, a highly ambiguous notion and possibly a destructive one. The above definitions are from the professional sociologist's point of view, and I think it is necessary to counterpose the perspective one gets from inside the movement in order to arrive at a workable understanding of a sociologist's role.

Before going any further, I must make it clear that I do not speak as a professional sociologist but as a political activist whose work involves a good deal of sociology. As a research associate of the Institute for Nonviolent Social Change, a component of the Martin Luther King Memorial Center, I have done, as much by necessity as by chance, a good deal of work that involves sociology.

The Institute, with Mrs. Martin Luther King as president and the Reverend Andrew Young as chairman of the Advisory Council, is essentially dedicated to continuing the philosophy and work of Dr. King. In the last year, as the Institute has worked on developing programs it has provided a unique vantage point for seeing what role sociology can, and cannot, play in the development of planning and strategy for a movement.

A further word of explanation is in order here. By concentrating on the area of program planning and strategy, I do not want to give the impression that this is the only, or best, area for sociologists to be involved in. Planning and strategy must be dealt with because sociologists tend to define them as their field. In a broader sense there is no problem defining the role of the sociologist in a mass movement. If he is seriously committed to the ideas and goals of an organization, he does whatever has to be done, whether it be handing out leaflets, running a mimeograph machine or perhaps something more related to his academic training. In short, his role is the same as anyone else's: to do whatever he can to aid the cause. Although many sociologists felt and still feel that licking envelopes is work for lesser mortals (the diplomatic phrase among social scientists is "being underutilized"), this kind of elitism is really incompatible with a serious commitment. If a struggle is worth writing position papers for, it is also worth licking envelopes for. Incidentally, for people seriously interested in working in a movement, it is worth considering the heretical notion that one should go out and learn the practical skills which are really needed. Depending on one's tastes and the needs of the group, such things as a knowledge of printing methods (how to run and repair a mimeograph machine, photo offset presses, etc.), accounting, fund raising, public speaking, and so forth will in general be far more appreciated than another comprehensive theory of social history.

Before considering a concrete example of program planning and strategy, it is necessary to make one basic point about the role sociologists have played in the black movement. The essential fact is that the really crucial developments of strategies and tactics came from the movement itself, and not from professional scholars. The insights and perspectives of the activists and the lessons of the struggle were the guide to action. The sociological understanding behind the key decisions and plans came from the evaluation of the practical experiences and active experimentation in the struggle, not intricate mathematical analyses of questionnaire data. It is worth demonstrating this in some detail because the still-popular romantic fantasy of intellectuals "doing the thinking" while activists simply carry out orders is far from the truth and prevents any more realistic view from being developed.

Perhaps the most striking example is the development of nonviolent mass action itself as a strategy for the black struggle. Although it has been largely forgotten, the early reaction of liberal intellectuals to Dr. King and the nonviolent philosophy was predominantly pessimistic about its potential. It was argued that the emphasis on loving one's enemy, nonviolent resistance, and redemption through suffering made it too otherworldly and demanded too much of the average black.

It was Dr. King and the other activists in the black communities of the South who, in addition to the moral issues, saw that, first, the growing concentration of blacks in southern cities made that community a basic part of the economic and social structure. This made a boycott not merely a moral gesture but also an economic weapon. Second, they saw that this concentration provided the social basis for a mass movement and that the crucial task was to define tactics which could involve masses of people. Third, they recognized that although superficially foreign, the Gandhian method met three decisive sociological criteria and was therefore particularly applicable in America. It linked up with the cultural tradition of the black church. It provided a way to mobilize the entire community in action. And on a psychological level, for all its seemingly otherworldliness, it constituted a vehicle for the assertion of black pride and dignity—a profound practical requirement of any movement at that time.

Thus, the development of nonviolent direct action was in part a sociological task and one which was conceived and carried out by the movement itself. It is probably true that if someone on the scene translated these ideas into the language of sociology and published it in a journal, bolstered by statistics, in later years he would have gained wide pestige as a social theorist of the first order.

The use of television to carry the movement's message and the development of tactics designed to win national support were also developed by the movement itself. While the "new" understanding of the power and influence of television is generally attributed to McLuhan, many key ideas were in practical use before he described them in an intellectual context. The concept that television delivers an image, an emotional valence quite apart from the content and often in opposition to it, was the basis for concrete day-to-day tactics in Birmingham. Activists used to refer to film clips of the daily news as "educational TV" and saw the very visual structure of the confrontations as ways to demonstrate clearly who is the oppressor and who the oppressed.

A last example is that Operation Breadbasket, perhaps the most successful and enduring method of struggle in the northern ghettos, was also developed out of the experience of the movement and not from outside.

This essential fact, that in a sense the activists themselves played the role of sociologists, is not limited to tactics in any narrowly defined sense. Rather, the experience of the struggle and the political conclusions drawn from it have been startlingly accurate as social analyses of America as a whole. While there are several examples, one of the most striking is the question of white working-class discontent.

Today it is becoming increasingly recognized that the euphoric notion of the affluent worker was largely a myth. The events in the last few years have made it impossible to ignore the real economic and social discontents of white workers and has forced the recognition that their political behavior cannot simply be dismissed as a product of ethnic status, lack of education, or any of the other clichés that were summarized as "white backlash" during the 1960s. The white poor and nearly poor are now accepted as a crucial subgroup of American society.

During the 1960s (say, through 1968), however, there was almost no sociological recognition or acceptance of this. Even the sociological journals collapsed working-class people into the middle class by the simple formula of calling them "lower middle class."

But startlingly, even though they were frequently in direct conflict, the movement was far more aware of this error. In a southern context, especially, there was always a clear vision of the position of the poor working-class whites and the way racism was used as a tool to deflect their attention from their own oppressed status, especially in relation to unionization. In 1968, when George Wallace shocked the intellectual community by making an effective right-wing appeal to manual workers, Dr. King and the Southern Christian Leadership Conference were already planning the Poor People's Campaign whose basic thrust was to relate to the legitimate economic grievances of *all* poor people. It is a sobering fact that the movement made far better use of a sociological perspective in anticipating the coming axis of conflict than did the professionals.

In all this work there were, of course, many social scientists, and sociologists in particular, who made real and enduring contributions to the movement. As we have seen, however, it was not in the paternalistic role of telling the activists what to do, or of making the basic strategic decisions. Rather, the sociologists who made real contributions were those who began with a genuine respect for the political wisdom of the people and the lessons of the struggle. They used that knowledge as the solid foundation of their own work. Many saw themselves as learning far more than they taught.

The area in which sociology made a contribution might be called professional expertise—the nuts-and-bolts skill of research and analysis—

which was needed to put the general understanding on a rigorous footing. While much of their contribution was in the ongoing aspects of the work—the preparation of materials for key court cases or in framing legislation—they also brought this nuts-and-bolts expertise to bear on programs and strategy. Essentially, what sociology could provide was its techniques and methods for practical answers, not some mandate for olympian pronouncements about the royal road to progress.

This view, which comes from individuals who actively participated in these struggles, is confirmed by my own observations of program development in the Institute for Nonviolent Social Change. Before describing this process, however, one point must be made. It is impossible to isolate the role or contribution of any individual in a process of this kind without giving a fundamentally distorted picture of what was "going on." Movement politics is an essentially collective undertaking with a constant overlapping and shifting of tasks and roles. While I was involved in essentially sociological work at many points, it was almost always as a part of some group or as one element in a larger whole. Therefore, to talk only about my role would inevitably take credit justly due many people and also provide a bafflingly incomplete idea of the role sociology actually can play.

Since the point of view being presented is that there is no simple, well-defined role for sociologists but a variety of tasks that sociologists can do well, to speak of my sociological role as though it were a clearly defined "thing" would be self-defeating. What is more valid, and of more interest to the reader, is the role university-style sociological knowledge did and did not play in the development of programs and strategy.[1]

The Institute for Nonviolent Social Change provides a unique view of program and strategy development for several practical reasons. Set up as an element of the Martin Luther King Memorial Center, it began fresh with no "old business" to complicate the picture. It was visualized by Mrs. Martin Luther King and the other people close to her and her late husband as a structure bringing together the people and movements who shared Dr. King's goals and were continuing some part of his work.

This resulted in the formation of an advisory council composed of figures from the nonviolent mass movement he led, representatives of other movements (peace, social justice, labor), and individuals from many fields who had contributed in one way or another to the struggle. It also meant that there was no clearly defined constituency with very specific goals, but a long-range, global kind of outlook.

1. Although it could legitimately be asked whether a professional sociologist with a Ph.D. and some years of experience might not find a clear role as "sociologist," whereas I would not, the role and experience of fully trained sociologists and other professionals is in fact no more defined or structured. If there is any status hierarchy in movement groups, it is based on proven competence in action, not on the number of articles published in the journals.

The development of programs by the Institute is a very practical and down-to-earth example of the relationship previously described between sociology and the movement. The first and basic step was a conference of the advisory council where, under the general heading of nonviolence in the 1970s, many activists and leaders of the movement presented a view and an assessment of their own practical work followed by a kind of projection of the future needs and goals.

One feature of this meeting was of particular interest. By leaving the agenda very flexible, asking other members for simple reports of "what you are doing," and allowing the discussion to flow freely, it was clear that the real intent was in getting the experience of these people as they saw it, and not trying to predetermine its form or content. The result was a startlingly effective exchange not just of points of view but of information.

In a very real sense the 250-page transcript of this conference was the basis for all later planning. The detailed programs that have emerged can all be traced back to the meeting and constitute the approaches and issues that continually reappeared in various forms throughout the conference. I will take two programs that have been developed and concretely trace their growth, illustrating the interface between the experience of the movement and professional expertise.

The first is a project referred to as the Boycott Resource Center. Its role is envisioned in the long run as providing various kinds of boycott information and resources for communities or groups that could not otherwise obtain them. Two key elements are developing an ongoing communications network of people and organizations from all across the country who would be ready to lend support to a morally justified boycott. The other service is specialized research and information on the practical economic, social, and legal questions that can aid in strategy. For example, the economic imperatives facing the company, policy differences between the national level and the local level, and the marketing strategy of the company should all be considered in evaluating a proposed action and the selection of tactics.

The beginning of this program can be very clearly traced back to two presentations given at the meeting of the Institute months before: the Reverend Andrew Young's and the Reverend Jesse Jackson's. Dr. Young, the executive director of SCLC and one of Martin Luther King's top aides, gave a detailed analysis of the 1963 Birmingham campaign. One point he emphasized was that although the confrontations with Bull Connor and the brutality of the police seized the national attention, these facts were underpinned by a powerful boycott during which the black community literally bought nothing but food and medicine.

Dr. Jackson, the nationally known activist who established Chicago's Operation Breadbasket and the Black Expo, dealt with the present crisis in the ghetto, focusing on the essentially economic nature of the problems. In the course of his remarks he both described boycotts actively in progress and offered his view that the boycott was a potentially key weapon, if used on a national level, for achieving fundamental change.

About a week later, in several conversations, Dr. Young, among others of the Institute, expanded on the role of boycotts, making two additional points. First, the support boycotts of Woolworths in other cities had a profound psychological and economic impact on the Birmingham campaign; and second, in a case in Atlanta, racist hiring practices in an auto plant had been reversed with a single phone call to the more public-image-conscious national office. Out of these conversations came the broad idea of a support center, a kind of resource for boycotts.

The next step was to pin down the idea specifically. In discussing the idea with people who had actually conducted boycotts, an idea was developed of some real needs; but the question was, What could realistically be provided?

One area, creating a communications network of groups and individuals, involved some fascinating considerations of applied sociology. Aside from researching and finding the names of people and groups already committed to the struggle and to the boycott as a weapon, it was necessary to think about groups or individuals who ought to be involved and for whom there were good sociological reasons for anticipating a positive response.

This question was complicated by the reality that there could be different levels of participation. Some people might be willing to boycott a product but not to picket a store or write a letter. It was necessary to define the population willing to give a certain level of support and then ascertain how to reach the maximum number with the slender resources available. Glib generalizations about liberal intellectuals or idealistic students are useless when one has to think in terms of expensive mailings and time-consuming telephone calls. Certain groups, such as black churches, socially conscious elements of the white church, and labor unions with a history of reliable support for the movement or large black memberships were obvious. Others, for example sympathetic individuals who are purchasing agents for groups such as churches, unions, or institutions, constitute a powerful force but not an easily defined or contacted one. All this had to be considered, and the number of people who could be reached and their probable level of support had to be estimated as a basis for any concrete program. As can be seen, it essentially amounts to a task of data collection, evaluation, and the prediction of behavior on a vast scale.

This fact notwithstanding, one small issue is of special interest here, as an example of the kinds of nuts-and-bolts problems that arise. In dealing with mailing lists, which range from a few thousand to over a hundred thousand, one problem was the obvious need to be able to reach specific subgroups with reasonable accuracy and speed. While there are completely computerized methods used by commercial firms, they are generally not economically feasible in a nonprofit operation. The less luxurious system used in mailing lists is a "memory" created by punching holes in a certain area of the card which several movable dowels on the addressing machine can sense and make a yes/no decision as to addressing the envelope. One common system provides the possibility of coding each name in sixteen ways and then offering the ability to select and print a subgroup chosen on any two factors. Selecting the factors so that the maximum flexibility is obtained, under these constraints, is a key task and one which is familiar to anyone who has planned and conducted survey research.

Another aspect of the project that required essentially sociological work was the area of analyzing corporations and proposed boycotts with an eye toward providing tactical information. This involved researching the kinds of actions that had been used in the past, such as the series of protests during the annual meetings of corporations last year. Also, areas such as market analysis and how to evaluate the economic position of the institution had to be studied.

After this investigation was completed, the idea was written up and sent or carried to many individuals seeking comments and suggestions. Although active work had begun, this is in a sense an unending process of improvement and refinement.

In general, in the area of practical analysis and evaluation there were a tremendous number of specific questions to be dealt with, all of which involved sociology, and more specifically, the skills and techniques of sociological analysis. It was only after analyzing these questions that attention could be turned to the details of financing and staffing with a confidence in the concrete feasibility and usefulness of the project.

Another program of particular interest is the project on violence in the factories, whose goal is to analyze the situational determinants of violence, both racial and nonracial, and seek nonviolent alternatives. This issue is interesting because there is little public awareness of either the size or character of the problem. Aside from the somewhat circumscribed view of the management magazines and a very occasional article in the press, the issue is almost totally ignored, especially in comparison to, say, violence in the schools.

The genesis of the project was in the recurring concern voiced in the conference of the advisory council about the growing polarization between black and white workers and what could be done. Dr. Jackson in his discussion made note of the hardhat phenomena, especially regarding blacks, arguing that there was no way to avoid clashes except by expanding the economic base so that blacks can find jobs while whites keep their jobs.

Later, after the Reverend James Groppi spoke, the issue of ethnicity came up, and Father Groppi expressed the view that the concrete economic and social discontents of the white working-class community he knew in Milwaukee was a far more solid organizing base than the cultural issues.

These remarks, along with several other factors brought up in later discussion, such as the growth of black caucuses within many unions, and the practical experience of both Mrs. King and Andrew Young with several unions, especially the hospital workers in Charleston and elsewhere, led to a feeling that this was an issue that could be tackled with useful results. The fact that so much attention had been placed on violence in the abstract in the popular press—with so little result—suggested that it was time to look at the question more specifically.

Two weeks, several major libraries, and many phone calls later, several very suggestive patterns appeared. First, there was almost nothing dealing directly with violence in the factories, especially from a nonmanagement point of view. Second, the specific information we did find seemed to indicate that while racial hostility and tension were evident across the country, whether actual violence occurred seemed to be very situation-specific and related to the social conditions of the plant and the community.

As with the boycott center, this was then discussed with the people in and around the Institute. One useful job was quite apparent: bringing together the experience of blue-collar workers, union leaders, management, black caucuses, etc., in dealing with the problem was something that had not been done. In addition, another long-range goal of the Institute, refuting the popular charge that the tactic of nonviolence is dead, was tied in. It was suggested that the varied materials the Institute had, all showing the power of nonviolent action in a very serious andconcrete way, ought to be made available, since many young blacks entering the factories had been too young to see the movement in action. The result was a research-action project with the twin goals of doing the first really comprehensive analysis of the problem and, secondly, seeking the way to replace violence with the nonviolent method in the search for improvements in this environment.

The development of both these projects illustrates the perspectives suggested in the beginning of his discussion. The basic strategy and perspective came from the practical experience of activists and leaders of real, ongoing struggles. The roles of the academic sociologists really came later, in the areas of detailed analysis and answering specific questions.

What this perspective actually implies is that the study of society is not the exclusive province of academic sociologists. The activist who has spent years in the streets talking with people, testing out tactics, and continually readjusting his vision in accord with the results is a sociologist. The understanding he develops of society and social change is not only legitimate, it is often a far more accurate guide to action than theories developed in isolation. It is both condescending and illogical to assume that simply because he possesses a Ph.D. the professional sociologist is inevitably more competent in understanding what programs people want and how to organize them to achieve their goals. The history of the movement suggests the opposite: the crucial tactics and strategy came from the movement itself.

The role that emerges from the examples given of the Institute is less exalted but actually far more meaningful. Like any applied field, a movement has areas of specialization, of concrete expertise, and sociology can validly find its use in many of them. While it is impossible to define such areas in the abstract, apart from the specific problem to be solved, it is clear that sociological training can provide many useful methods and insights.

One point should be made in conclusion. The deep paradox of the sociologists' participation in movements during the last decade has been that they have done more than ever before, yet at the same time generated enormous hostility in the very groups they wished to aid. The heart of this paradox lies in the issue presented above. Those who came simply to serve—in whatever way they could—made contributions both to the movement and to sociology. Those who came dragging their status as "sociologists," assuming they were entitled to lead, created only hostility.

For this reason, it is vital that one begin with the deepest respect for the wisdom of the movement and the activists who work in it. The masses of people in struggle have proved their understanding of society the hard way—by changing it. The professional sociologist should not assume that he is more competent than they are in this task until he has actually done the same.

"It's not the people in prison who worry me. It's the people who aren't."

—Arthur Gore, *New York Times*

part three

DEVIANCE

From the period of its origins in the early twentieth century, sociology has had a special concern for the alleviation of the nation's various social problems. Two of these, the rehabilitation of persons convicted of crimes and imprisoned, and the control of alcoholism, are explored in this section. Both problems have grim reputations for unimpressive social gains.

Even after the tragic loss of life in the Attica prison riots, and despite persistent turmoil in prisons across the country, the call for potent reforms in the goals and methods of managing prisons and prisoners is hesitant and undemanding. Meanwhile, the mass media keep before the public a general concern for addiction whether to alcohol or drugs, or to overeating or overwork, and the public longs for new advances in the art and science of addiction control.

The two essays included here speak to these concerns, the first cataloguing the many hindrances to any effort to understand better the deviant career of the addict, and the second advocating an effective new agent of social change in prison administration. Together these essays give some cause for hope and plenty of reasons for caution, pointing the way to possible additional gains and highlighting the hazards that lie ahead.

eight

FOLLOW-UP OF THE PHILADELPHIA SKID-ROW PROJECT
Leonard U. Blumberg and Thomas E. Shipley, Jr.

The rehabilitation of alcoholics has long concerned these two sociologists. In an earlier essay they reviewed the beginnings of a continuing project aimed at helping addicts leave a skid-row life style, and they explained the special contribution they made to the project as sociologists:

> *This included the importance of sampling procedure in order to permit generalization to the larger population of skid row; the value of comparison with the workingmen living in the "normal" community in order to put the skid-row men in proper perspective; the function of skid row as a service area for homeless and indigent men of the entire Philadelphia region, providing them with cheap lodging, cheap food, and work; the significance of the skid-row way of life as different in some ways from, but strongly reminiscent of, the way of life of the general unskilled working class, and the importance of downward class mobility into skid row for achieving that social alienation that sociologists have, since Durkheim, called anomie.*

Overall they advised that "action without research is a treadmill and research without action neglects important human values." Here they update the story, emphasizing the critical matter of follow-up evaluation research. Again we encounter the basic question of payoff, What

We would like to express our appreciation to Joseph O. Moor, Jr., and Leonard Moore for their assistance. The DRC/P is located at 304 Arch Street, Philadelphia, Penn. 19106; Irving W. Shandler, Executive Director. The projects discussed were made possible by the following grants: Demonstration Grant Project No. Pa. D-7, administered by the Urban Renewal Administration, Housing and Home Finance Agency, under provisions of Section 314 of the Housing Act of 1954, in cooperation with the Redevelopment Authority of the City of Philadelphia, the Greater Philadelphia Movement, and Temple University Center for Community Studies; and by the U.S. Department of Health, Education, and Welfare, National Institute of Mental Health, Project 15081, "A Study of the Prevention of Skid Row." The authors carry responsibility for the data and the interpretations of procedures discussed herein.

83

*difference, if any, has been made by the sociologist's planned intervention?
To assess that difference requires contacting the previous subjects, an
especially difficult task among the characteristically anonymous and
transient skid-row population.*

In an earlier volume we discussed our Philadelphia skid-row project and
the Diagnostic and Rehabilitation Center/Philadelphia, an agency created
to develop ways to assist skid-row men to relocate and to find social
services and health services in the community. As part of the Center's
activities we have undertaken follow-up procedures in order to assess the
effectiveness of relocation (1963–65) or material for a study on the
"prevention of skid row" (1967–71). Both these activities were clinically
oriented; that is, while we eventually planned to aggregrate the data for
statistical purposes, each man was followed up personally. In addition to
this clinical approach, we have also been concerned with a follow-up of
skid row in a more general sense. This was a part of a National Institute of
Mental Health grant which focused on questions such as, What is the
relationship of skid row to the larger community, and, Can skid rows be
prevented?

The present essay is not designed to review the data as such, but to
discuss some of our experiences with respect to the follow-up of skid-row
men and of skid row as a part of Philadelphia. We will first consider the
follow-up procedures and some brief recommendations that our experience suggests to us. Then we will turn to the societal and university
environment in which our work has been done and consider briefly some of
their consequences for us.

The Follow-up Procedures

Gillespie concluded that "Personal interviews are expensive and difficult, but yield more accurate data than that collected from secondary
sources." He further recommended that "researchers refrain from screening their samples and concentrate on alcoholic groups which are currently
under-represented in the literature, namely, the upper-upper class, the
lower-lower class, and Negroes." [1] In Gillespie's terms we were involved in
longitudinal "retrospective-prospective" research (before-after investiga-
tions over time in which base-line data was gathered about behavior before
entering the program and after leaving it) using personal interview, with
lower-lower-class persons.

---

1. Duff G. Gillespie, "The Fate of Alcoholics: An Evaluation of Alcoholism Follow-Up
Studies," in *Alcoholism*, ed. David J. Pittman (New York: Harper & Row, 1967), pp. 173–78.

Our initial plan was to interview men on the following schedule: one day after relocation; eight days after relocation; one month, three months, and one year after relocation. The interviews stressed residential mobility, employment history, health, and alcohol drinking behavior; they were carefully constructed to parallel information included in earlier interviews with the men. We underestimated the cost of these procedures. This can be put in terms of the much greater length of time needed to find a man and interview him once he no longer came to the Center, or it can be put in terms of the fact that the job as originally planned would have required a much larger staff than we had budgeted. We therefore limited the number of follow-ups for each man to a three-month and a one-year interview. In later NIMH-sponsored research we extended the same plan: three months, one year, and two years. We also developed a "pilot project" that was essentially a return to our original design. We hoped that these "intensive follow-up" procedures would reduce the dropout rate among men coming to the Center. Nevertheless, high turnover among the follow-up staff made it difficult to implement the research plan.

Parenthetically, we might note that follow-up contact with a skid-row population is extremely difficult and time consuming. Success depends a good deal upon the nature of the relationship that has been developed, not only between the man and the agency, but between the follow-up worker and the skid-row population conceived as a community. It also depends upon the circumstances under which relocation has taken place, if it has taken place at all. Thus, if a strong relationship (friendly, helping, trusting) had been achieved, and if the relocation had been to an alcohol-treatment program within an institution, the interview was relatively routine; on the other hand, if contact had been relatively superficial and relocation had been made to independent living in an isolated roominghouse, follow-up three months later was often difficult or impossible.

The following is a composite of procedures that have been used: During the relocation phase, all in-service counselors (caseworkers) reported to the research office all relocations as they were made, and the men's names were then placed on our list. After relocation procedures were discontinued, the caseworkers were supposed to notify the research office at the time that the case was closed—either the man broke contact with the agency or the client was sent to a hospital or treatment center. (Not all caseworkers lived up to the responsibility as well as we required, so that members of the research staff would review the files regularly to "take up the slack.") Shortly before the three-month follow-up procedure was to be instituted, the counselors were asked if they knew where the man had moved and whether they had any additional information on the man's current address. If indications were that a man had moved, a certified letter was sent to the last known address asking the man to come to the

Center or to let the Center know whether he could be interviewed where he lives. If the letter was returned as undeliverable, the man's name was forwarded to the Department of Public Assistance (many were receiving public assistance with Center help), and a call was made to the House of Correction (county prison for misdemeanants), the two most available additional sources of information. In addition, the constant circulation of men in and out of the Center and into several neighborhoods might be expected to yield some leads, although not all the men were helpful in giving information of this sort. The most effective person in getting this sort of information from clients was a mature caseworker who had had some years of experience with the men and who had taken a direct personal interest in them.

The follow-up worker went out to seek an interview with the man. Some of the follow-up men were very familiar with skid row because they had lived on or near it in the past. (We discuss this in greater detail later.) The interviewer made three or four attempts to find the man at the last known address. He would make inquiries of friends, former Center clients, and other acquaintances that he knew in and around skid row, at Alcoholics Anonymous clubs, and so forth. The effort to secure interviews took place at several times of the day; experience suggests that after six o'clock in the evening is a good time. Finding a man requires some ingenuity, however, for dwelling-unit entrances may be on a side alley or entered from a basement; a client doesn't always answer his door, even though neighbors will tell you that he is in fact in his room; the hotel clerk doesn't give the necessary information (unless he is given a small bribe); protective neighbors deny that they know the client—and this may be true since they may know him by another name or nickname only. The cooperation of landlords needs to be secured.

A monthly "lost list" was circulated to agencies such as the Department of Public Assistance, Social Security Administration, Veterans Administration Domiciliary, House of Correction, the largest of the gospel missions, the most significant and cooperative employment agency on skid row, the local hospitals which service the largest number of skid-row men (largely because they are located on the edge of the central business district). From time to time other Center staff workers who are also familiar with the local bars, restaurants, cubicle hotels, and roominghouses circulate through skid row in search of lost men.

Our intent was to saturate likely sources of available information, but contrary to procedures used in Saint Louis, there was no tie-in with the police department. Our successful contact rate was rarely over 60 percent at any time during the course of the several projects in which we used follow-up procedures. This is in contrast with Weber's reported 80 percent in Saint Louis. However, in addition to police assistance, Weber excluded those who did not stay for the full treatment period (normally seven days) and those who had not lived in or near the "greater St. Louis Metropolitan area" for about three months before admission to the detoxification program.[2] That is, those who were least likely to be found on follow-up were excluded from the beginning. We did have one singularly successful follow-up series which was a part of an intensive casework procedure. In this case the follow-up rate was higher than 90 percent. We attribute this to the relatively warm relationship developed during the course of the project. On this basis we might speculate that for people such as this, the follow-up rate may itself be a measure of the success of the treatment program. That is, those who are "successes" keep in touch with the program in some way because it is associated with later rewards, while the "failures" break it off and become "lost." Such speculations have a surface plausibility.

On the other hand, equally reasonable is the argument that those who have been able to find new nonskid-row friendships, or to pick up anew broken family ties, and also have been able to work out a relatively stable economic base, whether through a job, pension, or welfare assistance, may seek to drop their deviant past. That is, being "lost" from a research point of view would not then be a measure of failure of the program, but a measure of its success. We believe that neither is the correct position, but that some of both kinds of people are probably involved. Short of some permanent tagging of the population and a lifetime follow-up on a large scale (we are not advocating this) we do not at the moment see any resolution of this problem. Thus the problems associated with follow-up are likely to continue to be with us indefinitely.

Follow-up interviewing took place in the Center and "on the street." Men often returned to the Center some months after they had left the effective caseload (cases were considered "inactive" not "closed" during most of the period under consideration, and even closed cases were readily reopened if the man came into the Center). They might have been relocated under the demonstration grant; often they were not, but they returned because they were desperate and wanted help with a drinking, health, or housing problem. We made every effort to complete a follow-up interview when they were in the building.

The Follow-up Personnel

There were eighteen college-age men and women; some were in school, some were dropouts; we also had one high-school dropout, who has since

2. James M. Weber, "The St. Louis Detoxification and Diagnostic Evaluation Center: Final Evaluation Report," Social Science Institute, Washington University, St. Louis, 1969, chap. 2, p. 3; chap. 3, p. 3.

gone on to college. A majority of the college-age interviewers did their work within the Center itself, interviewed only a few clients, and therefore did not significantly contribute to the overall follow-up data. A minority of the persons of college age, all men, did their interviewing "out on the street" and, in general, worked full-time for the program, even though they were temporary employees (e.g., during summer vacation). They were highly motivated, approached the job imaginatively, and were able to complete a substantial number of interviews during the period of their employment, in spite of the fact that they had had no direct skid-row experience.

In addition to the college-age personnel, we employed about twenty persons beyond the college age as follow-up workers. A few were professionals or subprofessionals; e.g., a social worker with special competence and research experience with skid-row men, and a social-worker group therapist, but most were men with alcohol problems, whom we tended to think of as "indigenous workers." That is, they were "alcoholics" and presumably more likely to be understanding of and helpful to skid-row men. Actually, however, only perhaps one-fourth had had extensive skid-row experience, as far as we know, and as nearly as we can tell, being an ex-skid row man really did not make much difference in one's effectiveness in locating men who were on the follow-up list.

All the "alcoholics" interviewed both in the Center and in the field as a normal part of their jobs. Sometimes college-age people worked with them as a part of a team, but the alcoholics and the college-age people did not work together. In part we believe that this was a matter of youth vs. age, because the alcoholics were generally in their late forties or fifties, while the college-age persons were in their early twenties. In part, however, it seemed to be a result of class-education differences. While a few alcoholics had had some college background, most had only gone as far as high school. Furthermore, the college-age people mostly came from what might be stereotyped as middle-class background—white-collar and professional-family backgrounds. Finally, the alcoholics were seeking to solve a set of life problems that were radically different from those of the students; their sobriety was relatively new (under two years in almost all cases) and relatively shaky, so that alcohol was still the focal element of their lives; they believed that the students "did not really understand them." Sociologists who are familiar with "troubled people" will recognize that this is common. On the other hand, the college students were bright and brash; they saw the job as an evidence of their commitment to the sociopolitical activism of the era and, in some cases, they saw it as a kind of apprenticeship before moving into a counseling-casework experience with either alcoholics or with drug addicts.

The rate of success in finding men eligible for follow-up being what it was, there was a high potential for frustration on the part of the follow-up workers. The college-age personnel and the alcoholics tended to handle the situation differently. The college-age people felt relatively comfortable in discussing their problems with other members of the research staff, most of whom had similar backgrounds and were thereby able to get some perspective on their "inefficiency."

On the other hand, the alcoholics tended to seek solutions through working harder on the one hand and by keeping the problem to themselves, on the other; and this in the face of the fact that the statistics from week to week made it evident what was happening and the fact that we tried to convey to them that we did not expect them to be superproducers. That is, we tried to reassure the alcoholic follow-up men, but we do not believe that we were very convincing.

The consequence was that the alcoholics tended to seek ways out of the situation. A majority managed to shift to other parts of the agency, where they became involved in administration or in counseling others whose alcohol problem was more profound than their own. About one-third got drunk and had either to be let go or shifted to other responsibilities. As nearly as we can tell, one major factor in whether a man got drunk or not was the kind of social relationships he was able to establish and maintain. That is, most of those who got drunk seemed to be "social isolates" or to have interpersonal problems they were unable to resolve. Those who remained sober developed and maintained strong friendships often, but not always, tied to Alcoholics Anonymous. Sometimes the social tie involved a renewal of marital relationships. The nondrinking solution to the problems created by the difficulties of follow-up work, then, lay in participation in some posttherapy community of interest rather than accepting the difficulties as solely intrapersonal.

Some Recommendations

Social scientists engaged in action research will almost assuredly face the necessity of follow-up work and the need for follow-up personnel. The selection of such personnel will probably involve choices between college-age persons on the one hand and "indigenous" persons on the other. They will also face constantly the problem of the reliability and the validity of the data they get back. Depending on the kind of population involved it may not be feasible to reinterview a sample of those who have already been interviewed. We make the following suggestions:

1. A follow-up worker who has some life experiences that resemble those

of the clients would be our first choice. We see some elements of trade-off in this, however. At times the desires of such persons to assist those who they perceive to have an urgent problem may lead them to forsake their primary responsibility, namely, to administer follow-up interviews. This may mean lost interviews, or, even worse, "fudged" data. We have urged follow-up counselors to discriminate between those problems that urgently need immediate action and those that could be delayed in order to get the follow-up interview. We have urged the follow-up counselors to alert the man's anchor counselor (DRC/P caseworker) and, when feasible, to assist in following through with the anchor counselor's recommendations.

2. Given a choice between a marginally competent "indigenous worker" and a highly motivated and well-educated college student or graduate who is also sympathetic to the clients, the better choice would be the student. Here again there is a trade-off. The student's lack of experience may mean that he cannot test the validity of some responses through a comparison with his own judgment. If he stays on the job long enough, he will pick up some of this, however.

3. Follow-up work in our action research has been extremely difficult and time consuming. Gillespie, in summarizing twenty-two follow-up studies of alcoholics, reports the same thing. These people are often anonymous and highly mobile. Such a combination of attributes is likely to frustrate even the most diligent, dedicated, and emotionally stable follow-up worker. In the context of studies of alcoholics, the "indigenous worker" is not very far removed from the problems of his prospective respondent; a follow-up program using men with alcohol problems is likely to have instability as a major ingredient.

4. Many successful and unsuccessful follow-up workers moved on to some sort of casework-therapy situation in the Center or elsewhere. Their apparent success in a therapy capacity has led us to support the conclusion that it is reasonable for ex-alcoholics to want to move away from frustrating follow-up problems into more directly humanitarian casework and community-casefinding activity elsewhere in the Center.

5. We are still searching for a word or phrase that will convey to the reader our immediate emotions when we learn about or have a strong suspicion that we have been handed "fudged" data. We feel that these deviations must be detected and halted, but at the same time action-research agencies should modify their procedures in some way in order to manage the need that is evident rather than simply firing the worker because he has "sinned." In other words, organizational necessities do not necessarily take precedence over human (personal) ones. The search must be to find a successful combination of research procedures while enhancing human concerns.

A Wider Perspective

From the beginning of our research on skid row, we have been committed to the idea of "action research." [3] In its most dogmatic form this can be expressed as a slogan: No Action Without Research. Some of the difficulties in the implementation of this ideological position we have already discussed in the first edition of Sociology in Action. During the time that the program has developed, the larger society has also been developing, and the pressures placed on our specific academic context have changed as well.

For example, our position within our university in the period 1963–65 (the demonstration-grant period) is framed in the fact that the university administration was reluctant to accept presumed legal or financial risks that might be involved in the operation of an action agency as a regular part of its services. It became necessary to "spin off" the Center and to create an autonomous private agency in order to fulfill the action commitments of the ideology and to make its expansion possible as finances became available and as the need was recognized. That such a move was acceptable to the administration is evidenced by the fact that we have been able to undertake research within the Center as a part of our university responsibilities with the university being reimbursed for our released time from teaching. We believe that this model is one that other universities should consider, since it permits the service agency to respond to community need without the restraints of university politics and permits larger opportunities for the academic, while retaining his scholarly roots. Furthermore, it provides an answer to the controversy about university involvement: the university itself remains a center for scholarship, but its faculty may develop dual roots and find strength from both.

This is an important controversy for people who want to engage in action research. Since we began our work on skid row in 1959 there has been a crescendo of demands for changes in the larger society, and our university has not been immune to them. The war in Vietnam and the thrust for a redefinition of social justice in our society radicalized at least a minority of the university's students and faculty. One consequence is that work with skid-row men can hardly be considered "radical" even in the relatively conservative university environment, but at least such work is acceptable—provided it eventuates in publication. By the same token, the

3. Leonard U. Blumberg, Thomas E. Shipley, Jr., Irving W. Shandler, and Herman Niebuhr, "The Development, Major Goals, and Strategies of a Skid Row Program: Philadelphia," Quarterly Journal of studies on Alcohol 27 (June 1966): 242–58.

argument by radicalized students and faculty that the university should become "relevant" has not led to acceptance of action in the "real world" outside the university as a basis of rewards within the university itself. The university system has not changed very much from "publish or perish" even while it has been involved in the cooptation of "disaffected" classes of the general population. Nonetheless, the action-research agency provides a structure for accomplishing both real-world-oriented goals and university-oriented goals, although the high-risk nature of the action may mean that the university rewards may be slow in coming.

Finally, from time to time we have been asked about the significance of our work. This is a question of relevance, and often it is posed along the lines of traditional concepts of science and the scientific method. This is not, of course, the approach used by the politicized minority, who tend to rally around libertarian notions of freedom, and who may not see action research on skid row or about alcoholism as relevant because everybody should be able to "do his own thing." Our answer is that alcohol is a dangerous chemical that, when chronically used to excess, leads to a physically sick and unhappy person who is unable to make even moderately efficient responses to the problems posed to him by his environment. We believe that it is highly relevant to develop effective programs that will give that person whatever assistance we can so he can in fact "do his own thing."

Within the context of the traditional approach to theory we have taken the position that, in the largest sense, an action-research program should have some general conceptual undergirding. Insofar as we are dealing with real-world situations rather than laboratory ones, however, we have found it difficult to formulate our problems neatly, especially since the real-world situations are relatively unstable. Furthermore, insofar as the action research in which we are engaged is broadly "sociological" as well as clinical, we are seeking to understand (and hopefully) influence a metropolitan city. That is, our "follow-up" involves not only individual skid-row men, but large sections of the city as well. The related research problems are enormous.

One consequence has been that we have felt impelled to reconceptualize the meaning of skid row for purposes of urban social-welfare planning.[4] Another consequence has been that we have realized that our resources are not great enough to do the kind of thorough comparative study it requires. We have been forced to undertake pilot studies and to draw

4. Leonard U. Blumberg, Thomas E. Shipley, Jr., and Joseph O. Moor, Jr., "The Skid Row Man and the Skid Row Status Community," *Quarterly Journal of Studies on Alcohol* (December 1971): 909–41.

inferences from them rather than from the larger studies required. Thus, we have had to settle on comparative studies of one or two other American cities rather than a major study of what is happening to skid row in all the major cities of the country and Canada, let alone Europe. The question of the sociological significance of skid row has never been far from our considerations. Starting from a natural-area approach to skid row we have begun to evolve some theory centered on urban land-use politics, but our conclusions are rooted in the data; that is, they are inductive rather than deductive. We believe that such an approach will yield the general properties that we associate with "theory" along with a respect for the uniqueness of the Philadelphia case.

nine

SOCIAL-LEARNING THEORY AND SOCIAL PROBLEMS: THE CASE OF PRISONS
Michael J. Hindelang

The popularity of the Skinnerian psychology of behavior modification by means of rewards sharply challenges action sociologists. The techniques of behavior modification are somewhat opposed to a more holistic view of man, one that holds that to change behavior one must first change thinking and emotions. Instead, the Skinnerian approach deals immediately and directly with actions, with what the subjects or clients actually do. Variously called behavior therapy, behavior modification, reinforcement therapy, reward-and-punishment treatment, and behavior management, it has apparently been used successfully in the treatment of anorexia (loss of appetite), psychogenic seizures, autistic behavior, insomnia, tics, mutism, stuttering, vomiting, smoking, alcoholism, drug addiction, overeating, thumb sucking, academic anxieties, fetishism, exhibitionism, frigidity, impotence, sexual deviance, and so forth. Based on principles gleaned primarily from the controlled study of operant (Skinnerian) and classical (Pavlovian) conditioning, learning-theory applications of behavior modification appear limited only by the imagination of behavioral scientists. This essay reports on a successful application of behavior modification techniques at a boys' reformatory in Washington, D.C. The author's plea for more earnest uses of learning theory by action sociologists is an invitation to new successes in the field and a personal challenge to each of us.

The National Survey of Corrections conducted in 1965 revealed that the average daily population of those under the supervision of the American "correctional" system during that year was 1.3 million offenders, at an annual cost in excess of $1 billion; of these offenders, 425,000 were institutionalized [1] at an average cost of $1,905 per individual per year. Despite this vast outpouring of resources, it is difficult to find anyone who

---

1. Virtually all who were not institutionalized were on probation or parole.

is willing to argue that our system of dealing with offenders is successful. Of those incarcerated in federal prisons and reformatories, more than half have had previous prison or reformatory commitments. Of the male felons serving time in California state prisons, for example, about 90 percent have previously served sentences in state prisons, reformatories, or jails.[2] Obviously these are not enviable performance records.

Although recent catastrophes in a variety of prisons and jails have brought extensive publicity to the myriad problems in what has euphemistically come to be known as the correctional sphere of our criminal-justice process, these problems have long been evident to most of those who have come into contact with our penal system. The conditions in prisons are, of course, most cruelly and vividly evident to those who have become the victims of our crime of punishment, but they are not the only victims. For although an oft-stated aim of incarceration is to rehabilitate, there can be little doubt that our penal institutions— as they are currently operating— are quite debilitating; their dehumanizing effects are endured first by the prisoners, but they are ultimately felt and paid for by the remaining members of society, when the victimization chain moves full cycle.

Imprisonment involves several realities: removing an individual from his community (usually in an urban area) to the locale of the prison (usually in a rural area); stripping him of his personal identity—clothes, hairstyle, possessions, conventional roles; forcing him to maintain prolonged and intimate social contact with other inmates and to live a regimented existence for the sake of efficient control by the staff; denying him privacy, substantial communication with family and friends, and a voice in decisions that affect him; trying to control him through a system of punishments; making him almost totally dependent on the state to satisfy his primary needs; and generally treating him as less than human.[3]

Incarceration not only locks the prisoner in, but, perhaps more importantly, it locks his family and friends out; because of limitations in visitation rights and written communication, the inmate is even further cut

2. M. J. Hindelang, "A Learning Theory Analysis of the Correctional Process," *Issues on Criminology* 4 (1969): 43–58.

3. In a recent U.S. District Court decision, Judge Robert Merhige, Jr., enjoined the Virginia State Department of Welfare and its Division of Corrections from: (a) imposing bread and water punishment on any inmate for any infraction of prison rules; (b) using chains, handcuffs, hand-restraining tape or tear gas "except when necessary or required to protect a person from imminent physical harm or to prevent escape or serious injury to property"; (c) using physical force "against any inmate for purposes of punishment"; (d) placing more than one inmate in the same solitary confinement—Virginia's solitary cells are 6½ feet by 10 feet—"except in an emergency"; (e) interfering with or imposing punishment for efforts by inmates to file court documents, to have confidential communication with lawyers, even when confined to solitary, and to write legislative or other government officials. (Landman v. Peyton, Civil No. 170-69-R, U.S. Dist. Ct., E. D. Va. (Oct. 31, 1971)

off from his former social system. Many authors have written about the importance that the inmate social system takes on; for the inmate, the social system within the prison must somehow substitute for his former social system from which he has been isolated. [4]

From a learning-theory point of view, the importance of the inmate social system to the physical, social, and psychological survival of the imprisoned individual could not be more important. Brim and Wheeler have suggested that every group attempts to imbue new members with the values and norms of the group;[5] the inmate group is no different. The state, however, unwittingly contributes to, and virtually assures, the successful socialization of new prisoners into the inmate social system. By effectively severing the neophyte inmate's social ties with the outside world, by depriving him of his previous social status, by making the inmate social system his only source of social support, the state guarantees that the inmate social system will have substantial behavioral control over new inmates.

A related but distinct phenomenon is that of modeling. Albert Bandura, who is among the foremost researchers in the area of modeling, maintains that "virtually all learning phenomena resulting from direct experiences can occur on a vicarious basis through observation of other persons' behavior and its consequences for them." [6] That is, observers can acquire response patterns by observing the behaviors of others and the consequences of those behaviors for the actors. This means that, during incarceration, inmates will acquire new behavioral repertories via modeling processes. Unfortunately, because they have been almost completely separated from the outside world, inmates have only each other to serve as models. Thus, it is not difficult to understand why inmates learn primarily about criminal behavior and criminal techniques while incarcerated.

Social-learning theorists have noted that aversive control (punishment) is seldom employed as the sole method for modifying behavior, but when used in connection with reinforcers may hasten the change process.[7] Yet Sykes has insightfully observed that the system of rewards and punishments within our prisons may be ineffective because the reward portion of the system has been all but abandoned.[8]

---

4. See, e.g., G. M. Sykes and S. L. Messinger, "The Male Inmate Social System," in *Theoretical Studies in Social Organization of the Prison*, ed. Richard A. Cloward et al. (New York: Social Science Research Council, 1960); R. Giallombardo, "The Female Inmate Social System," in *Society of Women: A Study of a Women's Prison* (New York: John Wiley, 1966).

5. Orville G. Brim, Jr., and Stanton Wheeler, *Socialization after Childhood* (New York: John Wiley, 1966).

6. A. Bandura, *Principles of Behavior Modification* (New York: Holt, Rinehart & Winston, 1969), p. 118.

7. Ibid., p. 294.

8. G. M. Sykes, *Society of Captives* (Princeton: Princeton University Press, 1958), p. 52.

For example, many of the "rewards" which are controlled by the prison (e.g., visiting and mail privileges, the ration of personal possessions which the prison provides, "good time" which is automatically deducted from prisoners' sentences at the outset of imprisonment) are not made contingent upon inmate performance but rather are given initially regardless of the behavior of the inmate; in comparison to contingent systems of rewards, such noncontingent systems of rewards have been shown to be quite ineffectual in bringing about desired behavioral changes.[9] At the same time that a noncontingent system of rewards is operating, a contingent system of punishments is attempted; the result is that inmates come to view the rewards as rights rather than privileges[10] and when they are threatened with the denial of those rewards they become embittered. This embitterment may generate a substantial number of problems in the area of inmate control.

A final unintended consequence of our present system of incarceration is that by locking men up and making virtually all their decisions for them—where meals will come from, how lodging will be provided, what work they will do, how they will spend their free time, to whom they will write, what they cannot read, etc.—they become very dependent and probably less able to conduct the normal affairs of living on the outside. In the institutional setting, initiative, self-reliance, and self-determination, all deemed essential for postinstitutional success, are extinguished while more docile behaviors are positively reinforced by the prison hierarchy." [11] To thrust an inmate who has not had to provide for his own necessities for a period of months or years into a demanding and often hostile world seems doomed to failure; but it is under these circumstances that we expect parolees to be able to succeed.

The foregoing paragraphs have attempted briefly to point up many facets of our prison system that seem counterproductive according to some basic principles of social-learning theory. In order to illustrate ways in which rehabilitative programs based on learning theory can circumvent some of these difficulties, let us briefly review one of the earliest and most innovative such programs.

9. T. Ayllon and N. H. Azrin, "The Measurement and Reinforcement of Behavior of Psychotics," *Journal of the Experimental Analysis of Behavior* 8 (1965): 357–83; A. Bandura and B. Perloff, "Relative Efficacy of Self-Monitored and Externally Imposed Reinforcement Systems," *Journal of Personality and Social Psychology* 7 (1967): 111–16.

10. Whether these rewards *should* be viewed as rights or privileges is a separate issue. See R. K. Schwitzgebel, *Development and Legal Regulation of Coercive Behavior Modification Techniques with Offenders* (Washington, D.C.: Public Health Service Publication, 1971), for a comprehensive discussion of the legal issues raised by behavior modification techniques with offenders.

11. Bandura, *Principles of Behavior Modification*, p. 261.

Case Study

In *A New Learning Environment*, Cohen and Filipczak report on the CASE II—MODEL project (Contingencies Applicable to Special Education—Motivationally Oriented Designs for an Ecology of Learning) which they initiated at the National Training School for Boys in Washington, D.C.[12] The primary aim of the CASE II project was to increase the academic performance of forty-one young men between the ages of fourteen and eighteen who had been convicted of homicide, house-breaking, rape, armed robbery, and auto theft. Students worked on programmed courses and regular texts. Points (money) were earned by studying for an hourly wage and passing exams at a proficiency level of 90 percent or better. The points could be used to buy a wide variety of goods ranging from soft drinks and food to magazines and many articles from mail-order catalogs.

Students faced the choice either of going on relief or of becoming self-supporting. If they chose to go on relief they lived in a dormitory-type environment where they slept on bunk beds in front of an officer's station, were given a minimum of personal belongings, and were required to wear NTS-issue khaki clothing. It they chose to be self-supporting they could rent private rooms which they could decorate with items bought from the NTS store (pillows, pictures, *Playboy* centerfolds, etc.), buy civilian clothes, rent private shower stalls, wash their clothing in a coin-operated washing machine, rent books, pay an entrance fee and hourly charge for using the library or recreational lounge, secure private tutoring, pay for meals and recreation for Sunday visitors, open bank accounts, and so forth.

This was a token economy in nearly every sense; almost every activity had a cost. The boys studied and even worked at part-time jobs within the institution in order to avoid going on relief (which was equivalent to standard prison living conditions at NTS) and in order to acquire goods.

Allowing the students to purchase most of the goods they desired (and could afford) was not without its difficulties. It was quite customary for the boys to adorn their rooms with *Playboy* pinups which apparently pleased them and to which the CASE project staff was not opposed. After the chief chaplain of the Federal Bureau of Prisons visited the CASE project, however, the project directors received a call from the director of the Bureau of Prisons conveying the chaplain's shock at the pinups of nude women. The project personnel responded, in part, by pointing out traditional penal measures appeared counterproductive in preparing adolescents for life in a heterosexual, democratic society and furthermore

---

12. H. Cohen and James Filipczak, *A New Learning Environment* (San Francisco: Jossey-Bass, 1971). The following section paraphrases portions of this work.

that by punishing normal behavior regarding women and sex, homosexuality and homosexual rape would seem to be encouraged. Neither the chaplain nor the director of the Bureau was in touch with the project staff on this point again.

Social reinforcers, in addition to points, were programmed into the system. When a student performed especially well on an exam, his accomplishment was brought to the attention of his peers from whom he received recognition and respect. In addition to receiving points for studying, correctional officers were allowed to award bonus points to the students for exemplary behavior, such as keeping a very neat room. This moved the officer's role from one of aversive control to one of positively reinforcing control—a change that was welcomed by many officers and students alike.

Since all bonuses had to be recorded in the bankbooks of the students and in the officers' records, the behavior of the officers could be monitored. The officers were given the opportunity to earn extra pay by attending seminars during which they could learn constructive reinforcement techniques and could propose new programs of their own design. At least as exciting as the changes in the behavior of the students was the increased interest and the changing attitudes of the staff. The altered behavior of the correctional officers and the teachers had a marked effect on the attitudes of the students toward each other, the staff, and visitors. A student government served as an additional channel of communication through which staff and students could communicate their views.

Rather than making contact with the outside world difficult, the CASE II project encouraged it. The correctional officers and teachers established less-formalized relationships with the student; young, attractive females were hired as staff members so that the students would have an opportunity to learn how to act properly in their presence. Contacts with family and friends were facilitated through letters, phone calls, visits to NTS, escorted individual trips, town trips, and furloughs. Special prerelease programs were developed to ease reentry into society.

Within the institution, violent behavior lessened considerably in spite of a decrease in traditional punishments; in addition, the students accepted more responsibility for self-control.

Nevertheless, as noted above in reference to the pinup incident, the project did generate some difficulties. When the project staff began to run low on funds—because the students were working at a rate greater than anticipated—it was necessary to inflate the costs of goods within the project. Faced with wholesale devaluation of points, the students decided to go on strike and refused to go to work. This behavior, a perfectly acceptable sign of displeasure in our free society, is a federal offense in the regular NTS program. Because of the unique position of the CASE project as a separate community, prison officials did not enter the dispute. The CASE project director chided the students for their improper use of the strike:

> You guys . . . really blew it. I thought you had learned about the powers of government and the powers of protest, but obviously we failed to teach you the use of a strike as a weapon. The unions in America win their demands, but they don't do it by striking first and negotiating later. . . . The strike is the weapon and the last stage in a chain of events. I agree with your viewpoint, but since you've already struck, I have no reason to negotiate with you until after you've returned to work.[13]

The students returned to work and negotiations solved the crisis.

Overall, the CASE II students who generally had histories of learning problems showed a gain of nearly two grade levels per year as measured by the Stanford Achievement Test; 90 percent of the students showed a gain of the equivalent of four years of academic progress in at least one subject area within the first six months. A follow-up study showed that during the first postrelease year, the recidivism rate of the CASE students was two-thirds less than the NTS norm, but by the third year the recidivist rate for CASE students was near the norm. The program evidently delayed the delinquents' return to incarceration but they apparently required additional postrelease maintenance in the outside world to prevent recidivism after the first year. These recidivism findings, although somewhat discouraging, suggest that postrelease adjustment may be improved if the reinforcement contingencies can somehow be maintained after release. This difficulty in laboratory-to-natural-setting transition is not uncommon for new treatment programs; the solution may lie in trying to make the studying techniques reinforced during the program more intrinsically reinforcing and hence more resistant to extinction in the absence of external reinforcers. In any event, had the program been successful only in improving staff-student and student-student relations during incarceration, it would have had to have been judged a success.

Summary and Conclusions

The Cohen-Filipczak treatment program is encouraging because it provides a model in which many shortcomings of our present programs are circumvented.

1. The CASE II project encouraged interactions between the inmates and the outside world, including family, friends, and the project staff.

13. Ibid., p. 36.

2. In so doing it linked the inmates to social systems external to the prison and therefore provided them with a variety of sources of modeling.

3. The CASE II project replaced a "punishment only" system with an extensive system of rewards *and* punishments.

4. The project reinforced self-reliant behavior and extinguished dependent behavior; it reinforced the conception among students that they could be self-sufficient, that they could effect outcomes.

5. The project not only altered the institutional behavior of the students, but also altered the institutional behavior of the staff.

Whether and to what extent such token economy programs can be successful with adults—either in terms of institutional or postinstitutional adjustment—remains to be seen; since the inmate population is undereducated and has prior work experiences in more menial jobs than the general population,[14] it is certainly possible to apply the token-economy concept to educational and occupational improvement programs within institutions. It seems as though such programs could be used as vehicles for changing conditions that now exist in most prisons and that are incompatible with rehabilitative ends.

In the aftermath of the 1972 prison riot in Attica, New York, a glimpse at inmates' and correctional officers' positions is instructive. Among the demands of the Attica inmates one sees a thread which says "treat us as human beings." Why should inmates be cut off from family and friends by unreasonably limiting visiting and correspondence? Why should the inmates be isolated from developments in the outside world and sources of self-education by virtue of the fact that such readings as *Psychology Today*, *National Geographic*, Erickson's *Youth and Crisis*, Jung's *Man and His Symbols*, and Silberman's *Crisis in Black and White* are contraband reading in New York State prisons? Is it unreasonable to ask that brutality toward inmates cease and that correctional officers be prosecuted for acts of cruel and unusual punishment?

Among the correctional officers there was one oft-repeated observation concerning the cause of the Attica riot: a breakdown in discipline. Many correctional officers felt that because they had recently been restricted in their use of solitary confinement and the locking of inmates in their cells for long periods, their behavioral control over the inmates was reduced.

It can be seen that many of the demands of the Attica inmates are congruent with improvements in our prison system which are suggested

14. President's Commission on Law Enforcement and Administration of Justice, *National Survey of Corrections*–Task Force Report, Corrections (Washington, D.C.: Government Printing Office, 1967).

from a behavior-modification point of view. On the other hand, the "breakdown of discipline" theory advanced by the correctional officers seems to typify the reliance of prison personnel on punishment in the absence of an adequate system of rewards. While there is no guarantee that utilizing some principles of social-learning theory will significantly improve conditions in our prisons, there are many indications that this would be the case.

An extraordinarily large body of research has demonstrated the power of social-learning theory in comprehending and modifying human behavior. Sociologists have too long ignored its potential applications for the analysis of social behavior and the solution of social problems; it is time that applied sociology put learning theory more earnestly to work.

. . . it is only through the knife
of the anatomist that we have
the science of anatomy, and
. . . the knife of the anatomist
is also an instrument which
explores only by doing
violence.

> —Norbert Wiener,
> *God and Golem, Inc.*

part four

SOCIAL
CONFLICT

Among other applied sociologists, conflict-resolution specialists will see
a steady increase in the demand for their services as conciliators in

the 1970s. As we move from physical to verbal violence, and from blind hatreds to partially sighted hostilities, our styles of conflict change in kind: police dogs and family vendettas are replaced by cathartic personal confrontations and community exercises in renewing cooperation. We seek fundamental reforms in place of cosmetic treatments.

As the essays below make plain, the demands made of applied sociologists in these endeavors—demands for creativity, craft, and personal courage—are very great. In few other situations are the stakes so high, the risks so great, and the potential rewards so enormous. Conflict resolution as a calling of applied sociology is one that honors the profession and the action sociologist in a very special way.

ten

YOUTH RESPONDS TO CRISIS: CURAÇAO, AN EXAMPLE OF PLANNED CHANGE
A. Paul Hare

After the brickbats have been hurled and the buildings burned, after the catharsis of riotous destruction—then what? How do we put together a new and better society? How do we ensure that useful lessons are learned, that the pain, destruction, and even death have not been in vain? With memories of fiery Detroit, Harlem, and Watts, and most recently Northern Ireland, ever with us, we are pressed to find better answers to the question of how to rebuild after conflict. The following essay offers a model drawn from two vital sources: the values of Gandhian nonviolent direct action and the values of the radical critics of the social sciences. This model is oriented toward constructive follow-through, and it rests on a sound and productive theoretical foundation.

In May of 1969 there was a crisis on the island of Curaçao when rioters burned and looted part of the major city. The people of the island sought help from various sources to understand the social problems that had led to the riot and to promote a process of nonviolent social change. As one response a group of professionals, government officials, and businessmen joined with some consultants from the United States to form the Antillean Institute of Social Science, a summer institute held in 1970, which would provide a means for all citizens who wished to learn more about the economic, political, and social problems.

One of the courses planned for the institute was a workshop on Youth and Social Change. Since we wished to make the point that youth could play a valuable part in the process of change, we included on the American staff two men who were at the time both undergraduates at Haverford College: Frank Carney and Fred Ovsiew. Both men were experienced in the theory of nonviolence and the process of change in the United States.

In the pages that follow I first present an account of the development and the activities of the Institute, based on my report to the members of the Institute, which I prepared as the co-director.[1] This is followed by comments by Frank Carney and Fred Ovsiew on their role in the Institute and the questions this role raised for them as agents of change in another culture.

An Account of the Antillean Institute of Social Science

The first sessions of the Antillean Institute of Social Science were held on the island of Curaçao, Netherlands Antilles, during June, July, and August 1970. The Institute had been designed as an approach to nonviolent planned change as one response to the violent change that had occurred on the island on May 30, 1969, when rioting workers burned and looted in the town of Willemstad and brought down the local government.

THE RIOT A full account of the riot, including an hour-by-hour summary of the events of May 30, has been issued in Dutch by the Government Commission appointed to study the riot. In addition, a paperback book, written in Papiamentu in the form of a novel, illustrates the emotional involvement of those who participated in the disorders. At the time of the Institute, over a year later, little had intervened to dim the memories of the event. Unfortunately, few visible changes in the social structure of the island had occurred. Planned change was especially difficult because a formal local government for the Netherlands Antilles was not reestablished until July 1970. Nevertheless, basic governmental services were available during this period since the islands are in fact part of the Kingdom of the Netherlands.

In September 1969 Frank McDonald summed up the situation in a paper for the Institute of Current World Affairs. He said in part:

> A few months ago, no one would have thought that the Dutch government would be airlifting paratroopers to quell rioters in quiet, sun-soaked Curaçao. But on May 30 what started as a small strike directed against Shell Oil of Curaçao became an island-wide, $40 million insurrection. The immediate cause, a group of plumbers demanding higher wages from a Shell Oil Contractor (Wescar Inc.), was of course only a surfaced expression of the more serious economic and social woes in Curaçao. For behind the façade of some of the Caribbean's most glamorous duty-free shops, international hotels, and tourist resorts, lurk numerous pockets of poverty, vast numbers of unemployed, and a growing resentment of Dutch control of the island.[2]

1. I presented a similar report which I draw on here at meetings of the American Association for the Advancement of Science, Philadelphia, December 1971. Report completed under National Institute of Mental Health Grant No. 5 R01 MH17421-03 SP.
2. Frank McDonald, Letter for the Institute of Current World Affairs, dated 1 September 1969.

REQUESTS FOR EXPERT ADVICE   Members of the business community of Curaçao were accustomed to seek expert advice to solve management problems or introduce new manufacturing and marketing techniques. Many businessmen had already taken part in several management-training workshops with experts, primarily from the United States, who would come to the island to conduct a course. The fact that about a dozen modern computers were in use on the island was another measure of the community's success in keeping abreast of current business practices. Thus, when a major social problem erupted on the island, it was not surprising that these same men turned once more to outsiders for advice.

One group of businessmen from the Chamber of Commerce had read about the success of David McClelland's "achievement motivation" training which had been developed at Harvard University. A member of McClelland's applied-research institute (Sterling Institute) was invited to the island to conduct a survey and make a proposal for action. The proposal, which was accepted and implemented, called for a series of workshops to introduce business and government leaders to achievement-motivation techniques so that they in turn could conduct workshops for several hundred other community leaders. Concurrently, new organizations were to be developed to plan and implement change.

Although the Sterling Institute program and the Antillean Institute of Social Science program had independent origins in the United States, they merged on Curaçao in both intended and unintended ways. Some community leaders were eventually involved on the boards and committees of both programs, and the sources of funds were often the same and thus competing. Since the Sterling Institute arrived on the island first, the Antillean Institute was described at one point as a subproject of the Sterling program, to provide some necessary integration for the individuals involved as well as for the members of the society who sought to respond to both programs. The Sterling Institute program concentrated on weekend training workshops and long-range planning while the Antillean Institute concentrated on teaching and research, so the two programs were actually complementary.

The development of the Sterling Institute program is a story in itself. I will not attempt to give any more details here. Nor will I do any more than note that these were not the only individuals and groups interested in social change or research to visit the island after the riot. Nevertheless, the activities of the Sterling Institute and the Antillean Institute played the more prominent part in the efforts toward social change during the summer of 1970.

Concurrent with the inquiries to the Sterling Institute by the Chamber of Commerce, Victor Pinedo, Jr., a former Haverford College student, wrote to Dr. Peter Bennett, a faculty member at Haverford, to ask for the help of a research team to study the social-psychological aspects of the problems underlying the riot. Pinedo, a native of Curaçao, was at that time president of the Lions Club and the successful manager of a number of food and soft-drink companies, most notably Coca-Cola. To Dr. Bennett, Pinedo said:

> As a result of the riots a number of stores in the heart of the business center were burnt to the ground, 1,000 people will remain unemployed and about $50,000,000 of property was damaged. This is the first occurrence of its kind in Curaçao and the reaction of the people after the riots showed that there is a great deal of wrong in the values of the population.
>
> In view of the above, the community leaders feel that there is a big psychological problem in the population. As there are no experts on this island to point out where the problem lies and find its solution, I am writing you this letter to find out whether you know of any behavior scientist team which could come to Curaçao to make a study of the situation and advise the community as to what action they should take to remedy the problem.

Since I had had some experience doing research and working with the Peace Corps in the Philippines and doing research and teaching in Africa, Pinedo's letter was passed on to me. I suggested to him that one week be devoted to a preliminary survey of the problems on Curaçao as a basis for a proposal for research. During the first two days of the week I asked that we meet some people who might help us carry out any action research proposal we might formulate. We should also meet persons who could be potential members of the research or action team. Finally we should interview those who represented a cross section of the people who had been actively studying the riots or who were principally affected by them. By midweek we would stop and draw up a tentative plan; the remaining days of the week could be spent in determining the amount of interest in the plan.

STAGES IN THE DEVELOPMENT OF THE INSTITUTE The planning that eventually led to the first sessions of the Antillean Institute of Social Science passed through the four stages which have been observed in successful group development in many different situations.[3] In the first stage of *defining the situation*, the basic idea of the group is established. In the second stage of *gathering resources*, the resources necessary for the group task are gathered or manufactured. In the third stage of *defining roles and developing morale*, the roles for the leaders and other group members are specified and attention is given to developing group morale.

3. Paul A. Hare, "Theories of Group Development and Categories for Interaction Analysis," Nonviolent Action Research Project Report No. 4, Haverford College, 1970.

In the final stage of *group work,* the group members carry out the task that first brought them together.[4]

In the case of the Antillean Institute the first-stage activities were concentrated in one week of November 1969 when Pinedo and I developed the basic plan. The second stage reached a high point when I returned to the island in January 1970 with several colleagues to begin a major fund-raising drive for the $60,000 we had budgeted for the Institute. The third phase was again concentrated in a week in May when we recruited staff and worked out the details of the teaching-and-research activities. The final phase consisted of holding two five-week sessions of the Antillean Institute of Social Science during the months of June, July, and August 1970.

In many respects the Antillean Institute looked like any other summer institute in social science. There were courses, research seminars, public lectures, and informal gatherings. Some marked and dramatic differences were observable, however, and some of these can be traced to our efforts to be responsive to two sets of values, one set proposed by the advocates of Gandhian nonviolent direct action[5] and the other derived from the new radical critiques of social science.[6]

Gandhi's Principles: Truth and Love. The keys to Gandhi's principles of nonviolent change are to be found in two concepts, truth (*satya*) and noninjury (*ahimsa*). Gandhi called the power behind his approach *satyagraha* ("truth force") rather than "passive resistance" or "nonviolent resistance" because the earlier terms did not reflect the action and initiative of his approach. The truths he sought were especially about man's relation to his fellow man. He began his campaigns in South Africa where the European settlers placed severe restraints on the action and development of the Indians, Bantu, and other minority peoples. He continued his campaign in India where the caste system (and the British rule) placed restrictions on all classes of Indians. The main truth Gandhi sought was the sense of a wider identity which would allow groups, previously segregated by custom, to come together and work side by side as human beings. Truth was not simply reaching an agreement whereby the will of the majority would be accepted by the minority, but finding a new overarching sense of identity that would provide more freedom for all.

The concept of *ahimsa* in the Indian tradition means that man should not injure another living thing. The concept can also be said to stand for

---

4. These stages are referred to in functional theory as (1) latent pattern maintenance and tension management, (2) adaptation, (3) integration, and (4) goal attainment.

5. A. P. Hare and Herbert Blumberg, *Nonviolent Direct Action: American Cases* (Washington and Cleveland: Corpus Books, 1968).

6. "Some Radical Perspectives in Sociology," *Sociological Inquiry* 40 (Winter 1970): 1.

love. In this sense love means that we value our fellow humans so dearly that we would not only not harm them but also would accept "self-suffering" should they fail to understand and seek to harm us. Love also means a warmth and closeness of interpersonal relations which gives us a sense of community, allowing us to "live the revolution" now rather than postpone our involvement in life until some drastic, perhaps violent change has brought about the ideal society.

The Radical Critique of Social Science. The radical critique of social science has developed over the past few years as younger social scientists have challenged the older Establishment social scientists in confrontations at professional meetings and in articles in the professional literature. The advocates of the radical position suggest that professional social scientists should be willing to take stands on current issues of national importance and to do research on behalf of the people they study rather than on behalf of the government Establishment which usually provides the research funds.

Regarding research in a developing country, the typical approach has been for someone from a developed country to decide on a research problem without consulting persons in the developing country. The researcher has secured his own funds and staff, and has conducted the research using the persons in the developing country only as subjects. The data have then been taken home to be analyzed and published, some years later, in a journal or monograph that probably never reached the hands of the subjects who supplied them.

In many cases the research process still takes this form, but in others the process has evolved through a stage of participant observation to a stage of mutual cooperation between researchers from both countries, and finally to a stage in which the research becomes part of the process of social change rather than a preliminary step toward beginning the process. The research on Curaçao took the final form. Rather than respond to a request for research by simply sending in a research team, we evolved a process by which the members of the community could look at themselves while they were learning social-science theory and skills.

PLANNING THE INSTITUTE   By the middle of the week's visit in November, Pinedo and I had drafted an outline for a Summer Institute in Social Science. Our plan called for an Institute to be held during June, July, and August 1970 for from 100 to 300 students who would be primarily high-school graduates. (Since there is no formal education beyond high school in the Netherlands Antilles we were not competing with any local university.) The curriculum was to include general social-science courses as well as special courses in business and industry, Curaçao studies, and education. Each course or seminar was designed to meet some need identified by one or more of the community leaders interviewed during the first few days of preparatory work. We expected that the local government would provide classrooms and office space and that industry would donate computer time and other facilities. Our first budget of $60,000 would provide for a Curaçaon staff of at least nine persons, four senior professors from the United States, and four additional specialists representing the fields of journalism, computer programming, and youth work.

A single page was stenciled and given out on the island to members of the Lions Club and other community leaders who were asked to comment on the proposal. When a copy of the proposal was given to Stanley Brown he wrote the letters CIA across the top as part of his comment. Brown, a prominent member of the *Frente de Obrero*, a political party formed after the riot which identified primarily with the workers involved in the riot, was suggesting that we probably represented the Central Intelligence Agency. My response was, "Sure, Stanley, that stands for Curaçao Improvement Association."

I also took advantage of several opportunities to speak about nonviolence during the week, one of which involved a half-hour national television program where I was interviewed about Gandhi and his methods.

Our January visit two months later was designed to publicize the plan for the Institute as a prelude to fund raising and to recruit more teaching staff. This time I was accompanied by Harvey Glickman, political scientist, and Wyatt MacGaffey, anthropologist, both of Haverford, and by Lee Bramson, a sociologist from Swarthmore College, who were expected to be senior members of the Institute staff. Frank Loescher, sociologist and retiring director of the U.S.–South Africa Leader Exchange Program, also accompanied us at his own expense to see if he might be able to suggest some action possibilities based on his South African experience.

Pinedo had arranged a heavy schedule for us and had made good use of the news media. We were met at the airport by television cameramen. Our discussions and panel presentations were covered by the local newspapers. We appeared on the national television network with some of our Curaçaon colleagues. We also met representatives of the national and local governments. We presented our revised plans to our new Board of Directors with representatives of both the government and private sectors (since the project had already outgrown Lions Club sponsorship). We held a final press conference and left the island with the feeling that the project might well succeed.

During the weeks that followed the Institute staff on Curaçao sent out an appeal for funds asking local businessmen and government representatives to pledge $200 "scholarships" for students for the Institute. The call for contributions included a brief description of the Institute (now with its own Instituto Antillano di Sciencia Social letterhead), a list of the twenty-five members of the Board of Trustees, quotations about the Institute, and a pledge form.

At the same time I sent out written appeals or phoned to about a dozen foundations in the United States from a list supplied by the Development Office of Haverford College. Among others the list included Ford, Rockefeller, Shell, Kellogg, and the U.S. government AID branch. The letter asked for $25,000 to bring in additional specialists for the Institute. No foundation responded with a grant. Various reasons were given: some were concerned about their U.S. tax status if the project had political implications; and one foundation did not want to finance "gringos" who might meddle in Latin American affairs.

Fortunately, about $50,000 was pledged from sources on Curaçao so that we were able to go ahead with the planning by cutting out some of the special projects. As it turned out, not having U.S. funds made us somewhat less open to charges of being agents of the CIA, although this suspicion was never fully dissipated. Near the end of the project, after we had established ourselves as a going concern, we were still advised against bringing even one more American resource person to the island. The American influence was already seen as great enough by some Antilleans, and the extra person might just be the feared CIA agent.

During February, March, and April, members of the Board and staff of the Institute on Curaçao were very active. They prepared a questionnaire in both Papiamentu and Dutch which was sent to prospective students to determine the relative interest in a list of twenty possible courses. (We were considering up to twenty-five different courses at that time, but six were eventually dropped or combined. Professor MacGaffey received a grant to do research in the Congo and could not come. He was replaced by Vera Green who took over MacGaffey's courses as well as those of an Antillean sociologist who was not able to be on the island for the whole term. Other courses were dropped because they were judged to be too controversial for one reason or another.) Also, during April, the Institute was formally registered at a *Stichting,* according to Dutch law.

Final decisions about courses were made during my third visit to the island in May. This time I was accompanied by Professor Bramson who helped work out final details and made preliminary arrangements for a research project in education. Bert Kritzer, a computer programmer, also made the trip to prepare the computer programs for the courses on research methods and the actual research we planned to do during the summer.

Near the end of this visit a concern was expressed that the Institute staff was being dominated by the American group. In response we cut down on the number of courses to be taught by Americans, told a few additional Americans who were potential staff members that we could not use them, and did not use family members of the American staff as part of the American team. (Although my daughter, Sharon Hare, an anthropologist, assisted Professor Green in the anthropological research, she was not included on the payroll.) I also offered to step down as co-director to become the liaison with the American staff. My offer was not accepted, but the other changes were made. Since we did not hear about the final outcome of the deliberations of the Institute Board until after we had returned to the United States, we left the island on an anxious note. It was possible that the "revolution within the revolution" might bring the Institute to a halt.

It was little consolation that the revolt against the leadership typically takes place in the third phase in groups of many types. In theory, what we see happening is that members who might have gone along with the basic definition of the Institute (*defining the situation*), thinking that the Institute would never be able to raise the money and survive the phase of *gathering resources*, now find that they must settle any differences in the phase of *defining roles and developing morale* if they are to have any influence on the outcome. Once the group moves into the final phase of *group work* the major task becomes that of working toward the goal as it has been defined. Although minor revolts might be expected at the end of each phase, just before the group moves on to the next phase, the third-phase revolt often seems the most dramatic. Rather than revolt, some persons may leave the group at each stage. Thus, some drop out because they do not like the basic definition, some because they disagree with the allocation of funds, and finally some, as in this case, consider dropping out when they find they do not like the arrangements for leadership or for other member roles.

Formal specifications for the roles of the American staff were then expressed in Contracts for Services. Providing the housing called for in the contract turned out to be another difficult problem. Few houses were available during the ten-plus weeks of the Institute. As a result some American staff moved several times during the summer and others were unhappy with arrangements for various periods of time. This problem provides one of the main reasons for recommending a six-week Institute in the future, which would coincide with the school vacation when a number of teachers would be off the island. Providing services of all kinds turns out to be the major hidden cost of using expatriates as staff.

THE SUMMER SESSIONS Everyone who wanted to attend the Institute was allowed to register (269!). There were no fees other than for books, a practice in keeping with the other forms of public education on the island which have government support. Students could choose from nineteen different courses, with a few popular courses such as the introduction to sociology, introduction to anthropology, leadership and group dynamics, child psychology and youth and social change being offered twice so that the total enrollment in any one class could be kept to about thirty persons.

Each class met twice a week for one hour and twenty minutes over a five-week period. One set of classes was held Monday and Wednesday at 7:00 P.M. or at 8:40 P.M., and the other set of classes was held on Tuesday and Thursday at the same time periods. Jaap van Soest, the Institute administrator, arranged the class hours so that there would be a minimum of conflict in individual schedules, since most students were taking at least two courses. The first five-week session of the Institute was held from June 15 through July 17 and the second session from July 20 through August 21.

At the end of the first session several short summary reports were prepared for a meeting of the Board. A typical class, for example, was attended by twenty-five to thirty students. On the average, about 80 percent of those who registered for classes attended. Compared to other experiences with adult education on the island, members of the Curaçaon staff judged our attendance figures to be quite good. The majority of our students proved to be between twenty and thirty years of age. The majority were high-school graduates, with the younger participants tending to have a higher education level. This probably reflects a similar trend in the general population. Finally, of the 269 students enrolled, most were taking two courses. Almost twice as many students were enrolled for the First Session only (96) as for the Second Session only (51). The typical (modal) participant was either taking two courses in each session (42) or taking two courses in the first session and none in the second (50).

RESEARCH   Various research projects were conducted with active collaboration betwen American and Antillean staff. In some cases the research was conducted as a part of a seminar at the Institute, in others by a special project team or Task Force. In each case it was hoped that the Antillean members would be able to continue the same project or conduct similar projects after the Institute was over. We recognized that there would be a continuing need for accurate data about the state of the society and accurate measures of the effectiveness of programs for change.

The major research projects included:

> *Education.* Bramson and his colleagues prepared questionnaires to be given
> to a sample of approximately 500 teachers and 1,500 students in the
> secondary schools as a major study of education and aspiration on
> Curaçao. When completed, this study could be compared with a similar
> study conducted on the island of St. Croix.

Voluntary Associations. Green and her colleagues interviewed members of many voluntary associations on the island. These data will be compared with similar data from Aruba to show the role that voluntary associations play in the social system.

Labor Force. As a demonstration of the uses of sampling and computer-based statistical techniques, Hare and a Task Force of volunteers representing a cross section of the island drew a sample of every 30th person from the file of approximately 33,000 persons registered at the Government Labor Office. To this were added samples of employees from Shell, island and national governments, and other categories of workers not ordinarily carried in the government files. The data have been left in a data bank at the Institute and a few copies have been distributed. In addition to providing an estimate of some characteristics of different segments of the labor force, the project can serve as a model for analysis when Jan Spit, head of the government Labor Welfare Service, completes his projected total registration of all island employees.

Computer Programs. As a special project Bert Kritzer of the Institute staff and Paul Tevreden of the IBM Data Center adapted a set of statistical and data processing programs for use at the IBM Center. The programs include scoring and data screening and manipulation routines, and statistical programs for correlations, factor analysis, regression, analysis of variance, *t*-test, frequency distributions, means, standard deviations, and sums, and cross tabulation and contingency analysis. Each program, together with directions and sample data, is available at the IBM Center. Treveden and several other computer programmers on the island are familiar with their use and can help prepare data for analysis. During the latter part of the summer the programs were used for the Labor Force study, the research on the barrio of Santa Rosa conducted by the research methods class, and for an analysis of personnel ratings by a Task Force of representatives of Texas Instruments and Hendersons.

Political Analysis. During the second session Harvey Glickman interviewed a number of people on the island to identify areas for research concerning the partial dissolution of traditional patterns of leadership and support.

Economic Development Policy. Also during the second session, Sayre Schatz collected data for his "Report on Economic Development Policy for Curaçao" which has already been submitted to the Institute. His report includes sections on the nature of the Curaçaon economy, wage increases, and suggested policies for planning and foreign-exchange activities.

COMMUNITY ACTIVITIES   Several projects were related to the work of the students in the course on Youth and Social Change taught by Ger Van Atten, Frank Carney, and Fred Ovsiew. These included developing a proposal for an Antillean Youth Service Corps, conducting a two-week program to develop barrio libraries and reading programs, and working with a group of young men who were developing the Casa Manita as a youth center for the urban area. Another project enjoyed by members of the Institute and the community at large was the journal *Voz Di Inansiso* produced by the members of the workshop on journalism during the first session.

The project that reached the largest number of people in the Netherlands Antilles was the marathon "teach-in" organized by Harold Arends and other members of the Antillean staff. The teach-in began at 9:00 A.M. one Saturday near the end of the second session and lasted well into the early morning hours of the next day. Some people remained talking outside the Center for the Arts, where the event had been held, until three o'clock in the morning. The events of the day included a series of panel discussions on vital topics for the Netherlands Antilles: the Antillean identity, the state of the economic and political systems, and the values and aspirations of youth. After each panel, members of the audience could ask questions for as long as the topic held their interest. It was an exciting example of freedom of speech, and constituted the first time that there had been an open discussion of the problems and prospects of the Netherlands Antilles since the riot of May 30, 1969. The entire program, including one rather heated exchange near the end during which some persons left the main hall to meet in protest in the corridors, was carried live on a national radio station. At intervals, food and entertainment were offered in the lounge. In all it was a memorable occasion. Through it our "students" seem to reveal the fact that they had learned their lessons and were able to discuss the social problems they faced from new perspectives and with a new openness to the views of others.

PLANS FOR THE FUTURE   By the end of the second session we were already looking ahead to the possibility that the Institute might be held again the following year. A plan was submitted to the Board which called for a smaller budget for a single six-week session during the school vacation. More emphasis would be placed on the Antillean staff. Ideally, a small central staff would be able to continue some of the Institute's activities throughout the year. Since a successful weekend Institute had been held on Aruba in July there were plans for a similar Institute to be held on Aruba the following year. Each of the island Institutes might be combined in an overall Antillean Institute. Finally, I suggested some guidelines for planned change based on a functional analysis of social systems.

After the return of the American staff to the United States, the *Bryn Mawr–Haverford College News* carried an account of our experience. In that article I am quoted as saying: "The Institute grew out of the concern of members of Curaçao business, labor, and government to examine and accelerate the process of social change currently taking place on the island." All who had come from the outside had become very much involved in the process of change. We were thankful for the opportunity to use social science in the service of a group of people working together for a better society.

Appendix

OBSERVATIONS BY FRANK CARNEY   One of the greatest problems I had working on Curaçao was getting over the role I had anticipated for myself. I had seen myself working with people who had recently rioted to show their frustration about their social situation and who were ready to do things to solve some of their problems. This was a great mistake. The people in the course (Youth and Social Change) set up as a vehicle to organize work units were not interested in working. Difficulties also arose from our side: First, we did not speak Dutch or Papiamentu (their most frequently used languages), which made communicating hard. Second, we were viewed as American imperialists; the difficult part of this was that I agreed with them.

In light of these problems, we decided to set up the course so that the Curaçaons would dominate the sessions. This caused complete confusion. A few intellectual leftists took advantage of the situation to make our "American" presence more difficult. But, unfortunately, even their zeal was short-lived. In the end we abandoned the hope of inspiring working groups and decided to lead talks about Gandhi, Fanon, and Marx, et al., hoping at least to give the class a different perspective on society.

We were able to have some effect on at least two existing groups. One was a group that was trying to set up what would be the equivalent of a neighborhood recreation center. Our presence alone seemed to be the incentive for them to work harder. They were very Establishment-oriented. They seemed to be trying to impress us with their ability to organize. The other group was interested in reviving knowledge of the island's folkloristic traditions. They were very interested in what similar black groups in the United States were doing, so I was able to draw parallels with black activity on Curaçao and the United States for them. An interesting end to one conversation was that black people in the United States should emigrate.

The main difficulty that I had with redefining my anticipated role was that I lacked the skills the people needed, so I kept looking for a group that could use the skills I could offer.

OBSERVATIONS BY FRED OVSIEW   I have three points to make about what I learned in Curaçao. It is our learning that I must emphasize, for a number of reasons: We have had little feedback from Curaçao, and it would in any case be hard to evaluate our impact on them. But I must say right off that there are hard questions to be asked about the legitimacy of our going to Curaçao, earning large salaries, complaining about the lack of air conditioners, and then concerning ourselves with our learning.

This leads me to the first dimension that I want to discuss. I learned to ask, "Who's in it for what?" Each of us Americans was on a different trip. The youth workers, I think, had fantasies of leading a revolution of Third World people; another member of the team forthrightly was there to do research; and we were all there to take a vacation in the Caribbean and have an unusual learning experience. For anyone on Curaçao to evaluate our work intelligently, we would have had to expose our own hidden agendas. Perhaps more important, if we had wanted to avoid a haunting sense of frustration and failure, we would have had to be honest with ourselves about what we were all about. When we couldn't pinpoint these anxieties, perhaps we had a clue to unadmitted goals.

But we didn't own up, I believe, to all our hidden agendas. And thereby we kept ourselves from being confronted by our clients, or for that matter by ourselves or each other.

A second important dimension that I clarified for myself in Curaçao involves support and estrangement. We were, after all, working in an alien culture. At times we longed for more familiar surroundings, for at least the ease of communication that would come with speaking the same language. How did we handle the anxieties that developed in this situation?

I believe that we used a number of defenses. Most important, we stuck together. Like the Jews in Exodus, when confronted with a painful and ambiguous situation, we returned to the Golden Calf that we knew. On weekends we went swimming—with each other. We enjoyed talking with each other about Americana. Some of the Americans brought their families and made a home away from home.

We used other defenses. We idealized the people we were working with, who became for some of us gallant representatives of an assaulted culture; or alternatively some of us didn't work with them at all but chose to use Curaçaons as research material and assistants. We planned grand plans that seem in retrospect, at least to me, to be out of reach for and irrelevant to Curaçao.

I feel some anger about our using these defenses, because I think they made us come on more patronizing and less available. But, on the other hand, they helped us function. We all felt limits as to how far we could extend ourselves, and it wouldn't have been productive to venture too far and collapse. This, in any case, is a common phenomenon. One reason for the retreat of the young Left of the past few years into mountain communes is that people were burned out after years of struggle without support, in a foreign land called America. I am saying that this is a dimension that has to be considered in every effort at social change. And it is not simply a drawback that people engaged in making change have limitations. The lesson, it seems to me, is that we are human too, and our creative learning involves building a situation not so threatening that we must insulate ourselves from growth.

I would make one more observation. A great deal of what we were able to do depended on our entry point into the society. We had been invited initially through the Lions Club. Our first contacts were with important people in the business community; we had quick access to the key people in government and education as well. This worked both ways. Our access to resources that were unavailable to people who had lived their whole lives on Curaçao worked to the advantage of poor people on a couple of occasions. On the other hand, our credibility with some radicals was impaired. Yet, on the whole, they were very open to us, and were willing to accept us for what we actually did. What was more destructive was that quick access works both ways. We were not merely identified with the people who invited us, but were objectively most available and indebted to them. Naturally enough, the easiest people for us to listen to were the wealthy and educated: the people who spoke the best English had our ear. So when we were searching for a project, it was convenient to do some labor studies with the support and assistance of the personnel managers of the large (foreign) corporations. But the question must be asked of this, as of the whole project, Whose interests were served?

eleven

THE "LABORATORY CONFRONTATION":
AN APPROACH TO CONFLICT MANAGEMENT AND SOCIAL CHANGE
Irving Goldaber and Holly G. Porter

To resolve something as old and familiar as intergroup social conflict often requires something new and novel. This essay analyzes such a tool for conflict resolution. A field-tested innovation, "LABORATORY CONFRONTATION" challenges the conventional wisdom that holds that conflict can be resolved only by a loss of interest on the part of one of the antagonists, or by one antagonist overpowering the other. Instead, "LABORATORY CONFRONTATION" enables opponent groups to emerge either satisfied or contented, no small accomplishment when participants are angry minority-group members and city policemen, or school personnel and students, or prison administrators and inmates. Sociological sophistication is integral to the laboratory-confrontation process. Through that process, a firm groundwork is laid for continuing progress after the laboratory situation has ended.

Social conflict respects no boundaries of place and time. The sociologist functioning in the area of conflict management, therefore, operates without the restrictions normally imposed by the convenience of geography or the moment. The relationships of people per se are his concern, not the place where or the time when these relationships occur—even though factors of place and time are inevitably inextricably interwoven component parts of the conflict.

Furthermore, when conflict manifests itself as crisis—whether the occurrence is unforeseen or predicted—the sociologist is pressed into service instantly. Under this arrangement he does not have the opportunity to assess the situation in detail or to prepare the parties involved for the procedures he wishes to apply. As a result, the sociologist specializing in

Portions of this article are based upon material in Irving Goldaber's "Social Conflict Management and Social Change," *Journal of Social Issues* (forthcoming, 1974).

conflict management must be ready to utilize his skills anywhere, under any circumstances, and without delay. We have certainly found this to be the case in the work we have undertaken. In some instances we have luxuriated in the sufficiency of time necessary to secure cooperation and to establish a level of expectation for a successful outcome of the process we were about to pursue. In the main these were instances where governmental officials and community leaders had diagnosed the situation accurately and had expressed a willingness to engage in preventative programming to reach an accord acceptable to the conflicting parties.

Too often, however, naiveté, fear, indecision, or a determination to proceed along another route complicates the instant situation and makes the task of the clinical sociologist far more complex. Unfortunately, our work history also reflects this particular state of affairs. We have heard the telephone call in the early-morning hours summoning us to a distant city that has burst into civil disorder. Without the benefit of tool kit and gear, we have had to move to the task, our training, experience, and professional creativity leading us quickly to a valid analysis of and prescriptive approach to the problem. Critical in this, or in the far less frantic, far better prepared route mentioned above, is our special orientation and process, the "LABORATORY CONFRONTATION," which we explain now in detail. To place it in context we begin with an explanation of our guiding frame of reference—whether we be called months or hours before we go into action.

Frame of Reference

Typically, conflict arises between groups when a discrepancy exists between the availability of a commodity—however tangible or intangible it may be—and the intent of different groups to possess it. (Some examples of a tangible commodity are territory, goods, and services; examples of an intangible one are respect, authority, power, and exclusivity of possession.) When it occurs, conflict is handled by a process involving the interplay of competition and cooperation, and the outcome involves a vector of balance.[1] This may be created by an absolute possession of the commodity (with the deprived party accepting the situation), an even sharing of it, or a position somewhere in between. As long as both sides are either satisfied (i.e., with their wants and expectations having been met to the full) or

1. A simple illustration of this phenomenon is the sports contest in which two teams play against each other on the same field, with the same ball, with the same regulations, with the same referee. The two teams are in fact playing not against each other but with one another. Indeed the one team could not participate in the contest if the other didn't appear and agree to play.

merely contented (i.e., with their limited achievement keeping them from finding significant fault with the solution), the conflict and its attendant outcome serve to reintegrate the social relationship between the groups.

While conflict is a condition for integration, it is also a catalyst for change. It may appear that dormancy precludes conflict, but in actuality, dormancy exists only because there is an absence of visible activity.[2] Seemingly dormant situations are in reality being bombarded by variables seeking to dislodge the apparent equilibrium. Hence, conflict may be considered to be universal, and, there are no fixed, no permanent solutions to social conflict. There are only temporal accommodations—some, for one reason or another, of longer duration than others. The nature of group relations, if not the history of mankind, is that of a continual give-and-take which, in the final analysis, is precisely what constitutes the dynamics of the social process.

The "LABORATORY CONFRONTATION"

Our method of dealing with conflict provides representatives of antagonist groups with a procedure whereby they might negotiate their differences and join in a common undertaking to create the changes both groups seek. As the "LABORATORY CONFRONTATION" provides a functional solution to the problems facing adversary groups at any given time, the method may be utilized whenever the need recurs.

While nondirective in nature, the "LABORATORY CONFRONTATION" is a carefully structured arrangement. It seeks to offer a social-action alternative for energies bent upon creating changes—an alternative that enables the opponent groups to emerge either satisfied or contented.

How does it accomplish this? The procedure is based upon some critical formulations, namely:

1. Adversary groups are, in reality, interdependent. Their separate well-being is at most made possible and at least augmented by the reciprocal nature of their and their opponent's actions. The structure of the "LABORATORY CONFRONTATION" recognizes and promotes this interdependency. In fact the laboratory's progress is made possible by the symbiotic relationship of the opponent groups.

   Groups that are dedicated to the physical annihilation of their antagonists have no role in the "LABORATORY CONFRONTATION." Recognizing whether a group advocating destruction is utilizing rhetoric or describing a tactic is difficult, however. The former is too often mistaken for the latter, and, since those who deal in invective and threat normally

2. It may be postulated that a state of nonactivity cannot exist in reality.

exist in the population in fewer numbers than they appear to be, the mutual dependency obtaining between them and their adversary is obfuscated.

2. Conflict responds to the law of inertia. It both feeds upon itself and consumes variables relating to it. For this reason it is of a crescive nature. In a civil disorder, for instance, yesterday's actions are today's problems. Forgotten are the situations that initially triggered the disturbance; by-passed, too, are the opportunities of yesterday to reverse the direction of the clash or arrest its movement.

Conflict expands—slowly, perhaps, but perseveringly—either until one of the groups involved is eliminated from (or eliminates itself from) the conflict or the energies of both groups are coopted into a procedure for eliminating the cause of the conflict. When opponent groups deal with one another it is usually for the purpose of seeking to gain at the other's expense. Opponent groups very rarely come together for the purpose of reconciliation.[3]

The "LABORATORY CONFRONTATION" offers this precise opportunity. When the groups convene in the laboratory they have—unknown to themselves—taken the most decisive step in the direction of rapprochement.

3. Haves and have-nots prey upon one another. Either group is capable of becoming the protagonist when gain is to be accrued by an action. The action of one group, however, creates a reaction in the other.[4]

The "LABORATORY CONFRONTATION" is predicated upon an arrangement of equality. In the laboratory both sides share the same territory, have equal status and equal influence, and make decisions with equal power. This arrangement is followed to the maximum; the consent of each laboratory participant is needed every step of the way. (An exception to this total-consent procedure is made at the conclusion of the laboratory's deliberations; it is noted in the text.)

4. Reconciliation between conflicting groups is the product of a negotiation. The fluid nature of have/have-not relationships and the desire for at least a modicum of stability between the groups give rise to a somewhat continuous negotiation, informal though it is.[5]

3. This accounts for some of the reluctance displayed when the "LABORATORY CONFRONTATION" is proposed. Governmental and community policy makers simply do not possess a history in which conflict has been resolved through means other than the loss of interest by one of the parties or the overpowering, in one way or another, of one of the antagonists.

4. The direct-action strategy, both nonviolent and violent, of the civil-rights movement in the United States created a power shift among white and black groups in the population. While the whites for all purposes retained a grasp over the economic end of urban life, the ability of blacks to obstruct and demolish (even to destroy their own living areas) got their protests and demands taken seriously.

5. The subliminal nature of the negotiation will obliterate it from the view of the casual observer of group dynamics.

The "LABORATORY CONFRONTATION" merely formalizes this condition. It enables conflicting groups to move through a set of carefully formulated procedures, from positions of polarity to a working relationship based on admixture of expediency and trust.

THE PRE-LABORATORY It is necessary for a sponsor to supply the catalytic ingredient that brings the opponent groups together in the "LABORATORY CONFRONTATION." This is usually a third party with an interest in settling the differences, but it may also be one of the confronting groups. Needless to say, the sponsor must be acceptable to both parties.

The sponsor's role involves the legitimation and actualization of the process, the acquisition of the facilitator resource, the assumption of responsibility for administrative matters, the distribution of the recommendations emerging from the laboratory to potential implementers, and the submission of a report to the participants on the extent of the implementation.

The initial chore of the sponsor is the precise identification of the groups that are to confront one another. Securing an agreement to participate in the process from each of these identified groups comes next. The sponsor explains the purposes of the laboratory and the procedures to be utilized to available leaders from each of the groups.[6] These leaders serve as access routes into the groups involved. The sponsor does not deal with them as negotiators; they merely take the message back to their own group leadership and return with an agreement (or no agreement) to participate.[7]

Once acceptance of the project has been obtained from the groups involved, the facilitator resource is engaged. The location of the laboratory is decided upon; the place selected should be neutral, convenient, and comfortable. A decision as to whether the laboratory is to be nonstop or day by day is made next. If the latter, determinations are in order regarding the number of days, the number of hours each day, and the part of each day to be utilized.

Obviously the conflict's intensity will determine whether a nonstop or day-by-day model is selected. A raging conflagration of course requires a

6. Since these leaders are in fact only couriers, the sponsor need not be concerned about the representative nature of or basis for their leadership. It is important, however, that they carry out their assignment efficiently. Experience suggests that they will; even if they do not, the laboratory is nonetheless as valuable. At any rate, no more viable alternative is available to the sponsor.

7. A protesting group might feel that participation in the laboratory will not work to its advantage, that cooperation in the process will blunt its thrust. It is pointed out that participation in the laboratory does not subtract any tool from the protestor's arsenal; he is still free to avail himself of whatever activities he planned originally.

nonstop basis. Percolating, simmering, and quiescent situations may be handled on either basis. In the case of the day-by-day approach, the number of hours the laboratory is scheduled to be in session must reflect the intensity of the problem, the number of participants, and their ability to articulate. A duration of time is necessary for a laboratory to run its course, i.e., for coalescence to occur. The hours available should not be too few; in like manner, a too-lengthy laboratory is not good.

The selection of participants now takes place. The following stipulations should govern this process:

1. Each side selects its own participants; neither side has veto power over selections made by the other side.

2. An equal number of participants—not more than ten from each side—are selected. Names are written on charts and are placed on a wall of the meeting room.

3. The views of the individuals selected by each side should represent a cross section of the views held by that group which are concerned with or critical of the other side.

4. The individuals selected by each side should be those in the community who are considered opinion makers.

5. Those selected by each side subscribe to the position that their difficulties with the other side may be resolved or may be moved toward resolution through the give-and-take of frank and thorough dialogue between both sides' participants, through the subsequent joint development of proposals for implementation and, indeed, through implementation of a fair share, at least, of the recommendations.

Again, the guidelines for selection of participants are designed to create an awareness and a manifestation of equality. They also subtly seed the process with an expectation of success.

THE LABORATORY   The process utilizes readily acceptable procedures to move the confronting groups from their polarized positions to a state of workability. The movement spans the spectrum from a specification of concerns through a clarification of views, the emergence of understanding, and a manifestation of trust to the development of an ability to prepare together recommendations for change.

Grievances are specified by each group homogeneously.[8] The dialogue regarding them is conducted pursuant to the following ground rules:

8. The laboratory's participants sit in a circle. It has been our experience that the length of the diameter of a circle containing from fourteen to twenty participants maximizes the sociometric advantages generated by the group process. It would be of interest to research this hypothesis cross-culturally.

1. Every item any participant wants to discuss is in order.

2. Each person may speak as long as he desires.

3. Individuals will be recognized in the sequence in which they signal for the floor.

4. All discussion will cease upon a signal from a facilitator. This is designed to halt abruptly any speaking out of turn or remarks made simultaneously by several persons.

5. Each specified grievance remains on the agenda until all discussion regarding it has been exhausted.

While this process appears to thwart the possibility of a free-flowing conversation, it preserves the equality and the total-consent pattern of the laboratory. Groups manage to respond with ease to points made by the opposition; either individuals wait their turn or others who are already on the list of speakers use the opportunity to make the relevant remarks. As the laboratory progresses, however, a controlled back-and-forth dialogue arrangement is introduced.

The role of the facilitator(s) is rigidly set. His concern is restricted to the management of the circle in which the participants sit. His remarks are limited to the dynamics of communication and to group process. At no time does he articulate or indicate anything regarding the content of the matter being discussed.

A coin-flip decides which set of grievances is to be discussed first. Discussion of each grievance continues, as has been noted, until all comment regarding it has been presented. Sometimes agreement on the item will emerge; sometimes disagreement will persist—but the point will have been made that agreeable parties can disagree agreeably.[9]

When all items have been discussed, the participants are grouped heterogeneously. In these mixed groups they prepare recommendations dealing with the conditions and situations affecting them. These are suggested for implementation by various bodies having the power to effectuate the changes being sought. It should be noted that the recommendations prepared by the participants will extend beyond the area of the original grievances.

Recommendations prepared by the heterogeneous groups are discussed and placed together. A poll is taken to enable the participants to indicate

---

9. Observe that in its pure sense the laboratory represents a new society, a society without a history. This new society ingests the separate histories of the groups composing it and, as it incorporates these separate pasts into its present, it enables itself to work out an uncontaminated future. As grievances are dialogued, the complicating incrustation (created by misinformation, misunderstanding, and mistrust) is decorticated and the original discrepancy laid bare. The potential harm of this newly visible matter is often negligible.

their demurrers, if any, of particular recommendations. An exception to the total-consent arrangement is made here in the interest of retaining as much of the groups' product as is possible. The final package is then presented to the sponsor.

THE POST-LABORATORY The sponsor separates the recommendations and transmits each of them to the potential implementer. He requests a response for each proposal; namely, whether or not it will be implemented. In the case of a rejection, a reason for the action is requested.[10] When the responses have been received by the sponsor, he reconvenes the participants of the laboratory and reports the results to them.

Because the recommendations are drawn up after intensive discussion, and because the confronting parties will have brought a dichotomy of views to the laboratory, the recommendations tend to be relevant and balanced. And since the laboratory may serve to unite the two former antagonists against a third group, the recommendations may appear to set upon the third group with inimical intent. Should the third group feel that it is unable to implement these recommendations, a "LABORATORY CONFRONTATION" would apparently be in order between it and the two previously separated groups.

A *Significant Note.* While the negotiation may appear to be between the participants of each group involved (and indeed the experience in the laboratory is determined by the particular mix of individuals present),[11] the laboratory is a negotiating machinery that affects the populations outside represented by the individuals inside. This is made possible by the process which enables groups to select their own participants and which produces implemented recommendations bearing upon the total populations. The object of the negotiation is not to blunt or redirect the thrust of the change-seeker, but to enable him—once he has attained a level of either positive or negative power—to utilize a procedure collaboratively with his adversary, to reach an arrangement satisfactory to both.

Utilization of the "LABORATORY CONFRONTATION"

Obviously the "LABORATORY CONFRONTATION" may be used to advantage in a conflict between any two groups. It may also be used in a

10. Since the recommending groups do not have the sophistication of the implementer in the latter's areas of responsibility and competency, the implementation will oftentimes be a variation of what was actually proposed.

11. The question is often raised as to whether "the right people have been selected to participate." A selection made by the sponsor or a veto given to each side over the other's selection would undermine the foundation of the laboratory. It may be said that, in essence, those individuals selected are "the right people."

three-way or four-way arrangement when several groups are involved in the situation.

Community conflict lends itself to treatment by the process. So do difficulties between public (or private) agencies and the community groups they serve. Conflicting segments of agencies or of business organizations can benefit from an application of the process. The controlling guideline is basic: the "LABORATORY CONFRONTATION" may be used advantageously between groups that need one another but that do not enjoy a maximally positive relationship.

To date the "LABORATORY CONFRONTATION" has been used in cities in the midst of a civil disorder, in cities that have experienced disorder and must rebuild relationships, and in cities as a preventive technique to avoid a disorder by creating conditions and making changes agreeable to all. It has been used also, in a school system between faculty and students, in a prison between inmates and staff members, and in a business organization between board members and executives. The limit to its use is the boundary of the sociological imagination.

A Typical "LABORATORY CONFRONTATION" [12]

Location. The laboratory was conducted in Urban Center, a mideastern industrial city with a population of about 100,000, approximately 15 percent of it black.

Background. Urban Center had a history of racial segregation with all the resultant conditions that this arrangement generates. At the time of the laboratory the city was experiencing the effects of a growing black militancy. Deteriorated relations existed between the black community[13] and the police department. The police were intent on keeping the city lawful and orderly. The blacks complained, not about the need for law and order, but about the abusive and discrepant nature of the law enforcement.

Sponsor. Three private organizations—one concerned with civic affairs, one in the human-relations field, and one religiously based—joined together to sponsor the "LABORATORY CONFRONTATION." The sponsoring groups believed that a working relationship between the black and white communities had to be created. As a first step they reasoned that a

---

12. The description that follows is compiled from data from a number of "LABORATORY CONFRONTATIONS" conducted by Community Confrontation and Communication Associates. As a composite it is typical of the individual laboratory.

13. Of course, there is no single "black community." There is, however, the identification that blacks have with blacks as opposed to that which they have with whites.

"LABORATORY CONFRONTATION" between police and blacks would deal with the immediate crisis, reveal the sincere and reasonable natures of both groups, develop a cooperative relationship between police and blacks, and lead to laboratories between blacks and other elements of the white community including the business/governmental establishment. Funds for the expenses of the project were secured from a local foundation.

Confronting Groups. The participants of this laboratory, then, were members of the black community and members of the police department. The "LABORATORY CONFRONTATION" was held in the lounge area of a public housing project. It ran for four days of ten hours each. Ten police officers and ten members of the black community participated.

Concerns of the Black Participants. The following is a sample of the items of concern articulated by the black participants:

—Why do police respond to calls from the white neighborhoods much more quickly than to calls for help from blacks?

—Why are some police officers so unnecessarily rough with blacks?

—Why is there abusive language toward blacks and a lack of respect for them?

—How can you expect us to respect a corrupt police officer?

—Why don't the police do something about the dope being pushed on Main Street and First Avenue?

—How come the police are so quick to remove abandoned cars from white areas when there are so many more important jobs to be done in black neighborhoods?

—If a policeman has tear gas, why does he need a nightstick, a blackjack, and a gun?

—Policemen talk to us when something is wrong; why don't they try to be friendly when something is right?

—Why are there so few black police officers and why are the ones you have held down?

—Why isn't there enforcement of the loitering amendment that was passed?

Concerns of the Police Participants. The following is a sample of the items of concern articulated by the police participants:

—Why is there almost a complete lack of cooperation between the black community and the police at the scene of crimes within the community when the police are there only to help?

—Why do the majority of the blacks allow themselves to be used and put in fear by the few rabble-rousers among them, and not seek police help?

—Why is there such a complete unawareness in the black community of the function of the police?

—Why don't blacks want to join the police department?

—Why do blacks believe that rioting is a way to get what they want?

—Why do blacks teach their young to have disrespect for police?

—Why is there such a lack of respect for law and order?

—Why do blacks allow their housing to become run down?

—Why are police judged collectively rather than individually?

—Why is communication so difficult between police and blacks?

Recommendations. After the lengthy dialogue, recommendations were developed by the participants. The following is a sample of these proposals:

—A concerted effort on the part of law-enforcement agencies in the city to alleviate the drug problem and to investigate any tavern considered by police or community to be detrimental to the welfare of the community.

—Attendance by police leadership at community meetings.

—Evaluation of the police cadet-recruiting program so that greater numbers of young and eligible black men would be interested.

—The creation of a police–community-relations unit fully staffed and authorized to engage in a vigorous program.

—The complete listing of all governmental service agencies in the daily newspaper with emergency telephone numbers.

—Advanced education for police officers in areas of urban studies, psychology, and sociology.

—Cooperation by the black community in securing applicants for the police examination.

—Creation of a summer jobs program by the business community for young people of the community.

—Increased street lighting in both the downtown and neighborhood business areas.

—Additional "LABORATORY CONFRONTATIONS" between the black and white communities.

Implementation. At the post-laboratory session (two weeks after the "LABORATORY CONFRONTATION") the sponsoring agencies reported on the agreements they had received for implementation of the approximately fifty recommendations. Eighty percent were scheduled for implementation; 20 percent were rejected (with explanations offered regarding their unfeasibility). One of the implemented suggestions resulted in a series of "LABORATORY CONFRONTATIONS" involving many groups in the city.

Results. In addition to the recommendations implemented and to the further "LABORATORY CONFRONTATIONS" that produced more recommendations, many relationships between individuals in different segments of the city were formed and a standard was established, namely, that adversary groups could create a positive working relationship through a process of dialogue and negotiation.

The student of sociology desiring to work in the area of conflict management as a third-party facilitator must prepare himself for the task. He must master the theoretical aspects of group dynamics and familiarize himself with the intricate convolutions in the interplay of power. Along the way he must become proficient in maintaining a neutral stance—one totally uncommitted to the position of either disputant while completely dedicated to the necessity of treating the conflict.

As he gains experience the new practitioner will develop his own creative approaches to the procedures he has utilized. The technology employed in third-party conflict management evolves continuously, and new insights must be translated into new techniques. But through it all a singular reference point will remain: the basic integrity of the conflicting groups and the existence of conflict as the integrating force between them.

twelve

DIGGING TUNNELS ON THE PLAINS
Robert L. Herrick

*Many people think of the action sociologist as a harried, overextended
big-town dynamo frantically searching out "where the action is." However
true this unattractive image may be of some action sociologists, it is not
applicable to many, and especially not to those sociologists who labor
unknown on college campuses in small towns. In such communities the
problems and rewards for the action sociologist are quite different from
those found in larger cities. The characteristics of action sociology in a
small college community are analyzed and assessed in the frank discussion
that follows, a case study of the writer's efforts to bring sociology to bear on
war- and peace-related public-affairs activities. Throughout this essay one
senses an action sociologist remaining patient and responsible where his
big-town colleague might grow restive and impatient. This example from a
small-town setting plainly offers much to ponder and adopt in other
settings.*

I have not specialized in research on the subject of war; therefore it is
not surprising that I am not much in demand as a consultant to agencies
responsible for deciding policy on related matters. I am not even deeply
involved in citizen-protest activities; I am not an organizer, or a
sign-carrying marcher. These noncredentials have far less to do with my
feelings about peace and war than with my circumstances and personal
style. I plan to say some things here about the circumstantial. Other
sociologists are to be found in the same social situation and must also
contend with its constraints as they attempt to become engaged with such
large issues as "the war."

About three-quarters of all American sociologists are college teachers. A
goodly proportion of these teach in small private undergraduate colleges,
located in small towns. And those of us who do not work either in
universities or in colleges located in metropolitan communities are quite
aware of working in a situation that varies significantly from those who do.

One consequence of being in departments of one, two, or three persons is the sharp reduction in the number and range of supportive relationships with professional colleagues; this isolation is a major influence in determining the quality of one's off-campus activities.

Because the concern of this book is with how the sociologist fits into the issues and problems of modern society, I shall use the ecological word "niche." Sociologists located in nonmetropolitan areas and small colleges are not in a unique relation to the issues of our society and time, such as war, and it is not to be assumed that their extracampus "occupation" is different in any essential way because of their location, but it seems clear to me that their niche is smaller, less clearly significant to the resolution of such large problems, and that they have less companionate interaction with colleagues in the performance of their occupational niche.

The "small-niche sociologist" may find that he can select from the same range of alternative styles of action available to his university and metropolitan counterparts. Research, consultancy, social critic, activist—none of these are totally excluded by virtue of a sociologist's location. Nevertheless, in acting upon his selection from these alternatives, he is going to discover some frustrations directly related to the circumstances of his being in the small-niche situation. For the engaged sociologist in any location, "The important question is whether there is a role which utilizes the sociologist's technical skills more than just carrying a sign, but which involves more direct commitments than a genuinely neutral scientific observer is able to have." [1] I am going to argue that because of the circumstantial constraints against extensive involvement in either research or consultant behavior, the small-niche sociologist becomes more directed toward the social-critic role, if he is to maintain any significant involvement with large issues.

Before I proceed, however, I wish to register my belief that it would be unfortunate if it were assumed that these small-niche situations can be ignored or abandoned. It is an easy thought to hold. Even those in such situations are often prone to yield to such negating evaluations. Most of us were trained in the metropolitan areas and all received our graduate socialization in the university setting; as a result, we often regret not being "where the action is." But when we begin to wonder about the relevance of teaching undergraduates in "provincial" settings and develop an itch to "get back in the scene" we must be careful not to forget that, although

1. Jerome Kirk, in *Sociology in Action*, ed. Arthur B. Shostak (Homewood, Ill.: Dorsey Press, 1966), p. 139.

problems vary with the scenery, they don't disappear when it changes. For those of us who lament while we languish at being so far from the action, Lester F. Ward has a cautionary tale. It is about "the Scotch engineer whom some fortune transported to the plains of Kansas before the days of Pacific railroads [and who remarked] that there could be no railroads in that country, for 'where are the hills to put the tunnels through?' " [2]

It is possible for the small-niche sociologist to find himself in the role of consultant for a segment of the antiwar movement. Even small college campuses have students who wish to express themselves on this issue, and when they are in opposition to the national government's position, they too feel they are out in the boondocks and are likely to seek someone to advise them on how their few voices may be heard. If a sociologist is available and known to have sympathy for them, they may well turn to him. They are likely to view him as being knowledgeable about social structure and able to suggest ways to influence it. This consultative relationship is very informal, quite fleeting, and I have never gained much satisfaction from it, professionally speaking. Partly this is because sometimes when I have tendered the advice that I felt I could give *as a sociologist*, it has been rejected; and partly because at other times when my advice was accepted it was not particularly sociological, but something that any other educated person my age might have suggested to younger persons. The consultant role is extremely limited for the nonspecialist when the frequency of antiwar activities is small.

Of course, frequently this role of informal consultant is, or may be, transformed into the citizen-participant role. Even in small towns demonstration marches, teach-ins, and the tensions of campus confrontations have occurred. The multitude of emotional frustrations and satisfactions to be experienced in these are not different in kind from those of the nationally headlined instances. And one must not forget that in the major events, the really big ones, the means of national mobility and communication enable full participation by members of small-campus and small-town groups. Geographic location does not exclude one from the marches on Washington, political campaigns and conventions, and the like. But, as Kirk suggests, sign-carrying is not a talent peculiar to sociologists.

I am not a specialist in peace research, the military, or political sociology, but even for the nonspecialist, the researcher role may occasionally be open for the small-niche sociologist who seeks to make a professional contribution through research. Again, the nature of the

2. Lester F. Ward, *Applied Sociology: A Treatise on the Conscious Improvement of Society by Society* (Boston: Ginn, 1906), p. 97.

situation is not designed to inflate one's sense of worth to the cause. Several years ago I was asked to make an investigation for a group gathering data to support a bill in Congress on the economic problems of conversion from military to civilian needs. Surely this is a significant problem. My assignment was to gather information on the economic dependence of northwest Iowa (specifically the Sixth Congressional District) upon military and defense spending. I diligently made as complete a study as I could and supplied my findings to those in the university and metropolitan setting who had the responsibility for the total research program. Nothing startling was found, no great economic dependence upon the "war machine" could be identified in my region by such an investigation, and I doubt the sponsors of the bill were aided much by it. Not particularly exciting.

It is my belief that the most fulfilling, and probably most needed, professional activity that can be performed by the sociologist in the small-niche situation is that of criticism, both analytic and moral. It is not an easy contribution to make, however, and again I refer to Ward's story. Even those of us who during our graduate-study years were oriented toward an acceptance of social criticism as a valid expression of the profession of sociology will recall that our training was for drilling through intellectual hills rather than for sustaining a lonely drive across the monotonous plains. And when as a small-niche sociologist, you refer to some phenomenon as "fetishism" only to discover by the response of those about you that you have not made a critical statement but have simply failed to communicate, then you begin to realize the futility of using tunnel-building equipment out of its niche.

The role of social critic is not rejected in the hinterland environment, but it must be conducted in ways different from the manners of the university symposium. In fact, the educated nonsociologist is coming to expect this role to be played by social scientists and is puzzled when it is not. At a recent meeting of churchmen (clergy and laymen) for the purpose of previewing films on environmental problems which might be distributed to Methodist churches throughout the state, one short film on the topic of war was shown accidentally. In the discussion that followed this film it was spoken of as "sociological, not ecological." I found it interesting that those engaged nonsociologists so quickly and completely identified war as a "sociological problem," when war is so infrequently treated as such by sociologists in their ordinary professional pursuits. It is my impression that although it is becoming recognized as the responsibility of social scientists to provide social criticism, we have not yet institutionalized our fulfillment of this task. It is necessary that we move toward this as quickly as possible. For if basic *understandings* about such issues as war are not offered by social scientists in institutionalized ways (e.g., texts), then from where will citizens obtain their perspectives upon the matter? From those same channels used to sell soap, obviously.

One wonders if the lack of analysis by sociologists of war and military phenomena is a recent lapse. Probably not. Bowers reports a lack of sociological interest in the military establishment until the beginning of World War II.[3] Research projects for the military have increased since 1941, but the analysis based on such research has been generalized to problems other than those of war and peace: attitude research, socialization, reference groups, leadership, troop training, and organizational effectiveness.

The small-niche sociologist is likely to be isolated from colleagues who have specialized in the matter and so he finds himself leaning heavily upon columnists in daily newspapers, *Time* magazine "essays," and even articles in *TV Guide*, for journalistic gatherings of generalized data. These data are not always very comprehensive but one does with what one has. It is indeed as Gouldner has suggested: "applied social scientists are more likely to use the concepts than the generalized propositions of their basic discipline," and also, "When the basic discipline does not provide theoretical systems or concepts aiding the applied social scientist to deal with change, the latter will develop these himself."[4] These hypotheses hold not only for sociologists employed as agents of change but also for those in the position of seeking to clarify or interpret phenomena to nonsociologists.

The more I explored my own weaknesses on the subject of war, and pondered the difficulty in hammering out a sociological analysis of war on the basis of what I could find and have time to read, the more I became convinced that the lack of a general theoretical orientation about war is a common, not unusual, condition among sociologists. It was gratifying but not pleasant to find that others seemed to agree. Davison, for example, found that one reason the social sciences have so little influence upon the formation of foreign policy is that the researchers and consultants who are so employed lack a general orientation and a time consciousness. He stated that a "grounding in history and current international relations" during the training period for students would be corrective.[5] It may be that the lack

3. Raymond V. Bowers, "The Military Establishment" in *The Uses of Sociology*, ed. Paul Lazarsfeld et al. (New York: Basic Books, 1967), p. 250.

4. Alvin W. Gouldner, "Explorations in Applied Social Science," in *Applied Sociology: Opportunities and Problems*, ed. Alvin W. Gouldner and S. M. Miller (New York: Free Press, 1965), pp. 9–10.

5. W. Phillips Davison, "Foreign Policy," in Lazarsfeld et al., *The Uses of Sociology*, pp. 391–417.

of a generalist's orientation has inhibited those sociologists who do have special interests and knowledge in current events, so that they have not organized their knowledge in general terms. If this is true for consultants and researchers on foreign policy at large, then it would be true also for the students of war in particular.

Probably a significant change has begun to take place which will improve the situation. Olsen, in the first edition of this volume, referred to the use of sociology in a training program for persons who are engaged in "the peace effort." (But this, of course, is comparable to discussing the use of sociology in the training of clergymen, or insurance salesmen; it is an instrumental use of sociology in the service of *persuasive* aims. Has sociology no interpretative performance value so it can make contributions to the actual writing of theology, or of legislation, or of the critical analysis of war and peace?)

A more recent publication suggests that the "peace education" movement is progressing in desirable ways. Washburn estimates that there are "a minimum of 150 institutions that have courses related to peace." He specifically refers to projects at Haverford, Colgate, Pittsburgh, Colorado, William Paterson, Manchester, and Saint Louis University. Again, however, it appears that participants in such programs found they "had to learn the peace field basically from scratch." The involvement of the World Law Fund, and the Consortium on Peace Research, Education and Development (COPRED) have been influential forces, apparently, and these are multidisciplinary programs.[6] There surely are sociologists participating in this movement and perhaps it will influence the development of generalized propositions and concepts which will encourage an increased frequency of social comment on war by sociologists across the country, whatever their niche.

There is another aspect to social criticism which I perceive as a kind of "moral education." The small-niche sociologist is likely to do a lot of this, because the "house sociologist" is always on call for a "sociological opinion." It is a kind of behavior that is instructional or informative at the obvious level, but interpretative in function and moral in quality. (Sociologists need only be reminded that the word "moral" is a broader term than simply a connotative reference to the rightness or wrongness of behavior.)

As an example, I have found that my "interpretations" about antiwar behavior are frequently made in response to the question, "Why do they

6. A. Michael Washburn, "Peace Education Is Alive—But Unsure of Itself," *War/Peace Report* (November 1971): 14–18.

do that?" I am often asked to "explain" specific actions of one group to members of an opposing group. These actions to be explained are often ritual behavior or the violation of ritual. It is this form of social criticism that is required when one must point out the similarity and the nature of the differences between rituals such as playing the "Star-Spangled Banner" before a football game and the reading of a list of political criticisms before a track meet. Students who refuse to rise for the pledge of allegiance to the flag in an opening exercise preceding a debate on Vietnam ask me why the Legionnaires (who sponsored the program) got so mad. The Legionnaires wonder why the students couldn't have at least stood for the flag, since a spokesman for their views had a main part in the program. I have found, in such cases, that a discussion about ritualistic behavior and the sacredness of ritual items was necessary in *both* my responses. Obviously I was being asked to teach sociology, very *basic* social analysis, in such outside-the-classroom situations. Such instances are brief and informal but *very* frequent for the sociologist in the small niche.

I think of this as the use of sociology for "moral education." Archibald cites a publication of the Brookings Institution which puts it in these terms: ". . . social science has and will have, to the extent that it explains and justifies our policy choices, not just a clinical and a rejective function, but a *symbolic*, a *legitimizing*, and an *ideological* function." [7] In my small niche, I have found it so. There is a religious atmosphere about the reception of such interpretations as those presented above. When the interpretation (I prefer the word "analysis") supports the biases of the listeners, I am as warmly received as a preacher at the door of his church following a sermon in which he has helped the parishioners "go forth justified." When the listeners have found my analysis contrary to their values, they may be polite but the image shifts slightly; no longer legitimizing, the social-science view nevertheless retains the symbolic and ideological components and the religious aura surrounding it becomes more suitably that reserved for the "heretic"—or, depending upon the style, the fanatic.

In short, to the extent sociologists perform social criticism, they are going to be treated as spokesmen with a "religious" message—a message with moral quality. Indeed, it may be that we are beginning to be *expected* to offer moral guidance and judgments. I am not certain how sociologists in general are going to respond to such demands; certainly some will view them with repugnance, while others will welcome them. I am not sure why

7. Kathleen Archibald, "Social Science Approaches to Peace," in Gouldner and Miller, *Research for Public Policy*, p. 280.

this expectation is developing. It may be an indirect spinoff from a newly developing public view of society and its critical events, and sociologists are simply getting caught in that particular mode. Becker has expressed the belief that the topics we study "are seen by society as morality plays and we shall find ourselves, willy-nilly, taking part in those plays on one side or the other." [8] I find it amusing to contemplate that a society which secularizes traditional religions may yet come to view its major conflict situations as "morality plays" and may be moving sociologists (against their will) toward a Comtean role of more religio-interpretative functions than scientific-investigational ones. (Or, this may only be a passing fancy for a dreary afternoon!) Tumin also has spoken of a role definition such as I have felt thrust upon me in speaking on the major issues, such as war. He also, apparently, sees the sociological interpreter as a reconciling, mediating role with strong moral overtones.

> For our professional lives, we are enjoined to play a role that virtually no one else is capable of playing. . . . That role for which we are eminently and uniquely suited is to keep alive the possibilities of rapprochement and return among the warring and fleeing parties before the alienation and bitterness grow so intense that the terms of ultimate peace and return will entail destruction of much that is valued by everyone concerned." [9]

In closing, I want to raise the question of sellout. How does the small-niche sociologist avoid the responsibilities to provide social criticism, particularly with reference to the issue of war? What are the dangers with which he must contend? These questions should remain before us as we seek to extend our professional activity outside the classroom.

I find it doubtful that the small-niche sociologist has to contend with any special temptations, unless it is to allow his isolation to become a rationalization for inaction. But he will be freed from none of the pressures that confront any sociologist in action, although these pressures may take a different form in the small-niche situation.

Elsewhere it has been pointed out that one danger for the social-critic and consultant modes of applied sociology lies in "*professional parochialism*, whereby particular professional formulations, rather than the problem at hand, dominate in shaping the nature of the contribution." A variation of this to which the small-niche sociologist is surely susceptible is

---

8. Howard S. Becker, "Whose Side Are We On?" in *The Relevance of Sociology*, ed. Jack D. Douglas (New York: Appleton-Century-Crofts, 1970), p. 108.
9. Melvin M. Tumin, "In Dispraise of Loyalty," in Douglas, *Relevance of Sociology*, p. 163.

related to what I above called the "moral education" type of social analysis. When one is asked to interpret the mysterious (e.g., ritual commitment or ritual violation), one senses he is being given a respectful hearing. That feels good. The sociologist who develops a facility for interpreting the intransigence of ritualism by veterans of former wars, on the one hand, and for interpreting the profaning of rituals by contemporary protestants on the other hand, is in a position where it becomes easy to focus one's efforts upon filling the role of communicator between the groups. It is possible to work at interpretative mediation to such an extent that the *issue* about which the groups disagree remains unanalyzed, unclarified, and malignant.

Etzioni has suggested that sociologists have not been more involved in peace action because of "a fear complex regarding macroanalysis," "the fear of value judgments," and an overcommitment to the role of the sociologist to the exclusion of its complement or paired role—the intellectual.[10] For sociologists in small-niche situations, I might add, the environment may encourage a fear of being isolated if one is considered an "intellectual," and in the scarcity of other intellectuals, such an isolation can be an imposing threat. It is possible for persons in such situations to become preoccupied with finding ways to be an intellectual to one's own satisfaction, without letting anyone else know about it. The challenge of finding meanings for the events changes into a challenge of finding ways to express an intellectual perspective in ordinary language. The latter task may become so interesting that one neglects to apply that perspective to the issue—particularly those about which the emotions of one's listeners run high, or else one comes to speak to such issues in ways that will satisfy or entertain (there's a fine line between ironic wisdom and clever wit)—and thus pacify the audience more than enlighten or enlist their efforts.

Another constant problem is how to oppose what Slater calls "the Toilet Assumption—the notion that unwanted matter, unwanted difficulties, unwanted complexities and obstacles will disappear if they are removed from our immediate field of vision." [11] The small-niche sociologist has ever to combat being overwhelmed by the *absence of other people who naturally discuss major issues* on a critical level. If he is the only one in his environment who keeps a particular issue visible (e.g., by discussing Vietnam body-count statistics and the meaning of the orientations which

10. Amitai Etzioni, "Nonconventional Uses of Sociology as Illustrated by Peace Research," in Lazarsfeld et al., *Uses of Sociology*, pp. 832–34. This piece by Etzioni contains a section on "Sociological Perspectives" (pp. 824–29) that I found most stimulating.

11. Philip E. Slater, *The Pursuit of Loneliness: American Culture at the Breaking Point* (Beacon Press, 1970), p. 15.

produce them, when others would rather not consider the issue), then he may find the Toilet Assumption applied to him. He may be "flushed away" from situations in which his topics of conversation are considered undesirable. The peculiar salience of this for the small-niche sociologist is that it may be difficult to find alternative groups to which he may turn.

Finally, all of us need to fight a peculiar inertia that seems built into sociology, but to which the small-niche sociologist is particularly vulnerable—the seductive notion that "in *my* corner of the universe" entropy is so far advanced that one's efforts are bound to be futile. Who has the ego strength to believe he can reverse the second law of thermodynamics all by himself?

Nathan Glazer has recorded his belief that "the chief ideological function" of sociology is to expose the illusion-base of social phenomena and to undermine "the façade of society." This process must ultimately lead to "the chief illusion of sociology," namely, that "life is a fraud." Thus, while the ideological function of sociology attracts "the academic action seeker," it would eventually "unveil even the illusions of the action seekers. . . . At this point, some of the action seekers inhibit their true sociological imagination; they stop before unveiling some of the illusions." [12] In the small-niche situation the number of social scientists available to provide collegiate support for acting upon this "ideology" are few, the number and scope of the problems remain many, and the inhibition of the "true sociological imagination" of which Glazer speaks becomes very difficult to counter. But in the small niche, the inhibition may come not at the point short of exposing the "illusion" of the crusade, but at the point just before the perception that something is wrong which calls for a crusade. The lone crusader is perhaps less attractive and more to be feared as an identity than the lone intellectual.

It is essential that we both discover and beware of "that amused irony toward self which serves to make knowledge bearable. Silent laughter is an effective defense against the banality of one's own life, but it is also the enemy of evangelical energy." [13]

To return to Ward's story: Being where the action is has the advantage of finding exciting and clear challenges and discernible social rewards for mere effort as well as for accomplishment. The hills are obviously there, and it is clearly apparent when a tunnel is being dug beneath them. But in the small-niche situation, the challenges are so basic and elementary as to induce boredom, if not despair. The Plains may encourage farness of vision, but the goals appear so distant that even a very long walk does not

12. "The Ideological Uses of Sociology," in Larzarsfeld et. al., *Uses of Sociology*, p. 77.
13. Marvin Bressler, "Sociology and Collegiate General Education," in ibid., pp. 59–60.

appear to bring them closer. Nevertheless, it is possible to adapt to the problems of the Plains if one foregoes the excitement of conquering mountains, learns when not to depend upon tunneling equipment, and can somehow avoid the loss of energy.

FOLD, STAPLE, AND MAIL

DAVID MCKAY COMPANY

DESK OR EXAMINATION COPIES FOR

PROFESSOR LARRY L BAILEY
WESTERN ILLINOIS UNIVERSITY

322656 1 222
63560 051576

QTY.	NUMBER, AUTHOR, AND TITLE		SRC
01	SHARK	THE UNITED STATES	$3.95	
01	SHOST	PUTTING SOCIOLOGY TO WORK	$4.95	

THESE BOOKS ARE SENT TO YOU WITH THE COMPLIMENTS OF THE PUBLISHER. WE HOPE YOU WILL FIND TIME TO USE THE SPACE BELOW TO GIVE US YOUR OPINIONS OF THESE TITLES, AND TO LET US KNOW ABOUT YOUR PLANS FOR THEIR USE IN YOUR COURSES.

COMMENTS

MAY WE QUOTE YOU? YES ☐ NO ☐

FOLD STAPLE AND MAIL

"Be sure to get what you like,
or else you will have to like
what you get."

—George Bernard Shaw

part five

CLIENT PARTICIPATION IN ARCHITECTURAL DESIGN

Over and again we are challenged to maintain citizen power in a culture increasingly reliant on experts, specialists, and professionals. How are we, as laymen, to ensure that our wishes are know, respected, and taken into account? Action sociology, of course, has been deeply involved with just such issues throughout its twentieth-century development. But much remains to be learned, dared, and incorporated into the effort.

In this part we have two essays explicitly dealing with the issues of representation. In the first an architectural firm executive reports on his company's experimental employment of a client-sensitive action sociologist. In the second, this same sociologist reflects on other more innovative assignments he has undertaken in client advocacy since his original project with the architectural company. Together the two essays offer unique insights into interdisciplinary collaboration, one with significance far beyond the design issues immediately evident. For we are really grappling here with the fundamental dilemma of how—in a democracy—we are to keep the citizen and the expert in a mutually-productive relationship.

thirteen

WHEN A SOCIOLOGIST GETS INTO THE ACT
C. M. Deasy

What can sociology contribute to architectural and physical planning? And what if sociology raises more questions than it answers? These issues are considered in this essay, a rarity because it was written by the client of a sociologist. A progressive architectural firm contracted a sociologist whose "most persuasive statement . . . was that he wasn't certain the effort would produce practical results." Together, architects and sociologist faced up to problems that otherwise are not often considered in architectural planning. Striking is the emphasis on humane values—not always a prominent characteristic of new-building construction or of modern sociology. When put into practice, emphasis on such values seldom fails to work: "Recalling other experiments we have attempted, we would be happy if a fraction of them had turned out as well."

The sociologist who reports his observations on group behavior will rarely add footnotes suggesting that the information may have a bearing on building design.

Furthermore, it may not be at all apparent that the kind of group studied was very much like the ones we deal with in planning an employees' cafeteria or a dormitory lounge. It might have quite an effect, but the possibility that this data will fall into the hands of an architect, when he needs it most, is somewhat remote.

In view of the very substantial benefits that might be derived by incorporating this kind of knowledge in the planning process, and assuming that few architects have the time, energy or aptitude for mastering this field by themselves, it would seem reasonable for the profession to effect some form of liaison with the behavioral sciences and turn to them for advice. This, at any rate, was the course we pursued in an effort to include behavioral considerations in our own planning procedures.

149

The project in which we elected to test this idea was a new headquarters building for a savings and loan association in downtown Los Angeles. The development of a program of requirements, in the normal sense, had been completed. The building was under construction, an exhaustive analysis of departmental operations had been made, and schematic layouts for all the floors were finished. There were no particular problems in the client's operations that suggested the need for special consultation and no apparent reason why we should not proceed to complete the work on the basis of the information we had. We recognized, however, that a large number of people would be using the building and that anything we could do to ease personal strain and improve interpersonal relations within this group would be a worthwhile contribution both to the individuals and our client.

Consequently, we started a search for a consultant in social psychology that led us to Dr. Thomas Lasswell, professor of sociology at the University of Southern California. He had never done anything of this kind before, didn't know of anyone else who had ever tried it, but was keenly interested in the possibilities of this type of collaboration. His academic credentials were flawless, but the most persuasive statement he offered was that he wasn't certain the effort would produce practical results. Being accustomed to consultants who have a positive answer for every conceivable question, such candor was extremely impressive.

We reviewed our findings with Dr. Lasswell and, in effect, asked this question: "Given this data, can you, drawing on your knowledge of human behavior, advise us of behavioral factors we should take into account in planning these spaces to accommodate the needs of the people who will use them?"

His response consisted of a report which defined five social-psychological goals of the client, analyzed each department in the light of those goals, and concluded with some data on group interaction that was relevant to our planning problems. The report was in no sense a prescription for planning nor did it offer pat answers for our problems. For the most part it raised questions.

Raising questions may not seem to be a very useful contribution, but, in fact, it proved to be extremely beneficial. These often concerned matters that the architect is not normally aware of and for which his design solution provides an unconscious, perhaps inappropriate, answer. The general effect was that we as architects, and ultimately the management of the association, were forced to face issues we might otherwise have ignored. We had to define precisely what our objectives were in each situation.

The key to the value of the report lay in the statement of goals. Their simplicity was somewhat deceptive. "Maintaining the Value of the

Product" refers not only to the services the association offers its customers, a primary concern for any business organization, but also to the need of any individual or unit to feel that they too are providing something of value to the total organization. In a similar way, "Maintaining Control" is not concerned with policing personnel but to the far more subtle mutual-control effects resulting from the personal contacts between executives and employees brought about by patterns of movement within the building.

"Efficient Functioning" refers here to social-psychological considerations rather than traditional "time and motion" concepts. It recognizes that every individual has some personal goals that may, at times, be in conflict with the general goals of the organization. The individual's desire to get a good lunch, for example, may be in conflict with management's desire to have him return on time so that relief schedules won't be disrupted.

In Dr. Lasswell's words, "The object is not so much to design this building so that everyone in it will be happy as it is to design it in such a way that it is *possible* for everyone in it to compromise his individual goals in favor of the total organizational goals."

The body of the report analyzes each of the departmental operations in terms of the five goals. While it is not possible to review here all the issues that were considered, some generalized examples may clarify how this analysis affected our planning.

From an efficiency standpoint, the savings department would have elected to have the cages designed so that each teller could handle the maximum number of depositors in the minimum amount of time. The advantages in reduced payroll are obvious. The report indicated, however, that to many depositors the act of turning over their savings to a relative stranger was a rather important event and suggested that the association take steps to indicate that they regarded it as important too. Both goals are perfectly legitimate, of course, and this instance illustrates how easy it is to achieve efficiency from one point of view while losing it from another point of view.

Our solution offered one set of fast-service windows and another set where the customer sits in a high-backed swivel chair at what amounts to a private desk where he has the undivided attention of a teller who is also seated.

The analysis of the employees' cafeteria didn't present this kind of dilemma. It did point out that this was more than a money-losing fringe benefit. Under the right circumstances it could be a place where a good deal of interdepartmental liaison occurred almost unconsciously. The result was an employee dining room with some banquette seating but a majority of large round tables. It is quite unlike most institutional cafeterias and is intended to make it easy for new employees to be assimilated, minimize the formation of cliques, and encourage the mingling of people from different departments.

The problem of "mutual control" received careful consideration. While an executive exercises direct control over the people in his department, they also exercise a degree of indirect control over him, and this may affect his actions more than he imagines. When his office is located so that he knows what all his staff is doing and they all know what he is doing, this effect is strongest. Under such circumstances he may feel compelled to be at his desk, setting a good example, when the larger interest of the organization might be better served if he were out of the office learning new techniques or developing new business. Perhaps this explains the marked preference of most executives for completely closed offices with an "escape" door.

While there may be some employees who would be happy if they never saw their bosses, most of them want this contact. Isolated jobs are sometimes hard to fill, and part of the reason must be due to the fact that the employee who has no contact with management can hardly expect much recognition or reward for his diligence.

Our solution was to plot alternate paths of movement through the building so that no executive would be stuck at the end of a long cul-de-sac and no employees would be isolated. While the present plan accomplishes this, we are aware that modern business organizations change at a rapid rate, and it is not at all clear how these subtle relationships can be maintained.

In general, we used the data contained in the report as we would use any program requirements. Wherever possible, we accommodated the behavioral requirements. When they were in conflict with the operational requirements, we made adjustments that seemed to be in the best interest of the overall project.

The furnishings of the new accounts offices illustrates such a compromise. This is where a prospective depositor makes his first, and most sensitive, contact with the association. Dr. Lasswell suggested that the normal barrier between customer and staff—a desk—be eliminated here in order to establish the feeling that the new accounts officer was allied with the depositor in working out his problems rather than acting as the agent of an impersonal corporation. The operations of this department are such, however, that flat surfaces for the signing of documents are essential. As a consequence, we introduced a round table in the cubicle which will accommodate a group who might open a joint account and still permit the individual who wants a conspiratorial privacy to shift closer to the attendant.

The examples cited here are indicative of the types of questions that were raised and our efforts to resolve them. It does not cover the full range of questions by any means. We were, in fact, greatly surprised that so many social-psychological issues could be identified in what is essentially a normal kind of architectural project. Our surprise does not mean that we have ignored the needs of the people we were providing facilities for in the past. On the contrary, we have labored hard to resolve their requirements as we understood them, but it is now clear that good intentions and intuitive solutions are not an adequate substitute for systematic investigation.

While this study resulted in many detailed changes in our schematic plans and affected our design solutions significantly, it did not lead to any unique physical forms or arrangements. The visitor to the building will find it difficult to identify any unusual features that can be attributed to the social-psychological factors' study, though he may conclude that the overall impression is somewhat different than he is accustomed to seeing. The one exception would be that, regardless of department size, there is no area with more than nine employees in a group.

The division between groups may be subtle—a line of equipment, wall panels or a space frame—but nowhere will be found the open "bullpen" area so typical of the large corporate operation. These "imaginary" walls subdivide the floors into a series of interlocking spaces that permit movement in almost any direction. This solution is intended to provide a variety of traffic paths through the floors and resulted from the suggestion that the optimum group size to which an individual can relate comfortably ranges between six and nine. Beyond this size, groups tend to break into subgroups, regardless of management's desires in the matter.

Based on this experience, it is our feeling that a systematic investigation of behavioral considerations can be of real value in architectural planning. While this was something of an experiment with obvious weaknesses, it proved to be an extremely productive experiment. Recalling other experiments we have attempted, we would be happy if a fraction of them had turned out as well. Certainly the study would have been more effective if it had been started earlier in the planning process, before so many irrevocable decisions had been made. A far more important deficiency, however, is the feeling that we have not reaped the full potential benefit of this approach simply because we have not wholly grasped the implications it holds for architecture.

The positive results from the study are substantial. Not the least of these is the fact that the attitudes of *all* the people affected by the building were considered: public, management and staff. Even the custodian and the mailroom clerks were taken into account. This procedure has a remarkable effect in clarifying objectives. It called attention to the fact that "efficiency" may be seen in quite a different light by each of these three groups and establishes the alternatives from which a choice must be made.

The behavioral program hardly makes the architect's work easier. It offers no solutions, only a better description of the problem. There are more factors to take into account and more conflicts to resolve. These problems are offset, to some degree, by the fact that the purpose of design becomes clearer, the target in better focus.

One of the unexpected benefits of this study was the increased awareness of everyone involved in the project that architecture is primarily concerned with people, not things. If the task of the architect is construed to be perfecting space for human use, this, in itself, would have to be considered a development of substantial value.

fourteen

THE MEASUREMENT OF BEHAVIORAL SCIENCE INPUTS TO ARCHITECTURAL PROGRAMMING
Thomas E. Lasswell

*Like the preceding essay, this one considers what sociology can contribute
to architectural and physical planning. Here the perspective is that of the
sociologist consultant referred to by the architect writer of the earlier essay.
Lasswell relates how he met a brilliant architect relying on intuitive design
and how this chance encounter set him to pondering whether sociology
could give scientific aid. He considers conservative and radical models of
design, cultural and system strains, and certain aids to interdisciplinary
collaboration. This is a case study of sociological research in planning a
college student-union building; that research made possible the comparison
of the wishes of the different users of the proposed building. Concerning the
usefulness of sociology, the essay concludes that "the basic techniques for
making . . . a contribution have been developed, and the potential for
human betterment is great."*

About twenty years ago, the late Richard Neutra and I were spending an
afternoon together as guests of family members in the Tremaine house,
which Neutra had designed. As a young sociologist, I was (surprisingly to
me now) restricting my reactions to the house to an appreciative appraisal
of its aesthetic and luxurious qualities. Neutra interrupted my oh-ing and
ah-ing with a statement that he was getting ready to design some
apartments which would lower the probabilities of divorce for the people
who lived in them. As far as I can recall, that is the first time I ever gave
serious consideration to the possibility that an environment might be
modified *intentionally* to influence the nature of interpersonal relationships
of people exposed to it; at least, if I had thought about it before, it had
been at the level of fortresses, padded cells, dungeons, and execution
chambers as places where people could be controlled.

Fascinated by Mr. Neutra's project, I began immediately to ask
questions about his procedures. I found that the established genius did
much of his architectural programming by "sympathetic introspection,"
taking the roles of his clients and their families on the basis of letters from

155

them and long interviews with them as well as direct observation of their habits, life styles, and objects that had special salience for them.

How scientific, I wondered, could sociological programming for architectural design become? Could objective procedures be set up for identifying and observing variables relevant to desirable environmental modification? If so, it might be possible for architects and planners to rely on principles of design derived from behavioral science even as they were currently using principles of construction derived from physics. Architects and planners might then be freed to some extent from their dependence on intuitive geniuses for bridging the gap between human values, goals, strains, sentiments, and design.

Some time later, I received a telephone call from Neil Deasy, another architectural genius, asking me what information I could give him about people and their patterns of interaction in order to help him design a building that would permit the organization which it was to house to accomplish its goals. It was an opportunity for which I had been waiting. Immediately we set about to work on his particular problem and, more important, to devise a procedure for incorporating sociological inputs into architectural programming. (A report of Deasy's reaction to our teamwork appears elsewhere in this volume.)

It seemed logical to begin our joint endeavor by attempting to define operationally some existing sociological phenomena of the populations likely to be affected by an anticipated modification in the environment. A *conservative* model for such populations might assume that an anticipated modification will (1) be congruous with the existing relevant values of the populations involved; (2) not impede the existing individual or collective *goals* of the populations; and (3) not introduce strains which do not presently exist nor aggravate those which do. A *radical* model or a *radical* design, in contrast, focuses on *changing* the existing values or goals of the involved populations, removing or alleviating strains, or in changing quantities or characteristics of the populations themselves. The conservative sociological climate of a building is defined effectively by the responses of every person who engages in interaction with others as a result of that environment. Radical sociological models, on the other hand, are effectively defined by architects, planners, and their clients. Normally the client is considered to be the person who employs the architect or planner to modify an environment. In a traditional legitimation pattern, it is the client's prerogative to specify or to select radical models to be used.

Often in the past, clients have ignored sociological considerations altogether, leaving it up to the architect or planner to introduce any radical features of this kind into the program. In the long run, of course, any benefits that the client might accrue from "good" sociological design belonged to him (e.g., he was under no obligation to reward the architect further if radical features introduced brought him increased profits), and on the other hand the client accepted the costs of a "bad" sociological design. It seems much less likely at present that a client could successfully sue an architect for malpractice for poor sociological programming than that he might if physical features were designed in some defective way.

A rather gross example of a personal strain produced by design might be seen in the location of a "powder room" to be used by guests so that it opens directly into the living room and is not perceived as soundproof by its users. More common examples might be: shower heads so high that women cannot shower without drenching their hair, or so low that the tallest member of the family cannot wash his hair comfortably in the shower; the lack of mirrors or illumination appropriate for shaving (e.g., one cannot see his face without bending over if he is tall or myopic; the light source is above or behind the head of the shaver and there is no reflecting surface which illuminates his beard area). Examples of *cultural* strains might be: violations of the aesthetic values of persons exposed to the environment; room shapes or sizes that will not accommodate conventional furniture; or any feature that impedes enculturated response dispositions. An example of a *system* strain in a school or college setting would be the classroom designed so that the teacher must rearrange the furniture daily in order to carry out his educational goals while the custodian must rearrange it nightly in order to clean the room. Some strains seem inevitable; others seem capable of rather simple resolution.

In larger projects, it may be difficult to determine who the client is. In the student-union project described herein, some candidates for the position of client could have been the current student body (who committed the funds for planning and building), future students (who would use the building and who would pay off the obligations incurred), the college administration (who committed the space, among other considerations), the governor of California, or the people of the state. In such a case, it is difficult for the planner to know where to turn for the legitimation of a proposed radical sociological design. In many similar instances in the past the architect himself may have made such decisions (either consciously or unconsciously) without discussing the issue with anyone else.

Since 1965, conservative models of values-goals-strains complexes have been developed jointly by myself and several different architects for specific projects either already completed, under construction, or projected; still others are in the "talk" stage. These include a savings-and-loan-association building, an architect's home office, one floor of a university administration building, a student union, a black ghetto school, an enormous multiple dwelling and a commercial complex, a planned unit development, and some public libraries. In most cases where the study progressed beyond the talk stage, radical programs were made of ways in which the values-goals-strains complexes might be altered by new construction. Nevertheless, the present article is limited to a discussion of the development of conservative models, since it is not a part of the role of the behavioral scientist to make policy decisions.

Perhaps it will be most useful at this point to report the application of the technique described to an actual case. In 1968 a study was made for the behavioral-science programming of a student union to be built by the Associated Students of California State College at Los Angeles (CSCLA).[1] Several populations were identified as being concerned with the proposed student union. Random samples of summer students, fall students, faculty and alumni of CSCLA were interviewed. Purposive samples of administrators, staff, and community influentials were also interviewed during the same period. The first six populations will be easily recognized; the "community influentials" were drawn from San Marino, . lhambra, and East Los Angeles, using a procedure for selecting fourteen members of each community from predetermined categories of influentials. The communities chosen were ranked as upper class, middle class, and lower class, according to a system devised for ranking the social areas of Los Angeles by Marcia Meeker for the Welfare Council of Metropolitan Los Angeles.

Face sheets enabled the research team to break down student responses by such variables as age, academic load, paid work, time spent on campus, distance of residence from school, marital status, and study habits. This information was intended in part to supply the eventual policy makers with data from which radical models might be constructed. For example, if the policy makers decided to encourage students to spend more time on campus than they were spending in the existing (conservative) environment, they would have the values-goals-strains profiles of students who spent different amounts of time on campus to use, either to attempt to influence the behaviors of students through radical environmental design or to recruit desired types of students by differential appeal through either a changed public-relations program or perhaps through some kind of environmental design.

The basic interview schedule consisted of seven sequences of eleven to

1. This study, as well as a study for a black ghetto school, was financed by a grant from The Educational Facilities Laboratory of the Ford Foundation and by Deasy and Bolling, Architects.

twenty-six Likert items each. The first sequence, which dealt with collective goals, was presented with instructions for the respondent to rank each of the eighteen items on a five-point scale ranging from "a primary goal for CSCLA" to "an undesirable goal for CSCLA." Some of the items included were: "to provide a general education in letters, arts, and sciences"; "to provide professional training for students enabling them to become teachers, social workers, engineers, nurses, etc."; "to bring together a faculty of mature thinkers and scholars so that they will have a maximum opportunity to explore new ideas"; and "to teach people a philosophy of life." Similar Likert-type scales were devised for rating individual goals, values, strains, tastes, images, and specific desiderata. The completed instrument contained 128 Likert-scaled items, 18 closed questions and 13 open-ended questions to be answered by all respondents, with students being asked to complete the face sheet previously mentioned in addition.

Modal responses were recorded for each scaled item and the items in each sequence were ranked for each population. Spearman rho correlations were then computed for each pair of populations for each sequence of scales, so that it was possible to measure the overall similarity of value-goal-strain models between each pair of populations as well as their characteristic differences.

A summary of the high points of the findings showed that all populations agreed on certain values, goals, strains, images, desiderata and tastes. These areas of agreement were called the conservative consensual model. As expected, this model turned out to be in favor of home, apple pie, and motherhood, so to speak, and against earthquakes. Briefly, it revealed that CSCLA was an institution dedicated to providing a general education and professional or preprofessional career training for qualified students.

The conservative consensual model indicated that all populations believed that students actually came to CSCLA primarily to train for a chosen career or to find one rather than for a general education; that noteworthy architectural design, functionality, and efficiency were highly valued; that the proposed union should facilitate informal meetings among students and faculty; that the image of the union should be foremost one of congeniality; that it should not be presumed that the student who comes to the union will have much money to spend there; that, if possible, the less-vocal students should be made to feel that they are being properly attended to; that CSCLA should encourage "retreads"—people who wish to change or better their established careers or learn new skills. The union, according to this model, should be a comfortable place where students and faculty can meet and talk without either interfering with the work of the other.

The consensual model, then, does not contain many surprises, although some items do indicate definite philosophies for programming when they are considered in the light of their alternatives. This will be seen more clearly in the following models constructed from the responses of particular populations.

The conservative *student* model revealed that students see the cultivation of a faculty of mature thinkers and scholars as irrelevant to the institutional goals of CSCLA. Generally, they found the existing architecture more appealing than the other populations, although they concurred on which was the least appealing building on campus. Students were more concerned than the other populations with service facilities (barber shop, snack bar, recreational facilities) and with space for para-academic activities (student government, newspaper offices, displays, bulletin boards, and student organizations), while most resistant to the use of any part of the building for classrooms or administrative offices. They did not want sexually segregated lounges or study areas (that is, separate "women's areas" and "men's areas" somewhere in the building). They expressed neutrality toward the union's projection of images of good citizenship, but rated an image of freedom as "extremely desirable." They indicated that fraternities, campus organizations, and departmental divisions created no strains, nor did authority conflicts between students and employees of the college.

The conservative *alumni* model differed from some other models on several points. One of these, for example, was the emphasis placed by alumni on providing good facilities for guest speakers to use. The conservative *faculty* model also differed from the other models on several points. They saw (predictably enough) a primary goal of CSCLA as bringing together a faculty of mature thinkers and scholars. Faculty also differed from other samples in their belief that *most* students came to CSCLA to study a particular discipline.

The conservative *administrative* model did not differ from the conservative consensual model on collective and individual goals. Administrators did differ from the other populations, however, in their tastes in architecture, rating every existing building listed on the interview schedule as "unappealing" with one exception. Administrators differed from the other samples, too, in rating as "extremely desirable" that the union should be used to gain public recognition as an asset to CSCLA.

The *staff* sample included personnel from maintenance, the stenographic pool, food service, custodial staff, engineering staff, landscaping, and so forth. Like the faculty but unlike the students, the staff rated as a primary goal of CSCLA the bringing together of a faculty of mature thinkers and scholars. Almost diametrically opposed to the administration, they rated ten of the eleven reference buildings listed on the questionnaire as "appealing." They expressed "some concern" over the divisiveness of fraternities, student organizations, and academic departments.

The conservative *community-influential* model tended to follow the consensual model with a few notable exceptions. They gave a top rating to the desirability of having an informal meeting place for students and faculty in the proposed union. They expressed extreme concern over the perceived strain between freedom and responsibility on campus.

In addition to the preparation of a conservative student model, the student populations were analyzed by comparing the scale profiles for a number of subcategories. Married students were compared with unmarried students, for example, and those married with children were compared with those married without children. Summer students were compared with fall students. Employed students were compared with students who were not employed. High participators were compared with low participators; students over age forty were compared with students under the age of forty; males with females. A long series of Chi-square tests was used to single out each item on which a special category of students differed with its counterpart or with the total sample of students as a whole. Although the findings in general showed fewer differences than were expected, significantly different items were included in the report to the architect in case they were suggestive of a radical design. For example, far more part-time than full-time students attended no meetings on campus ($p = .005$); Protestant Anglo students are less likely to be full-time students than black, Mexican-American, Jewish, or Oriental students ($p = .05$); and more full-time students are concerned with activities centered around dating and "marriage prospecting" than part-time students ($p = .01$). It is entirely possible that the union might be designed with the specific intent of altering the part-time or full-time students' attitudes toward the college.

When the new student union is constructed on the CSCLA campus, embodied in it will be many features that will affect the sociological and social psychological climate. A major purpose of this study was to call attention to the values, goals, strains, images, and tastes of the various populations on campus who will be affected by the new union. The results of the policy decisions that are made will be reflected in the building. The architect will be more aware of the behavioral-science decisions he is making. He, in turn, has an enormous pile of data with which to defend his decisions to other policy makers, or to present to them in requesting that a decision be made. Through this process, he may also be better able to define precisely who his client is.

This procedure may not produce sociological and psychological climates that are any better than an architectural genius such as Richard Neutra could produce intuitively without it. It does, however, offer two distinct advantages over intuitive design: (1) it forces behavioral-science issues in architectural design to the conscious attention of policy makers, and (2) it provides a thorough record of the sociological and social-psychological inputs into the architectural program so that systematic studies of cause and effect can eventually be made, enabling behavioral-science programming to be more scientific and therefore eventually more predictable in its effects on the behavioral science climate of the modified environment.

It is appalling to me to recall my afternoon with Neutra and to realize that my advanced education in sociology had not given me the slightest inkling of the contribution that the discipline might make in applications to architectural programming. The basic techniques for making such a contribution have been developed, and the potential for human betterment is great.

He that leaveth nothing to
chance will do few things ill,
but he will do very few things.

—Halifax

part six

NEW TOOLS FOR RESEARCH

Educational gaming, applied mathematics, and computer dialogues—these
three recent additions to the tool kit of the applied sociologist are

discussed in this section. The essayists, each a pioneering innovator working on the frontiers of a new specialty, encourage trying first one application and then another. Again and again the point is made that applied sociology can be strengthened if we will school ourselves in the powerful innovative techniques available to us.

The difficulties of learning new techniques are not nearly as great as they may appear from our less-daring side of the divide; and the potential returns to applied sociology are far greater than nonusers of these new techniques can imagine. All three essays remind us that our profession requires risk taking and open-minded experimentation with these innovations.

fifteen

GAMING AS APPLIED SOCIOLOGY
Cathy S. Greenblat

*Whether in Monopoly™, chess, ROTC war games, or Tactics II, all of us
have participated in games that are facsimilies of the real world or of a
special part of it. Not many of us have become proficient in the
social-science adaptation of these games—the simulation game. Part of our
methodological arsenal for nearly twenty years, simulation games represent
an important breakthrough for social analysis. This essay presents not only
the academic side of the subject but it also relates experiences that action
sociologists have had in bringing gaming techniques off the campus and
into the community. Some educators are helping laymen gain a deeper
understanding of urban processes; others are using games to train people in
political methods. Games frequently provide training in complex strategies
and opportunities to assess novel alternatives to the status quo. Many
participants, in playing with strangers or even with antagonists (police and
militants, for instance), gain new friendships. But, this gets ahead of
Professor Greenblat's story of the excitement, discovery, and fun involved
in simulation games.*

In the midst of a heated debate at the recent National Gaming Council
meetings, one member of the audience began his attempt at reconciliation
of two seemingly diverse positions with the statement, "I want to try to
narrow the gap, so we can leap over it." This paper has a somewhat similar
purpose: to propose a way of narrowing the gap between the things
sociologists know about and do in the classroom or research center and the
things they might do in the community.

Even those sociologists who are "sure-footed" in their research and
teaching capacities often find the jump to the out-of-class community too
big to allow them to land on their feet. Many questions present problems
to those who want to take their ideas beyond the ivory tower: How do you
get across an understanding of social organization, community development, problems of diverse subgroups, to an audience that is not as
"captive" as students? How do you transmit an understanding of the

167

dynamics of interpersonal and intergroup relations in terms that assist people in learning to assess their position and their opposition, to develop effective organization, and to exercise greater control over their lives? How do you get groups in conflict to become more aware of how the world looks and feels to those with whom they are embattled so some reconciliation can be approximated? How do you help people expand their horizons concerning available alternatives and their costs and rewards so they can make choices about their lives? The difficulties of response send many scurrying back to familiar territory in haste.

Changes in Games and Players

Simulation games are operating models of central features of real or proposed systems or processes. Scenarios are developed, roles are defined in interacting systems, and players are given goals, resources, and rules. Then they make the system work, trying out alternative strategies within the system constraints presented.[1]

War games have been played for centuries, not simply by those seeking "fun," but often by those who later would put what they learned in the exercises into practice in real-life military operations. Both the Japanese and the Americans used the technique extensively in the pre-World War II and during the war days, and the U.S. Joint Chiefs of Staff still "game" a number of military and diplomatic situations.

In 1956 the American Manufacturing Association developed the first business game—a training device to develop management skills through practice and subsequent analysis of various strategies where the costs of real-life errors were absent. Within a few years, more than two hundred companies were utilizing business games for training in marketing, production, investment, organizational decision making, and other business problems; for the identification of potential management skills; and as part of their larger programs of general education for employees.

Movement of games into the schools followed somewhat later. In the early 1960s social scientists at Johns Hopkins University started work under James Coleman to develop game models for teaching sociological and political science concepts and theories; Abt Associates in Boston began developing a number of games with simulated environments; and Project SIMILE at Western Behavioral Sciences Institute moved from early

1. For elaboration, see Cathy S. Greenblat, "Simulations, Games, and the Sociologist," *American Sociologist* 6 (May 1971): 161–64; and John Raser, *Simulation and Society* (New York: Allyn & Bacon, 1969).

work using Harold Guetzkow's *Inter-Nation Simulation* (ins)[2] for research purposes to the development of simulation games for teaching. If participants in the research endeavors became so involved and excited during the experience, they reasoned, could not some of these interest and motivational outcomes be brought into the classroom via games?

Since that time numerous developments have taken place in the field of education. Individuals and companies all over the country are developing and disseminating games for teaching and training in a variety of disciplines.[3] Elementary and secondary-school teachers and college instructors are turning to the use of gaming as a means of developing interest and motivation, promoting cognitive learning, bringing about affective change concerning oneself and others, and changing the structure and climate of the classroom.[4]

The next step seems to be one of moving the gaming technique into the community, and this has already begun. Despite the fact that the purposes for which these endeavors have been undertaken are those sociologists speak of, most of those who have started using gaming in the community seem *not* to be sociologists. Rather, some community organizers have "discovered" gaming as an effective tool for transmitting understandings of urban problems and developing skills; numbers of ministers and church people have found them good ways of opening channels of communication; and others have found different gains. The city of Plainfield, New Jersey, hired a psychologist in 1970 to run a Community Relations Training Program for city employees and interested citizens; two or three days of the five-day workshop were spent playing William Gamson's simsoc[5] and discussing the questions it raised about the relationships between individual, local and national needs, the relationship between alienation and deviance, and a host of other issues.

My own work with games has been limited largely to the classroom, and discussions with others in the profession reveal similar limitations of locale. Surely some sociologists have made important strides in the use of gaming in the community. In exploring game use in the out-of-class context,

2. Guetzkow, Harold et al., *Inter-Nation Simulation*. Available from Science Research Associates, 259 East Erie Street, Chicago, Ill. 60611.

3. For a list of available games, see David Zuckerman and Robert E. Horn, *The Guide to Simulation Games for Education and Training* (Cambridge, Mass.: Information Resources, Inc., 1970); or Cathy S. Greenblat, "Partial Bibliography of Games and Simulations in the Social Sciences" (Rutgers University, 1971; mimeographed).

4. Cathy S. Greenblat, "Teaching with Simulation Games: A Review of Claims and Evidence" (Douglass College, Rutgers University, 1971; mimeographed); Sarane Boocock and Erling O. Schild, *Simulation Games in Learning* (Beverly Hills, Calif.: Sage Publications, 1968).

5. William Gamson, simsoc: *Simulated Society* (New York: Free Press, 1972 Edition).

however, I have found sociological enterprises, but not sociologists. What I shall try to do, therefore, in the rest of this paper, is to describe some activities of people whose work seems to represent "sociology in action," and then review the lessons these vignettes offer for sociologists interested in using games to "make a difference" in the off-campus world.[6]

Larry McClellan

Many of Larry McClellan's endeavors in designing and using games in the community have had the dual function of giving people more holistic notions of cities, communities, colleges, and other social systems, and of training people in the political skills of negotiating, strategy planning, forming coalitions, and the like.

Larry was an organizer in Cicero, a white working-class neighborhood in Chicago, and in several affluent white neighborhoods, when he and three fellow students in divinity school played Allen Feldt's *Community Land Use Game* (CLUG)[7] in a course on metropolitan planning. The others had had experiences in Chicago working with poor blacks, running coffeehouses, organizing in other communities and so on, and they found CLUG an exciting experience related to their concerns. Some of the problems they were involved with, however, were not dealt with in the game, and they thought that a simple modification might bring these concerns into the play experience. Nine months later and with another recruit to the design process they completed *Urban Dynamics*.[8] They report:

> I think a large part of our impulse in putting the thing together was our frustration, particularly in dealing with affluent suburban whites and working-class whites, in trying to give them "handles" on the city. Most whites don't understand the internal dynamics, let alone the hassle that poor blacks go through—they just don't have a perception. We believed that blacks in Chicago are powerless partly because of overt racism, but largely because of certain kinds of structured, institutional relationships. So we wanted a game that would help people realize the institutional and group dimensions of poverty and other urban problems—about the relationships between individuals and systems.
>
> Our original concern was with that teaching function. Ideally we'd really want to get whites spending six months working on the streets, but that's not

6. These accounts present only a small piece of the work being done by these individuals. The selections have been chosen to accentuate different utilizations, but all are using games for several purposes, are in touch and share ideas, and use some of one another's games from time to time.

7. Allen Feldt, *Community Land Use Game*. Available from Environmental Simulation Laboratory, 109 East Madison, Ann Arbor, Mich. 48104.

8. Larry McClellan et al., *Urban Dynamics*. Available from Urbandyne, 5659 South Woodlawn Avenue, Chicago, Ill. 60637.

a very practical alternative; and the game we developed seemed to create a very intense, dramatic situation in which people started making discoveries. Those caught up in the individualistic ethos began to realize that no matter how good you are, if you're caught up in a group with limited resources you have real constraints, which they hadn't recognized before playing. *Urban Dynamics* was based on the city of Chicago and the kinds of inequities that existed there between the different economic and racial groups, but as we played it elsewhere it became clear we had built a more generalized model. People in New York and Rochester and Cleveland were all saying, "Yes, this is really true, this is the way it is."

After using *Urban Dynamics* a number of times, Larry and his colleagues in Urbandyne, a company formed by the five designers, began finding out that the process of playing had other consequences than the learning of content.

Players really struggled with questions of decision making, organizing, negotiating, getting things together, and for many of the groups that was the real value of playing: struggling with the problems of community organizing in a simulated urban context as a way of developing these skills for application in the real world. In doing so, we've had some groups that have really faced up to their own disorganization. For example, I ran one game for a planning group and they just couldn't get themselves together. I found out after the game that this staff group was going through a great deal of administrative difficulty, but nobody had been able to talk about it. In the game situation the same difficulties emerged. These problems were analyzed in the debriefing, and later the players were able to draw parallels to their actual organizational dilemmas.

We've also discovered that people started using the game as a broad kind of strategy tool. For example, they say, "What would happen if you divided the resources up differently?" and then do it and play and see what the consequences are. Also, we have had some groups who asked, "How could you equalize suburban-urban development?" and then used the game for exploring the possible alternatives.

Much of this work in using games for pedagogy and as deliberate organizing tools has proceeded with *Urban Dynamics*. The Urbandyne staff, however, have developed and used several other games. *Edge City College*[9] is a simulation of a college. It developed from a concern about how to get people to understand the dynamics of a college campus, and has been used with high-school students and incoming freshmen to illustrate some of the nonclassroom aspects of a university and the way it

9. Urbandyne, *Edge City College*. Available from Urbandyne, 5659 South Woodlawn Avenue, Chicago, Ill. 60637.

functions. De Paul University used it two years ago for orientation for approximately 500 incoming students, and last year as part of the orientation program for 700–1,000 incoming students. Larry reports that the president of the student body indicated she believes that playing the game politicized the students to the nature of the university, and that they have been involved in the life of the university in a far more significant way as a result. In a postgame questionnaire, 87 percent of the participants indicated that playing had bettered their "understanding of the structures and processes of the university." Other evaluations were also positive. I asked Larry if he thought the game's contribution was in increasing knowledge of what the system is like, or in increasing students' sense of efficacy within it, and he could not be sure. Whatever the source of its effectiveness, the game was suggested as an essential ingredient of future orientation programs by the student participants.

Learning A&M

The Learning Activities and Materials Cooperative is an informal group of people—most of them students and faculty at the University of Michigan—who share an interest in games. Michael VanderVelde explains:

> The games that excite us are those that get people to share *themselves* as well as a common experience. We just finished a few weeks' work designing and running a gerontology game for institutes of gerontology all over Michigan. The game we developed was a loosely structured one used to get participants reacting to gerontology problems as they ordinarily do. Then through postgame discussion we tried to get them gradually to talk about the issues that are affecting them and their ways of dealing with them. It's the same philosophy of gaming coming through in all our work: the people bring whatever it is, but use the gaming device as the *vehicle* to get talking about things.

Bob Parnes points out that Learning A&M is primarily concerned with designing and disseminating games that are easy to construct, demolish, and redesign.

> Social-simulation gamelike exercises—that's how we've come to define what we're doing. I think probably one of the things that symbolizes our group more than anything is that we don't think people learn very much from playing games, but that they learn a lot about themselves and the systems they're working in by taking a game and redesigning it for their own purposes. So some of the games we have allow the group to play many versions of it—to just play around *with* it.

One such game, developed by Fred Goodman, a professor of education and member of Learning A&M, is *Policy Negotiations*.[10] In the basic version the content concerns a series of educational issues that players must deal with through influence allocation. Variations have been developed and used as training and educational games for university students, church workers, police, social welfare workers, and others. When I spoke with Michael VanderVelde he was beginning work with the nursing staff at a local hospital, developing a variation to show how hospitals run, what the power structure is and how it works, who the people are and what kind of influence each would have on various critical issues. Then they'll have student nurses play. The important thing about *Policy Negotiations* is that it's a "priming game"; once it has been introduced and played, it can be revised easily by participants to reflect their own system's issues, constituencies, and agencies. Thus, instead of a game director redesigning the game, the participants can do so. This process of articulation and analysis of system components may have important consequences for heightening awareness and understanding of the system in which the player-designers live and work.

They Shoot Marbles, Don't They?[11] is an experimental, experiential game designed by Goodman, in which players build a community. A few rules are given and participants make up the rest in the course of play, experimenting with different forms of government and of social organization. People from Learning A&M have "gone off with the game—some to schools, some to churches—using it with kids and with adults." Bob talked about Wes, who is interested in playgrounds and in kids' play, and wanted to get a feel for how kids would respond to the game.

> This summer every afternoon he would dress up in as "non-grown-up" clothes as he could possibly find and go out to playgrounds. It's funny, because Wes is about six foot six—a big black guy, a football player in college—and here he was carrying around his little "Marbles" game and trying to get these five-, six- and seven-year-olds to play. And it wasn't anything formal at all; he didn't ask for an invitation. He'd just walk onto the playground and get kids to play. Why? Well, it's fun to play and we think it's a great way to start discussions, and that's an important aspect of learning—people sharing experiences with each other.

10. Frederick Goodman, *Policy Negotiations*. Available from Environmental Simulation Laboratory, University of Michigan, 109 East Madison, Ann Arbor, Mich. 48104.

11. Frederick Goodman, *They Shoot Marbles, Don't They?* Available from Environmental Simulation Laboratory, University of Michigan, 109 East Madison, Ann Arbor, Mich. 48104.

R. Garry Shirts

As director of SIMILE II, Garry Shirts has worked extensively with games for education. He has designed several games dealing with international relations, domestic politics, city problems, stratification, race relations, etc.; he runs workshops on simulation use and design for teachers, researchers, community workers, and interested others; and he often runs game sessions in schools. Some of Garry's work in out-of-class settings has entailed use of games for education; for example he has used games for teaching purposes with police groups throughout the state of California, focusing on such problems as the pressures and problems of minority groups.

Some of his other endeavors, however, do not involve games for transmission of information. Rather, games are utilized to facilitate communication between antagonistic groups of people who have difficulty talking and relating to one another. In these cases the games are not the end and the content is not relevant; the games are employed to set a climate, a stage, that permits other things to happen later. The game-play is thus task-oriented: its function is that of changing group dynamics and processes. Garry says:

> Let me tell you about two different experiences that we had. An organization had been trying to develop a program to get blacks and whites and browns communicating with one another. They had run a series of discussion sessions, but these tended to break down, to develop into encounter-type sessions which completely polarized the groups. The blacks ended up browbeating the whites and the whites felt guilty and then more guilty and then finally became angry and fought back. The sessions exacerbated racial tensions rather than improving them.
>
> I received a call asking me to design a game to help facilitate communication. I told them that since they knew the specific problems better than I did, I thought it would be better if I came and taught them how to build a game themselves. They agreed, and put together a group which included members of the university community, the police, the white community, the militant minorities, and the moderate minorities. We set up a three-day program to help them design a game, and the program consisted mostly of having them participate in and discuss a variety of existing simulations.
>
> The first night the militant black faction announced they wouldn't play. They said that their problems were real and they weren't interested in playing games, but wanted to talk about pressing issues. We asked them to go along with our plan for the one evening and they agreed. In the game that night, one militant got in a position of power and took advantage of the other groups. The other militants challenged him on this and said, "Here you are always complaining about the white Establishment and as soon as you get in

power you do the same things they do. You're really no different than they are." That turned out to be a very real experience for him. From then on there was nobody who didn't want to participate and who didn't see the games as important. We played several SIMILE II games, including *Starpower*,[12] *Sitte*,[13] and *Napoli*.[14]

After the three days there was an incredible amount of rapport between the groups. Initially, when coffee and meal breaks came, the blacks went out with the blacks, the whites with the whites, the police with the police, etc. At the end, everybody went out together. One policeman said that for the first time in his life he was able to respond to a black person as a person rather than as a stereotype, and that type of feeling was expressed by several of the people.

It was an extraordinarily emotional experience for me, seeing the change from a group in desperate positions and highly antagonistic, to a group that communicated in a way that you see only after the very best of encounter sessions. We tried to analyze what had happened and why, and it seemed that maybe the games did several things. First, by participating on teams, players formed new in-group relationships. If you have people from groups A, B, C, and D on a team and they get a sense of working on a team, then they develop a sense of themselves as a group. They can communicate with each other instead of A only being able to talk with other As, etc. Second, participation allowed them to begin communicating with each other in nondefensive ways. They were able to learn how a person responded to authority, how well he was able to persuade, how well he spoke in public—so many things they were able to learn about each other in that amount of time. While they never found out about personal hangups and the other things you learn about in encounter groups, they did learn a lot about one another—the same kinds of things they would find out about if they were to work side by side for an extended period of time. The third possible explanation is that I think participation in games provided a common experience which not only helped to solidify the group, but helped them to communicate with each other and to make sense to each other. Previously when they talked, for example about "power," they all meant different things. We played a game about power, and then they had a common referent.

We got a chance to try these ideas out when we got a call from a California community with a serious problem. An interracial incident had polarized the community, and the work of the Human Relations Commission which was set up immediately afterward had exacerbated the situation. Every time they interviewed someone, the person was suspected of being racist, and charges and countercharges flew.

12. R. Garry Shirts, *Starpower*. Available from SIMILE II, 1150 Silverado, La Jolla, Calif.
13. SIMILE II, *Sitte*. Available from SIMILE II, 1150 Silverado, La Jolla, Calif.
14. SIMILE II, *Napoli*. Available from SIMILE II, 1150 Silverado, La Jolla, Calif.

After three months of this, we were called in and asked to run a conference. We decided to try out what we had learned in the earlier experience, for it was clear that the community was torn with dissension and that the community leaders gathered for the conference would be unable to work together. We thus spent the first morning and part of the afternoon having them participate in a simulation (*Sitte*). Our aims were what we discussed before: to break up in-group relationships as the only mode of relating, to help them to become acquainted with each other, and to give them a common experience that would unify the group and help them develop a common language. After the simulation, we had a working situation in which we had them look at some broad goals for the community and devise ways to attain them, instead of looking directly at the racial question. They outlined a series of steps and assigned responsibilities for executing them. It went remarkably well, and one year later essentially all these goals were met and the racial situation had substantially subsided.

We can't be sure what effect the simulation game actually had, but before playing these people were unable to work together on anything, and afterwards they functioned beautifully as a group and accomplished the things they set out to do. Original in-group ties no longer hampered cross-group cooperation.

Some Out-of-Class Uses of Games

The foregoing accounts suggest several uses of games in working in out-of-class settings.

First, games may be important tools for teaching in the community. The same kinds of outcomes cited for games in the school context may be found in these situations: learning of principles, processes, structures, and interrelationships; development of empathy for and understanding of the predicaments, pressures, and problems of real-world role players; a stronger sense of efficacy. Particularly with an audience not used to being "lectured at," the approach of teaching through play of a high-verisimilitude simulation game and postgame discussion and analysis may be a far more potent way of getting across information and ideas than is the more traditional lecture. Thus, those working to increase the information and understanding of general citizens' groups or special-interest groups may find gaming a valuable tool for transmitting ideas.

Second, gaming may provide a training device for those who wish to help develop skills. Businessmen and diplomats have been using games to cultivate abilities of persuasion, bargaining, and strategy planning; police, minority-group members, commissions, and the like may derive similar benefits from the technique.

Third, games may be good vehicles for social planning or "future testing." Using some games, players can try out alternative forms of social organization, resource allocation, communication, etc., within a simulated context to "test" the efficacy of their ideas, the costs and rewards of various options, and the difficulties of going from the present structure to the desired future one.

Fourth, games may be good vehicles for helping individuals and groups to explore values, ideas, and behaviors—for making explicit what has been implicit. This is a general communication function—leading people to a better understanding of themselves and others, as has been discussed in the account of the activities of Learning A&M. In a somewhat similar vein, Peter Stein, Norman Washburne, and I have been exploring the uses of our newly designed *Marriage Game*[15] for counseling purposes. Although we designed it for teaching about marriage as a social system, discussions with marital counselors suggest that participating in the simulation (which involves much of the decision making and interaction typical of real-life marriages) may prove to have heuristic functions. Analysis of game behavior may be a less threatening way to begin exploration of marital difficulties than "jumping right in" to look at the real-life, emotion-laden situations and behaviors. Again, the aim is to use the game to elicit perspectives about "the way the world is" and one's place in it, as a means to begin to develop new modes of relating and of problem solving.

Finally, the fifth use is clearly exemplified by Garry Shirts' report of games for dealing with problems of conflict resolution. Here the aim is to use games to facilitate communication between disparate, antagonistic groups so that other tasks can be undertaken more effectively. The game is employed as a vehicle for changing group structure and the work climate, opening new channels of communication; thus the game-play is for naught if other activities do not follow. Game use is preparation for more serious endeavors.

Gaming as Applied Sociology

How, then, can sociologists use gaming to "make a difference in the out-of-class world?" First, they can work on the *design* of games, particularly those to be used for teaching purposes, which require high verisimilitude. The translation of sociological theory and data into the game format would create new and better tools for use in teaching community groups. Games seem to have real potential for increasing people's understanding of the nature of alternative social environments

15. Cathy S. Greenblat, Peter J. Stein, and Norman F. Washburne, *The Marriage Game: A Simulation of Marital Decision-Making* (New York: Random House, 1972).

and the consequences of living in them. If sociologists could translate their research findings into games, people could then play to learn about the costs and rewards of living under fascism, democracy, or socialism; in monogamous marital arrangements or in communes; in the mainstream of contemporary American society, in minority groups, or in groups that have deliberately relinquished some of the technological accoutrements. Thus the sociologist-game designer could give people greater opportunities to make decisions about their lives and their worlds.

Second, sociologists can use some existing games in their attempts to teach community groups. The most important part of gaming is the postplay discussion, and the sociologists' expertise could help to make postplay discussion and analysis a rich learning experience.

Third, those sociologists interested in helping create new relationships, new patterns of communication, new skills for those they are working with, might well consider the other uses of games described in this paper. In such ways, perhaps the community role of the sociologist will become more vital.

Gaming is relatively new in academic quarters, and as is typical of many such enterprises, research lags behind the innovation. Hence, although numerous claims are made for the efficacy of games for cognitive, affective, and behavioral learning, the empirical status of these claims is fairly low. Anecdotal evidence abounds—all of us who have used games in and out of the classroom can offer examples of significant happenings, important changes in individuals and groups, major insights gained into oneself, others, or social systems. Reports of those who have run or participated in games are almost always highly enthusiastic. The experience is involving for both participants and directors; the games raise many questions and present operating relationships rather than static elements for later analysis. The interaction during play creates new relationships between those who otherwise may see fellow students or workers simply as faces, names, or numbers.

Unfortunately, most anecdotal reports are not yet backed up by research findings proving them to be prevalent outcomes rather than singular occurrences. If your decision to try gaming is attendant upon a body of "hard data" from research, therefore, this is not the time to begin. On the other hand, where is the demonstrable evidence that more traditional approaches bring about these results? The *general* paucity of evidence in social science and in education must surely be kept in mind in looking for evidence for gaming. In addition, although there is little "proof" that participants learn more via gaming, there is no evidence that they learn less. Games seem to be at least as effective as other modes of teaching when tested with standard measurement devices; yet the types of learning that gaming seems to best promote require new tools of measurement.

Of course it is to be hoped that further research will be undertaken to discover just what games do, under what conditions, and for whom. Until such data is available, however, those willing to gamble and join the search for better, more involving approaches to teaching will find gaming filled with excitement, discovery, and fun.

sixteen

ON STRENGTHENING APPLIED SOCIOLOGY WITH APPLIED MATHEMATICS
Robert Busby

Mathematics and the computer offer extraordinarily powerful tools to the developing sociology of the 1970s. As we strive for more scientific, more verifiable, and more respectable methods, as we wrestle with staggering quantities of data, as we grope for measured estimates of probability when critical information is unavailable, and as we cope with increasing time pressures, we will rely on high-speed computers and more and more refined methods of mathematics. Applied sociologists are not uniformly cheered by these prospects, and they disturb particularly those (like this writer) who have a long history of profound mathematical ineptitude. All the more valuable, therefore, is this essay by a mathematician impressively self-taught in sociology. He believes that action sociologists can, should, and will profit greatly from collaboration with mathematicians who share their social concerns. His reassuring counsel gives us new reason to hope for increasing mathematical competency among sociologists in the years immediately ahead.

While mathematics is employed to some degree now in sociology, I believe that a substantial increase in the quality and quantity of mathematical involvement will be quite beneficial to both disciplines, is a likely development in the 1970s, and is very much in the interest of applied or action sociologists. Moreover, I think this increase will be significantly promoted by action sociologists. Many such social scientists understand even now that an action requirement may well require more (and perhaps new) mathematical techniques, or at least the sort of deductive organization characteristic of mathematics.

For example, suppose you, as an action sociologist, find yourself involved in the practical process of trying to aid minority mobility into the executive levels of industry. Now, granted you may find that attitudes and economic practicalities are the most intractable obstacles, but you must also have a firm grasp of the mobility mechanism and how it functions if you are to make effective attempts at altering the status quo. The regression analyses of trends (which have been numerous in mobility) give some information on flows into and out of fixed positions, but shed little if any light on the underlying mechanism of these flows. Thus they are of virtually no help in this practical endeavor, although they are of some theoretical interest. In this case you could consult the recent excellent study by Harrison White[1] on the mobility mechanism in a system of fixed jobs. You would learn how the opportunity to obtain a particular position is strongly influenced by the vacating and filling of other positions throughout the organization. This would provide a better picture of what factors are and are not subject to arbitrary control, and could pinpoint the effective organs of change with the organization. White's study is definitely mathematical in orientation (although it is not highly technical) in that it attempts to model systemic behavior and isolate causal factors. Similar efforts at the same and even at greater levels of sophistication, in areas such as social mobility, aspects of the criminal-justice system, questions of social causation of political attitudes, and the like, would surely be of help in practical efforts to alter or improve concrete social situations, by identifying the mechanisms of causation and change. Mathematics, perhaps of advanced and abstract type, will be a great ally in these efforts.

The second way in which mathematics can be useful in applied sociology is in the solving of specific problems that arise at an operational level. Problems in optimal distribution, decision making with and without complete information, and the like, have been widely used in such fields as engineering, business, and economics. Such problems have not been of particular concern to sociologists in their academic interests, but they will surely arise in numerous practical situations, and action sociologists will need access to solution techniques which are tailored to their interests.

Let me illustrate with a hypothetical (somewhat stylized and oversimplified) practical example. Your wish to effect changes in a group to which you belong. Policies of that group are initially screened in a policy committee of 15 of the total group of 51, and by majority vote are or are not recommended to the total group. The larger group then votes (majority wins) with the committee's votes going in a bloc according to whether or not the measure was approved by the committee. You can join the policy committee, which has been conservative in the matters where you favor change. You estimate that they will approve the measures you favor with probability 0.5 (50–50 chance) while the rest of the group will vote "yes" (based on past performance) about 7 times out of 10 (0.7 probability). Should you join the committee or not?

1. Harrison S. White, *Chains of Opportunity* (Cambridge, Mass.: Harvard University Press, 1971).

By joining, you help sway the voting in committee and you might gain 14 extra votes. But victory in committee is harder to achieve than in the general body, and if you lose in committee your vote must go against the measure you favor. The question is whether the prospects for approval of the measure you favor will be increased or decreased by joining the committee. This particular type of risky decision was considered in James Coleman's recent paper, "The Benefits of Coalition" [2] and the techniques developed there will allow you to make the decision (which, in this case, is that it is better not to join, but if the committee had 17 or more members it would be in your interest to join).

I am not making any particular claim of relevance for this example, and in fact it is clearly a contrived exercise, but I am saying that more protracted analyses of this sort might well be useful in affecting change by political action in organizations such as the school boards or business organizations. More importantly, I am making the point that effective action in specific situations often requires analyses which cannot easily be made at an intuitive level. The well-developed practical techniques for optimal decision making should prove invaluable in social action especially when they are extended and interpreted in social and political situations, as illustrated in Coleman's paper.

Finally, as an action sociologist in many concrete endeavors, you will find yourself flooded with data of all sorts. Some of this data will be of the type traditionally of interest to sociologists and some will be grease for the wheels of various bureaucracies, but in any case you will be increasingly besieged by information. It is definitely in your interest to be at least casually acquainted with modern methods of processing, retrieving, and analyzing data.

Many social scientists have some training in statistical methods for data analysis but the full impact of modern computer technology has yet to be felt. The advantage of computer methods is that they permit previously unmanageable quantities of information to be stored in an accessible place, sorted into categories, and systematically examined. The prospect of sorting through census, health, crime, and voting data at the large-city level, and digging for correlations with the usual statistical tools, is already unthinkable without computer aid. Moreover, the flexibility of the computer will allow methods of processing that would have been completely impractical before, even with moderate-size data (e.g., individual comparisons which require an iterative examination procedure and thus mean searching through the data a large number of times).

The implications are many for action sociology as well as for social-sci-

2. James S. Coleman, "The Benefits of Coalition," *Public Choice*, 8 (Spring 1970): 45–61.

ence theory. For example, it is feasible to process large quantities of voting data and correlate this with the more customary sociological data at various locations throughout a community. Conceivably, if enough data are used, this could yield important information on the attitudes of people (as expressed in their voting preferences) on various sociological questions, which information in turn is often a necessary preliminary to instituting social change.

Applied mathematics can thus aid the action sociologist in his attack on a social problem at three levels, which might be vaguely categorized as strategy, tactics, and reconnaissance. It aids strategy in that underlying structure of aspects of the operation of certain social processes can be exposed, thus allowing identification of causal factors, areas amenable to change, and likely consequences of proposed changes. Mathematics aids tactics by providing important tools for concrete problem solving and decision making. Finally, reconnaissance, in the sense of perceiving various aspects of the problem through available information inputs, is aided, and in some cases made possible, by modern methods of data processing and analysis.

What steps do I recommend in order to realize the potential of applied mathematics to action sociology? First, it is essential that there be more communication between mathematicians and social scientists. While it is true that there are mathematical sociologists with an excellent grasp of technical tools, and true that they have made excellent studies, it is almost certainly true that the developments which I discussed earlier will require the continuing involvement of mathematicians in sociological theory. This is so because no one sociologist (or even mathematician) can have command of the full range of tools that the mathematical community possesses, and recent work has begun to suggest that the mathematics which may be appropriate may be quite different from that previously used in social science. Moreover, many sociologists who will be involved in action projects will have virtually no experience in mathematics at all, and it would be virtually impossible (and wasteful of their talents) for them to try to develop the needed technical skills.

Thus, I think that interdisciplinary cooperation is needed if the action sociologist is to benefit from the potential outlined above. The mathematician may be equally lost and inexperienced in sociology, but at least sociological results are largely written in conventional language, and so he can grasp much of their essence. To me this means that the first step in this cooperative enterprise must be taken by the mathematician who wishes to involve himself in social science. I feel that this step should be actively encouraged by the applied sociological community, and that this particular kind of sociologist should endeavor to make relevant sociological results readily accessible and intelligible to outside technicians. At the same time, of course, sociologists who feel that they can benefit from this joint cooperation can make some personal efforts to cultivate at least a beginning technical competence.

A beginning introduction to abstract mathematical thinking may be had by going through some elementary books on linear algebra, abstract algebra, or topology. This may be a much more appropriate beginning for ultimate communication with mathematicians than the usual process of learning calculus and similar analytic tools, because it will facilitate familiarity with the language of mathematics. After this a text on applied probability and maybe a simple text in FORTRAN programming[3] would be good follow-ups for those with little experience in these areas. I know that the ranks of those mathematicians who are willing to cooperate with social scientists are swelling, due both to an increase in personal awareness of critical social problems and to the effects of changes in national research priorities. The prospects for valuable cooperation in action as well as for theoretical projects are possible and even likely, if members of both communities are sincere in their desire to work together and in their attempt to view one another's specialties from a sympathetic point of view.

3. For example, Herbert S. Wilf, *Programming for a Digital Computer in the* FORTRAN *Language* (Reading, Mass.: Addison-Wesley, 1969).

seventeen

SOCIOLOGICAL APPLICATIONS OF INTERACTIONAL COMPUTER SYSTEMS: TOWARD A DIALOGICAL RESEARCH MODEL
Robert Johansen

How to get in touch, how to stay in touch, how to be available to one another—these are critical problems for action sociologists who seek continuous communication with clients, with other action sociologists, and with a wide range of specialists. Exciting advances in communication are being made possible by the high-speed electronic computer, a fundamental tool whose creative possibilities action sociologists have barely begun to explore. This essay by a pioneering specialist who is also an experienced applied sociologist opens up a new world of communication possibilities. The case study shows many ways in which computer-based interactional systems can alter action sociology—provided that we undertake substantial work in this area. The call for "an openness to technology" and the warning that anything less threatens us with dues too high to pay leave us much to ponder.

Applied sociologists have long relied uncomfortably on the questionnaire to provide still another valuable flow of data. Their discomfort rests with the fact that its drawbacks are so conspicious: the public is weary and wary of this overused tool. Many doubt that the questionnaire is reliable and valid enough to really register their personal perceptions. And few respondents (previously called persons) really expect to see the results, or, in such a rare instance, can recall whatever it was they once answered to the fool questionnaire to begin with.

A potentially better instrument is now becoming available for use by action sociologists, and I should like with this essay to help it gain the attention and acceptance it merits. The better tool might be called Computer Interactional Research (CIR) and is grounded in advanced computer technology. Where the public seems to be weary, the new tool offers novelty. Where the respondent could be wary, the new tool as yet has no special negative connotations (e.g., security checks) attached to it. Where the public is inclined to doubt the data-collecting finesse of the traditional paper-and-pencil instrument, the new tool is dynamic enough to permit the user to question the questions as they unfold, gain clarification, and even alter the shape of the questions being asked. Finally, where the respondent often expects no feedback from the average questionnaire campaign, CIR can offer a kind of dialogue process. Using charted comparisons, graphs, or a variety of other formats, CIR can provide personal feedback to each participant showing his or her relationship to others in the sample or in comparative groups.

How does it work? How might a creative sociologist put it to work? Some insight here is available from the fictional scenario below, modeled on an extension of NET's weekly TV show, "The Advocates." The show viewed controversial issues in a courtroomlike format, and the viewers acted as jurors, sending in postcard "verdicts" that were then tabulated and sent to the germane public agencies (e.g., Senate, President, or whatever). Weakened by all the limitations of traditional data-gathering, the TV show could have profited immensely from the adoption of a CIR format:

"Tonight ladies and gentlemen," the television announcer began, "The Advocates will begin what may become a new era in human communications. Following our usual format of debate on a current social issue of pressing importance, we will ask for your opinions immediately via the recently expanded International Cable-Television Network. As you know, simple computer keyboards are now installed with all television units, making it possible to literally talk back to your television. The Advocates is proud to be the first show to test this exciting new communications network.

"Rather than wait for your postcard votes to reach our studios, we will ask each of you to vote on the issue: 'Should the United States Support the Proposed World Federation?' through your own television consoles. Your votes will then be compiled through our Central Computer with general results tabulated before the show is over. As has always been our policy, results will then be forwarded to all congressional and executive bodies.

"If you wish to have the results categorized further so that you can compare regions, etc., you will of course to able to do so. The interactional language LINGO will allow you to make any requests or comments in normal English. And now let us begin consideration of this critical issue. . . ."

This vision of instantaneous survey methodologies is far from science fiction. Though the possibilities for linking to cable-television networks are uncertain, computer systems that actually implement the input-feedback process described in the scenario (and more) are already in operation.

If computer terminals are readily available, the subject of the action-sociology project need only sit down at a console and call the appropriate program. The console may be connected via telephone lines to a computer in a location which is perhaps miles away (or in the next room). There is no necessity for prearranged administration times, mailing or circulating questionnaires, scheduling interviews, and so forth. The subject merely signs on at his or her own convenience. Of course this process will become progressively easier as the availability of terminals increases, perhaps to the point where they will be basic parts of every home and office. Plasma screen terminals[1] make this kind of proliferation a much more realistic possibility for the near future, particularly around schools and universities. Expanded facilities such as these will form an unprecedented sociological and human resource which could become essential to many new types of social inquiry and action sociology.

From the perspective of the time-harried sociologist, much of the busywork of test administration and organization can become automated with an interactional system. Responses are stored (usually on a tape or disk pack) as they are given according to a programmed format designed by the researcher. Comments and reactions of the participants can be recorded in a similar fashion. This data can then be retrieved periodically by the sociologist in whatever format is most usable to the ongoing purposes of the project. Some systems can automate this to the point where the data would be reported on punched cards, ready for detailed analysis. At the very least, orderly summaries of the responses can be available at any time to the researcher or (to the degree determined by the researcher) to each participant in the project.

The CIR format is already in the field, and every passing month sees improvements being made in it. In the action-critical field of Future Studies, for example, CIR underlies an exciting variation on the RAND-developed Delphi technique, a crude pioneering means of projecting possible alternative futures. Normally the technique involves sampling experts in an area and pooling their opinions as to the probability of particular events. The research sequence often involves a series of rounds where the experts can change their rating in an effort to reach some kind of presumably more valuable opinion. Murray Turoff, using CIR, has attempted to circumvent the tedious round structures of Delphi with its multiple mailings, sluggish time constraints, and awkward data analysis.[2] He has developed instead

---

1. Plasma screens combine low cost and simple construction with potentials for color display, audio capacity, drawing of lines, display of slides, etc. Donald Bitzer, head of the University of Illinois PLATO project, is the designer of the unit that will be marketed in the near future. Bitzer predicts a total user cost of fifty cents per hour, including the cost of the terminal and computer time.

2. See particularly Murray Turoff, "Delphi Conferencing (i.e., Computer-based Conferencing with Anonymity)," *Journal of Technological Forecasting and Social Change* 3, no. 2 (1971); Thomas W. Hall, "Implementation of an Interacting Conference System," Proceedings of 1971 Fall Joint Computer Conference, University Press of New England, Box 979, Hanover, N.H. 03755. This last article lists recent references for similar Delphi efforts.

what he calls the Delphi Conference (also called Continuous Automated Delphi, or CAD). Each participant is linked to the group (no matter how far away) through a teletype, offering information and giving reactions at his or her convenience. The information is then stored for compilation and display to later participants. In this way it is possible for loosely structured groups—even if they are far apart from one another—to participate in an ongoing conference session. Dr. Turoff has conducted at least one major experiment with the method and seems generally encouraged by the possibilities for further development. The system was also used in the administration of the recent price freeze.

Another application of special interest to the action sociologist involves the work of Stuart Umpleby and Valarie Lamont through the PLATO System at the University of Illinois.[3] The PLATO System is perhaps the most advanced interactional system in the world. Near-future plans (perhaps four years) include the installation of a statewide network of terminals connected to the central computer by closed-circuit television. Using the original plasma screen terminals (designed by project director, Donald Bitzer), the potentials for low-cost and efficient operation are startling. Already research programs in operation on the PLATO System include a citizen sampling of general alternative futures, a future of the university program, and an ecological simulation. Unfortunately the university has been less than supportive of the possibilities for PLATO in interactional and futures research, so that the future of the Umpleby-Lamont project seems unclear. Their efforts, however, are quite creative and seem to foreshadow possible directions for operationalizing a general dialogical research model of unestimable value for action sociology.

Other alternative applications of interactional research to applied sociology concerns have been suggested in such areas as individual-placement testing and perhaps even some types of counseling. Wayne H. Holtzman has edited a book called *Computer-Assisted Instruction, Testing, and Guidance* (Harper & Row, 1970) which contains specific articles in these areas. One of the more interesting propositions (suggested by Frederic M. Lord in chapter 8) calls for computer-based testing that would design specific tests through an ongoing analysis of the individual responses of the test takers. Based on the general rule of giving a harder item after each correct answer and an easier item after each wrong answer, the ideal would be a perfectly adapted and concise test of each person's specific

3. For further information, contact the Computer-Based Educational Research Laboratory, University of Illinois, Urbana, Illinois. Stuart Umpleby's most recent article on the subject is "Structuring Information for a Computer Based Communications Medium," Proceedings of 1971 Fall Joint Computer Conference, University Press of New England, Box 979, Hanover, N.H. 03755.

needs and abilities in certain areas. Questions would be drawn from a large pool of possibilities available to the computer for construction of each tailored test. Such application could become a potentially humanizing alternative to the present maze of standardized tests which are arousing increasing hostility as their dehumanizing impact becomes clearer.

Where I am writing from, at Northwestern and Garrett (both on the same campus and affiliated institutions), we have been experimenting with interactional computer systems in several exciting ways. Perhaps the most interesting where action sociology is concerned is in the area of curriculum evaluation and feedback. Garrett's three-year Master of Divinity Program operates under a dynamic model of learning—ungraded, process oriented, etc. Thus the question of curriculum evaluation is a very difficult one (e.g., there is no precise "end product"). Traditional research techniques are difficult to apply to this model of education, and there is a somewhat high degree of distrust among personnel toward questionnaires in particular and sometimes toward research in general.

In attempting to develop a curricular feedback network within this kind of environment, it has become clear that flexible research methodologies are very important. Thus we began experimenting last year with interactional research models involving a future orientation. The general purpose of the project has been to develop channels of feedback within the curriculum in such a way that evaluation becomes an ongoing process, rather than a series of separate (and often unrelated) research efforts. Evaluation of this sort must involve more than examining what has been done in the past; it must probe alternative future directions and blend them with a concise analysis of what has gone before. Thus there is a strong need for the method of evaluation to be consistent with the goals of the evaluation process. Since in this case the project goals were dynamic, a methodology was needed which would provide insight about the process of education—not freeze the process so it was more suitable for dissection than for meaningful social analysis and action applications.

Early efforts to establish the curricular feedback network relied upon carefully designed paper-and-pencil instruments, but we realized from the start that this format could not be a final answer. Since an interactional computer system was being considered for other applications within the curriculum, it seemed appropriate to explore possible applications of this system in the area of curricular feedback.

We then began designing programs which could be used to facilitate this kind of a process. The first programs were modifications of the RAND-Turoff Delphi technique, which asked for ratings on the desirability of specific events as well as the probability that they will occur by a specific date in the future. Each person's responses to our computerized questionnaire are recorded, compiled along with earlier respondents, and the participant is able to get immediate feedback on group reactions to each event. Also he can ask to be compared to previous groups that have participated. (The question of how much feedback to give and at what point to give it is one with which we are still struggling.)

The first program was based on thirteen possible futures for Garrett (e.g., merger with other schools to form a new theological center, quarter system eliminated) which each person was asked to consider. The actual choice of events, however, took on such an importance in itself that we decided upon a more open-ended format where each person could add new events which would become a part of the program for future participants. Thus it also became possible for various smaller groups to use the program by considering only issues specifically relevant to them (these were then stored on separate computer tapes by the system). Committees and task forces which met very irregularly could then transact some parts of their business at their own speed via this program. Furthermore they considered long-range possibilities which time constraints would have made impossible through normal committee channels. (This application is still being developed, however, and we are just beginning to get feedback as to what effect this program has on group decision-making process, member deployment, etc.)

Most of the development thus far has been at the level of planning and experimentation. A major problem is, of course, funding the rental of the necessary hardware. As a temporary move, we have now set up a kind of "world game room" at Garrett containing a portable computer terminal (from another project) which is available at established times. Our goal is to encourage students and faculty to use the interactional system in as many different ways as possible (CIR being one of these uses). Students in a sociology class that I am teaching, for example, are now designing their own simulations on the interactional system, as even nonprogrammers can computerize their simulations when that is desirable. Also, when adequate funding for permanent computer terminals can be arranged, computer resources will become a part of the library system. At that time, a specific concerted effort will be made toward developing individualized learning programs in various areas of university concern, on and off campus, with applied sociologists looked to for a very considerable imput.

The general idea I wish to convey is simply that interactional research via computer systems has numerous appealing possibilities and an almost equally large number of untested effects which demand to be explored. It seems, though, that the promise of a dialogical research model merits the effort necessary to develop reliable means of operationalizing the model. If it all seems very uncertain, recall the uncertainties of questionnaire surveys. There may yet be a better way.

I am not unaware of the probability that many persons to the "soft" side of computer sciences will discount CIR systems as expensive novelties that play pretty good games of chess. This seems at least unfortunate to me, and is perhaps a major reason why I am writing this article. We are at a point in history where the technology-humanity gap is dangerously widening. The social sciences, supposedly something of a bridge between the two, often become intrigued with only one side of the chasm. No matter which "side" it is (human or technological), one choice without the other seems particularly dangerous to me in our era.

Regarding CIR systems, it seems that they will become an important technology involving social systems in the near future. Hopefully this article has hinted at the ways in which interactional systems might alter the modus operandi of social inquiry and applied sociology. Yet, at present, the major efforts at developing social applications for CIR-like systems is coming from the military and from the "hard" sciences. Thus far the potential for humanistic and self-actualizing applications of CIR systems has been largely left undeveloped by social scientists. Perhaps the neo-Luddite (named after the Luddites who smashed machines in the nineteenth century) instincts within us are shading our views of possible applications. I would contend that, given the already successful implementation of several systems with CIR potential, the question is not *whether* they will be developed, but *who* will develop them.

My hope is that the "soft" sciences will work together with the technicians in the development of future systems. This is already happening at some locations (e.g., PLATO) but it needs to be a much broader and more experimental network. Interactional languages are already developed to the extent that one need not be an expert programmer to write successful programs for action sociology projects. One needs only the hardware facilities and the motivation to take a chance with a system which could basically alter specific portions of the field of social science, action sociology, and human communication in general. The implications of the development are simply too great to default experimentation and control to military mindsets alone. Sociology in action during this period of history demands an openness to technology and a willingness to develop whatever expertise is necessary to have a significant effect on new technologies. CIR systems are in need of precisely this kind of creative sociological exploration.

"The most incomprehensible thing about the world is that it is comprehensible."

—Albert Einstein

part seven

APPLIED RESEARCH

Possibly the weakest "link" in action sociology is one labeled *research*. Our mistakes here are numerous: We research faddishly and unevenly, without continuity, follow-up, or long-range design comprehensibility. We research tiny and fragmented puzzles, responding far too eagerly to the proclivities of financial sponsors or the ready accessibility of data. We research alone, as if oblivious to the enormous potential of team research. And we research without vision or poetry.

Not all of us are misguided, but far too many of us may sometime fit the caricature above. Helpful therefore are the two essays below, each of which struggles constructively with some of the various issues now raised. In the first, Professors Sally Bould Van Til and Rafael Valdivieso suggest a larger context we might employ as a guide to our choice and direction of social research. In the second Mrs. Sarajane Heidt explains the origins, programs, problems, and prospects of one of the freshest, most dynamic, and most socially-concerned of the large research centers in America. Together the two essays offer reason to hope that the entire "chain" will soon be stronger for new strength in its critical and controversial research link.

eighteen

THE SOCIOLOGY OF SOCIAL POLICY: PATHS THROUGH THE MORASS
Sally Bould Van Til and Rafael Valdivieso

How does the overall direction of American social policy influence our effectiveness in action-sociology projects? How do our projects, in turn, relate to our sociological theories? And finally, how might we go about learning the sociology of social policy? These research-oriented questions lead to the three major value perspectives in contemporary social policy, or the perspectives of the conservative-elitist, the liberal, and the radical. Exploring all three in depth challenges us to claim more carefully than ever our own value preference in the wide-open matter of policy and research perspectives. Above all, however, this essay makes a strong case for applied social research freed from a debilitating insistence on value neutrality, and finally equal to the overt-values stance long overdue in our profession.

After three decades of regrettable attempts to sever the relationship between sociology and social reform, certain sociologists began in the 1960s to reenter the arena of social action and to encourage their students to do so as well. Together they asked whether the traditional classroom setting could serve as a basis for understanding the noncampus arena of social action. This paper argues that the academic setting *can* provide a forum and a frame of reference for academics *and* nonacademics involved in the processes of social change. We call this setting the "sociology of social policy," which, in our definition, includes a range of perspectives on domestic social issues from that of radical social-protest action through the social-policy "planning" of elites.[1]

Our own involvement in social policy arose out of concrete experiences. In the 1960s, one of us was involved in trying to find jobs for poor people; the other was attempting to obtain adequate incomes for poor people. While such involvement sensitized us to unmet needs among poor and

---

1. Our use of the term social policy includes not only social welfare policies but also the broad spectrum of economic policies.

minority populations, we also realized that simply finding a person a job or obtaining welfare benefits for a poor mother was not going to bring about the social changes we desired. Furthermore, the problem lay not with an individual's motivation to achieve the minimum necessities of a comfortable life, but with the overall direction of American social policy. What was required was an analysis of these policies: what sorts of policies were being proposed and implemented in American society, and why?

While the sensitivity obtained in field experience is invaluable, it is not sufficient to enable most students to develop optimum sophistication in the complex arena of social reform. Popular slogans and a sympathetic point of view remain no substitute for the difficult task of analyzing social policies. This was brought home in recent discussions with certain poverty workers and social workers convinced from their field experience that a "culture of poverty" thesis provided an adequate conceptualization for social policies dealing with poor people.

It was impossible in a few short discussions to convince these workers that whether or not the culture-of-poverty thesis was a valid one, it necessarily implied a frame of reference aptly termed by Ryan as that of "blaming the victim." [2] The poverty programs of the 1960s had clear historical antecedents in the repressive Industrial Poor Laws of the nineteenth century; characterizing the poor as caught in a "culture of poverty" rather than as indigents with defective moral characters places the blame no less squarely upon the poor themselves. Accordingly, it is both possible and desirable that the classroom setting provide the needed mechanism to translate sensitivity into sophisticated comprehension of current social policies and their historical antecedents.

Nevertheless, the question of the legitimacy of the sociological study of social policy is inevitably raised by traditional sociologists. Here we can only point to a growing number of established sociologists who have seen the arena of social policy as of sufficient intellectual and academic import for them to devote their time, both in discussion and publication, to this question. Political scientists Edward Banfield and Daniel Patrick Moynihan have similarly devoted considerable attention to the issues of social policy, and academic economists have been involved in debates over social policy since the 1930s. No less an Establishment sociologist than Edward Shils devotes considerable space in an article to sociology and policy.[3] Nathan Glazer and S. M. Miller and Frank Riessman have also discussed social class and social policy.[4]

2. William Ryan, *Blaming the Victim* (New York: Pantheon, 1971).

3. Edward Shils, "The Calling of Sociology," in *Theories of Society*, vol. 2, ed. Talcott Parsons et al. (New York: Free Press of Glencoe, 1961), pp. 1432 ff.

4. Nathan Glazer, "The Limits of Social Policy," *Commentary* 52 (September 1971):

In spite of this involvement of leading sociologists in social policy analysis, a division still remains between social science in the classroom and social action in the streets. For us the resolution of this traditional split was prompted not merely by our rejection of the hackneyed two-role model (sociologists as scientists vs. sociologists as citizens), but also by the realization that a social-science perspective could better inform our actions. And, conversely, we realized that the arena of social action could contribute substantially to our understanding of man, institutions, and societies. Although this latter contribution could be made in many ways, we here focus only on two.

First, social action provides for reality testing of sociological theories formulated in the detached world of academia. For example, in the 1950s and early 1960s, sociologists and political scientists formulated a theory of pluralism to explain the American political scene. The United States was conceptualized as a pluralistic society where interest groups could mobilize political influence to obtain action for their concerns. Lack of mobilization was construed to indicate "satisfaction." By the mid-1960s this theory was put to the test with the mobilization of thousands of poor people in local community groups, people who aimed to obtain greater influence over the decision making that directly affected their lives. From the results of mobilizations by the Citizens United Against Poverty in San Francisco, the Welfare Rights Organization in New York, the Child Development Group of Mississippi, and the Blackstone Rangers in Chicago, among others, pluralism did not operate for low-income groups; mobilization did not result in influence. Moreover, in the process of mobilizing, new and potent barriers were uncovered that limited the access of poor people to even traditional avenues of power and influence.[5]

Second, involvement in social action invariably raises relevant research questions often overlooked by academic sociologists. Again, to cite but one example, over fifty years ago Weber identified the nature and dangers of the bureaucratic structure. Nevertheless, we know little more today about how to make our bureaucratic structures any more responsive to human needs. Faced with the contradiction between the huge welfare bureaucracy in New York City and the large degree of unmet needs among the poor, Cloward and Piven have developed the tactic of overwhelming the bureaucracy by encouraging the needy to apply.[6] While this tactic has

51–58; S. M. Miller and Frank Riessman, *Social Class and Social Policy* (New York: Basic Books, 1968).

5. See Jewel Bellush and Stephen M. David, "Introduction: Pluralism, Race, and the Urban Political System," in *Race and Politics in New York City* (New York: Praeger, 1971), pp. 3–24.

6. Richard A. Cloward and Frances Fox Piven, "The Weight of the Poor: A Strategy to End Poverty," *Nation* 202 (May 2, 1966): 510–17.

produced some changes in providing more money to poor people, the welfare bureaucracy, buttressed by the political system, has nevertheless been able to continue its traditional antihuman practices. This painful experience of the Welfare Rights Organization in New York, in addition to raising questions about tactics for changing bureaucratic structures, laid bare the strong interrelationship between bureaucratic structures and political systems.[7] The issues raised by this struggle are critical for action sociologists, but they are also relevant for the discipline of sociology itself.

We must respond to the question, How does one go about learning the sociology of social policy? After a number of years of struggling with this question, and participating in numerous seminars specifically designed for that purpose, we can assert that the going is rough, the routes consist of mazes, and the terrain is slippery. We have still much to learn, but it may be useful to identify three approaches to the study of social policy that we have tried and found lacking.

One such approach is the traditional sociological tack of studying social problems. As they have traditionally been viewed by American sociologists, social problems are thought to be forms of social deviance and social disorganization. They are seen as embodied in inadequate socialization, conflicting values and norms, and situations characterized by anomie. Implicit in this approach is the whole concept of functionalism: social problems are dysfunctional in that they disrupt social order. Moreover, sociologists have pointed out the latent functions of deviant behavior; e.g., the institution of prostitution contributed to the maintenance of the traditional family structure. As Durkheim first said, deviant behavior provides for the reaffirmation of traditional values and norms by the collectivity.[8]

While the social-problem approach is intellectually fascinating and has been broadened in recent years to include the discussion of solutions, it is nevertheless limited by its ties to functionalism. The functional framework is more adequately suited to the analysis of the persistence of social problems rather than the mechanisms for long-range structural changes that might reduce or eliminate them. Merton and Nisbet describe this perspective in their statement, "Owing to the systematic interdependence among the parts of a social structure, efforts to do away with one social problem will often introduce other (either more or less damaging)

7. Richard A. Cloward and Frances Fox Piven, "The Professional Bureaucracies: Benefit Systems as Influence Systems," in Readings in Community Organization Practice, ed. Ralph M. Kramer and Harry Specht (Englewood Cliffs, N.J.: Prentice-Hall, 1969), pp. 359–72.

8. Emile Durkheim, The Rules of the Sociological Method (New York: Free Press of Glencoe, 1950), pp. 70 ff.

problems." [9] Furthermore, the emphasis upon deviance and social disorganization lends itself to focusing solely upon the deviants themselves, a focus all too compatible to the perspective of "blaming the victim."

Instead, what appears needed is a broad-based approach to the study of social policy. This would provide a larger framework within which action sociologists can explore the historical and immediate aspects of problems, and learn how to put their academic training to use in their current and future off-campus involvement. After a frustrating search, however, we have concluded that a general and broad-based approach to social-policy research is likely to be too far removed from the specific needs and interests of the student and thus fail to become a useful guide. The problem is exemplified by Etzioni's concept of societal guidance.[10] The limitations of such a grand theory of social policy are analogous to the limitations of a grand theory of sociology that Mills so cogently outlined;[11] when specific questions are asked or specific applications are needed such a theory cannot provide a useful frame of reference. It may be that such a grand synthesis is simply premature.[12] The amorphous nature of the study of social policy, however, may be such that systematic conceptualization, even in the long run, will limit rather than enhance.

The third approach to social policy which has been used most widely in both the academic study and in the policy-making arena is that of the economic model. In contrast to the problem of the grand synthesis, which attempts to cover too broad a range of social reality, the economic model is too limited. It focuses on economic policy, with social policy regarded as merely a residual category. Its goals are assumed to be given, and its solutions are seen as a choice among means based upon technical efficiency. For example, the economic model often focuses upon "rational" technocratic methods such as cost-benefit analysis and systems analysis. Action sociologists invariably question the assumptions made here about human behavior, assumptions based solely, or primarily, upon economic motivation. Neither are they content to define decisions about goals as outside their purview, nor do they accept the principle that the choice among means is merely a question of rational decision making.

The three approaches outlined above suffer from a still more critical limitation. For the student attempting to make sense of social policy, each

9. Robert K. Merton and Robert A. Nisbet, *Contemporary Social Problems* (New York: Harcourt, Brace & World, 1966), p. viii.

10. Amitai Etzioni, *The Active Society* (New York: Free Press, 1968).

11. C. Wright Mills, *The Sociological Imagination* (New York: Oxford University Press, 1959), pp. 25–49.

12. Martin Rein, "Social Policy Analysis as the Interpretation of Beliefs," *Journal of the American Institute of Planners* 37 (September 1971): 297.

fails to deal with the inevitable intrusion of social values. The contribution of social science to the arena of social action lies most critically in "making the values underlying social policy and human behavior explicit." [13] As Martin Rein has stated, "the study of social policy involves the interaction between values, operating principles, and outcomes." Furthermore, he contends, and we would agree, that "ideology and beliefs attach to means as much as to ends." [14] Social policy is, in essence, politics. In the Spanish, French, and German languages this inevitable overlap is recognized by the use of one single term; unfortunately, in English the distinction between "politics" and "policy" lends itself to the illusion that the two can be separated.

We suggest, then, that three major value perspectives dominate the arena of social policy: the perspectives of the conservative-elitist, the liberal, and the radical.

The conservative-elitist approach is based on the assumption that the ideal system leaves all policy decisions to the mechanism of the free market. Because of the cyclical nature of the capitalist economy, however, and especially the experience of the Great Depression, conservatives have modified their free-market view to include minimal intervention by the state in order to alleviate the most negative consequences of capitalist economic policy. The notion that the market mechanism is the best system for the distribution of rewards, as well as for the protection of individual liberty, has thus been modified slightly to include conservative reforms, designed by professionals, that enhance social stability during times of economic crisis. The analysis of social problems and remedies proposed for reducing or eliminating them is viewed as a technical rather than as an ideological matter. The economic model, discussed earlier, is often employed by conservatives.

The liberal perspective focuses more on social justice. It would operate by opening up the opportunity structures within the existing societal arrangements while providing for "decent minimum living conditions for all." [15] Furthermore, the implementation of these policies is viewed as the task of government. The government's investment in social justice is seen to pay off not only in the rehabilitation of the individual as a human resource, but also in the greater social stability of society as a whole. Liberals argue that social justice is necessary and also efficient, since a more just society will have to contend with fewer social problems. Liberals even go so far as to advocate some conflict and certain kinds of protest, but

13. Louis Wirth, "On Making Values Explicit," in On Cities and Social Life (Chicago: Phoenix Books, 1964), p. 157.
14. Rein, "Social Policy Analysis," p. 298.
15. Glazer, Limits of Social Policy, p. 51.

only where such conflict appears to lead ultimately to the resolution of issues and the reestablishment of the stability of society.

Liberal programs that do not provide for social stability and are not capable of producing contentment on the basis of their greater social justice become the foils for the conservative as well as prompting the retreat of liberals from their own social programs. Thus, liberals fear that social policy as "an effort to deal with the breakdown of traditional ways of handling distress" through the family, the ethnic group, the neighborhood, and the church will only encourage further the weakening of these traditional mechanisms.[16] Liberals, then, wish to avoid dramatic new programs that might cause major economic and social dislocations and prefer what Lindblom calls "the incremental pattern of policy-making" or "muddling through." [17]

From the radical social-policy perspective, social problems are viewed as the inevitable consequences of the institutional arrangements and class structures of the society. Moreover, the predominant social policy in the society is seen as a reflection of the dominant political-power relationship in that society. Government, then, cannot be viewed as a mechanism for social change, since it is not independent of these relationships. Social policy is, in fact, politics in the broadest sense—the analysis of the struggle over which groups get what and why, and not just the formulation and execution of policy by government. The overall objective of social policy for the radical is directed toward creating conditions of equality as distinguished from the liberals' goal of equality of opportunity. In focusing upon the relative differences in life chances and well-being of different strata, together with the institutional arrangements which work to preserve those differences, the radical concludes that such differences are inevitable without profound changes in the structure of the society. Economic policy, therefore, must be subsumed under overall social policy, and that social policy cannot be characterized by the timid "muddling through" approach of liberals.[18]

While the action sociologist must become sophisticated in the analysis of values and operating principles inherent in social policy, perhaps the most critical contribution of the study of social policy to social action lies in analyzing the outcome of social programs. There is no simple one-to-one connection between the original values and operating principles of a proposed policy and the actual outcome. This is especially critical for those

16. Ibid., p. 52.
17. Charles E. Lindblom, "The Science of 'Muddling Through,'" in *Social Welfare Institutions*, Mayer N. Zald (New York: John Wiley, 1965), p. 225.
18. See Howard M. Wachtel, "Looking at Poverty from a Radical Perspective," *Review of Radical Political Economics* 3 (Summer 1971): 1–19.

who endorse the values of a radical social policy but have seen both historically and in our own experience that radical social programs are often manipulated for their own use by conservative elitists, with the result invariably being a conservative outcome. As Michael Harrington has indicated, "proposals of impeccably leftist origins—radical or liberal—are now being systematically re-designed to serve the cause of sophisticated conservatism." [19]

The recent Nixon economic plan is only the latest example of this redesigning process. In his dramatic shift toward a WPA-type program in the Emergency Employment Act, the President called for an investment of $2.25 billion in the creation of 150,000 public-service jobs. This is an echo of an old socialist demand that social policy be directed toward providing work for all who wish it.[20] There is little evidence, however, that this program will make a dent in the 5 percent unemployment rate; nor will it be a boon to the poor who cannot qualify for the $12,000-a-year jobs it creates.

Similarly, when the New York State legislature voted for the less paternalistic flat-rate grant in public assistance, their aim was not to give welfare clients the right to spend their grants as they saw fit but rather to destroy the special grants that had been used as a basis for organizing the Welfare Rights Organization in New York City, and thus to enhance the legislators' chances for reelection. There is nothing new in this adaptation of liberal and radical programs for conservative political ends. The history of this adaptation goes back to Bismarck's implementation of social insurance as a means for removing the basis for union organization in Germany during the time when the socialist unions posed a threat to the established order.

While certain recent events lead the radical social reformer to despair, radicals have on occasion translated liberal reforms into far more radical outcomes. One recent such translation involved the "maximum feasible participation" clause of the Economic Opportunity Act of 1964. Liberals were shocked when the clause was used by radical reformers as a basis for mobilizing poor people into politically cohesive groups. The Syracuse University Community Action Planning Center was criticized by the executive director of another community-action program for "looking at poor people as a class-poor people rising as a class. We're thinking about making opportunities for individuals." [21]

19. Michael Harrington, "Government Should Be the Employer of First Resort," *New York Times Magazine* (26 March 1972), p. 44.

20. Ibid., p. 44.

21. Quoted in E. Knoll and J. Witcover, "Organizing the Poor," in *Poverty American Style*, ed. Herman Miller (Belmont, Calif.: Wadsworth, 1966), p. 248.

For the action sociologist of any persuasion, a serious problem remains in determining how best to analyze the relationship between values, operating principles, and outcomes so that when a plan of action or program is proposed and implemented, the results are in conformity with the original goals. For the radical reformer, however, this becomes a question of whether or not such actions will lead to cooptation without significant social change. In the short run, liberal and radical aims may coincide, for example, by providing some economic break for poor people, but in the long run the liberal wishes to provide for a better functioning of the existing society. This latter goal is also adopted by conservatives in the short run, which explains why Nixon chose to implement his Emergency Employment Act; but in the long run the conservatives have no desire to maintain an ongoing program of publicly supported jobs, for in the long run the goal of the conservatives is to return to the free-market mechanism.[22]

Radicals, liberals, and conservatives may all adopt a short-term policy of "buying off the poor," but the operationalization of these policies is very different in the long run. In times of crisis, conservatists seek to buy off the poor for the cheapest price possible. The Nixon Family Assistance Plan proposed to buy off the poor at $600 per person or $2,400 for a family of four for an entire year. Economist Milton Friedman, who pioneered this approach, also proposed removing all social services from the public sector and moving them into the arena of the free market. Liberals, who are more disturbed at the thought of human misery, are willing to pay a slightly higher price, and are also willing to sustain programs of social services on more than a crisis-intervention basis. They nevertheless expect that in return for these efforts the poor will respond with the appropriate social behavior and attitudes, while leaving the bulk of the administration of the program in the hands of professionals. For radicals, the price is one of continuing escalation: to wrench a community park out of the hands of Bethlehem Steel was merely the first step of an escalating program for the community organization of Pike County, West Virginia. The long-run radical goal is a transformation of society itself.

Perhaps, however, the most telling difference in the potential outcome between the various social-policy perspectives lies in their view of citizen participation. The extent to which citizens participate in the initiation and implementation of programs determines to a large extent the nature of the program. For poor people, citizen participation is especially critical, since history provides abundant evidence that programs for poor people are generally poor programs.

22. Frances Fox Piven and Richard A. Cloward, *Regulating the Poor* (New York: Pantheon, 1971).

In the conservative-elite model, citizen participation is interpreted to mean the participation of prominent citizens or elites in direction of the programs. Professionals are used to provide technical assistance for the goals of the program. When the goals of the program are directly related to the interests of the civic elite, as with urban renewal, one can describe the elites as the actual clients of the program. The poor are the products; one is even tempted to say, the waste products. In Forrester's model they are relegated to what is euphemistically termed "the limitless environment." [23] In programs such as public assistance, where the interests of the elite are less directly involved, it is the interest of the middle-class clients and the arena of legislative reform where the participation of citizens is deemed relevant. Again, the poor are the objects upon which the program attempts, with the aid of professionals, to effect changes.

In the liberal model, political participation is given greater emphasis, and it is generally broadened to include participation not only of the middle class but also of the poor, since the stress is upon social justice; but the poor are expected to participate on an individual basis only and not as a collective group. The participation of the poor in the implementation of programs is justified both by democratic principles and efficiency; thus, services can be delivered more effectively if poor persons serve as interpreters to professionals. The goal is to improve the circumstances of individual poor people, but the client, in the liberal perspective, is still the larger political and social structure of the society.

The radical attempts to shift the model so that the poor in fact become the clients. Poor people lack not only the financial resources of traditional middle-class clients, but they are also limited in their access to knowledge which might permit them to organize more effectively.[24] In this situation they are very vulnerable to cooptation. The only path of influence is often the one of protest and disruption which can be aided and abetted by their ability to mobilize themselves. While radicals agree that poor people should be represented on policy-making boards, they view such procedures as counterproductive if the representation is merely "window dressing" for the implementation of professional programs. They reject the liberal emphasis upon the value of poor people interpreting "poverty" to middle-class professional groups. For the poor to have a real program input, representatives must represent organized client groups. Ultimately, however, the poor and other minority groups must achieve not mere representation in, but control over those institutions that purport to

23. Jay W. Forrester, *Urban Dynamics* (Cambridge, Mass.: MIT Press, 1969), pp. 116 ff.
24. Harry Brill, *Why Organizers Fail* (Berkeley, Calif.: University of California Press, 1971).

provide for their needs, as well as equal access to society-wide decision-making processes.

In sum, then, sociology, we feel, presents a unique discipline for the study of social policy; it is less limited by traditional boundaries and permits its students to examine legal, historical, and economic perspectives as well. In addition, more than any other social science, sociology has focused most explicitly upon questions of values and their analysis. A clear understanding of the implementation of values in social programs is critical in order to make sense out of social policies.

In employing a sociological perspective, however, the student oriented toward radical social change must remain alert to its conservative tradition. In recent decades sociologists have often focused on problems of improving the functioning of the social order, maintaining traditional values, and achieving social stability. Sociology also provides support for the apparent intransigent nature of societies, while radical social change is always on the verge of utopianism. Nevertheless, students of radical social action must not let the evidence that societies, institutions, and individuals are difficult to change deter them from their search for processes and variables which are important in creating change. To paraphrase Frances Fox Piven: we may well be pessimistic about the likelihood of change, but that is no excuse for refraining from the attempt to change.

nineteen

THE CENTER FOR POLICY RESEARCH: ITS PROMISE AND PROBLEMS
Sarajane Heidt

Is it possible to begin from scratch in action sociology? Can one collaborate with other sociologists, and, with a clear conscience, find paying clients to work for with a fair hope of having a positive impact? These fundamental questions are not easily answered, but this account of a vital new enterprise in collaborative applied sociology is encouraging. To get started in action sociology, Heidt finds philosophic commitment, professional role clarity, protracted sacrifice and patience, and hardheaded realism all indispensable qualities. The experiences of the Center for Policy Research, as she explores them, provide a proven model that could be replicated anywhere.

As a graduate student in sociology at Columbia University during the 1960s, I became increasingly dismayed by the chasm between sociological research and societal reality, between sociologists' personal concerns and their professional interests. Other students shared my dismay, and the question of the proper political role of sociology and of its practitioners was much debated, in class and outside. Although this debate was never resolved and continues, the unappealing majority position can be summarized, fairly I think, as follows: As citizens, sociologists are free to take whatever political attitudes and actions their souls or self-interest dictate. Professionally, however, sociologists must be "objective." This view of sociologists, it can be argued, is essentially a dehumanizing one in that they, as well as their work, are considered tools which can be applied to any problem or project. Like a hammer, a sociological method or theory can help in the building of a pleasant park or an inhuman prison. Objectivity has come to mean such self-estrangement, a necessary lack of involvement, a view of oneself as object.

This, to me, was an eminently unsatisfactory position. Its implication that a professional concern with the state of the society is inherently biased seemed ill founded. None of us was arguing for a lowering of scientific criteria, a falsification of findings or a sloppiness of method, an adjustment of results to support a political value or voice. None of us, to use a phrase which was to have its heyday a few years later, had advocated "selling out."

Amitai Etzioni, one of the few faculty members who shared our perspective, began to meet informally with a few of us to formulate alternatives to the majority position summarized above. Hundreds of cups of coffee later, the Center for Policy Research was incorporated in August 1968. We deemed it essential that the kind of policy-relevant research we advocated take an organizational form primarily for two reasons. First, we wanted to increase our number, to draw like-minded social scientists into the group, and this is more easily accomplished if there is an organization in which to participate. Moreover, we wanted a milieu in which sustained interaction was encouraged; coffee klatsches are simply too irregular and informal. Second, an organizational context identified with out viewpoint was much more likely to become visible to policy makers and granting agencies, and the need for such visibility was inherent in our approach; it was a prerequisite for the influence we hoped to have.

We believed quite strongly that sociologists qua sociologists can work to effect social change without sacrificing the quality and rigor and intellectual interest of their research. In the choice of the issue to be studied, the data to be used, and level of analysis adopted, the statement and communication of findings—in all these facets of work, the sociologist can opt for the most policy-relevant approach.

Moreover, sociological training may result in more than the learning of specific theories and techniques, modes of analysis and methodologies. It can provide what C. Wright Mills called a sociological imagination, what I will call "a good eye" for uncovering the underlying dynamics and developments of seemingly disparate and varying social situations and structures. While no one would argue for anything even approaching a congruence of views among sociologists on most theoretical, methodological, or substantive issues, I think a case can be made that there is at least fairly wide agreement about where to look and what to attend to in particular situations. Thus, apart from specific studies, we felt that this sociological judgment could and should become available to the society.

Implicit in our orientation are, of course, notions of how social change can most effectively and easily be brought about. In this sense, it can be said that those of us who formed the nucleus of the Center in its earliest days share a theoretical stance toward society. That is, although our personal social and political views can and do differ on particular issues and problems, we generally agree about the location of the strategic sites for social action.

This stance was set forth by Etzioni[1] and has essentially the following features:

1. It *is* possible for societies to orient themselves toward fundamental but peaceful change in the direction of a greater realization of their own basic values. On this point, we are in fundamental disagreement with our more radical confreres. It almost goes without saying that we see basic changes in societal structure as absolutely necessary; that is, our disagreement with the conservative position is even deeper on this point. In other words, we maintain that the basic values of our society, e.g., equality, freedom of expression, have been nowhere near fully realized.

2. Politics is the major locus of such change. That is, while more "basic" economic and social processes and forces have major significance, the political system is the place where social change can be effected most consciously, quickly, and responsively. Unlike our colleagues who emphasize those attributes of the social structure which are very difficult to alter, for example, socialization patterns or individual sexual preferences, we concentrate on such *relatively* malleable political variables as level of mobilization and decision-making strategies. To say it more abstractly, we maintain that the political structure is at least partly independent of the society which it represents and to which, to varying degrees, it must respond. And it is here where leverage for change can most readily be applied.

3. At the same time, this control structure must take into account, and indeed have built-in mechanisms to this end, the needs, values, and interests of those affected by the decisions. Not only do we maintain that the political system *ought* to respond to the needs and values of those over whom it exercises authority, but that in the long run it *must* do so if it and the society of which it is a part are to survive. Thus, we do not hold simply another elitist political theory.

This theoretical stance, we suggest, is necessary to policy research in the Center's terms. And it impinges considerably upon the kind of work we do.

Policy research is concerned with mapping alternative approaches and with specifying potential differences in the intention, effect, and cost of various programs. It differs from applied research in much the same way that strategy differs from tactics; it is more encompassing, longer-run in its perspectives, and more concerned with the goals of the unit for which it is undertaken; that is, it is more critical.

Policy research differs from basic research as strategy differs from theory. It is much less abstract, much more closely tied to particular actions to be

1. Amitai Etzioni, *The Active Society* (New York: Free Press, 1968).

undertaken or avoided. While basic research aims chiefly to uncover truth, policy research seeks to aid in the solution of fundamental problems and in the advancement of major programs.[2]

Thus, what we mean by policy research can be seen to follow directly from the theoretical orientation so briefly sketched here.

While we are not arguing that policy-makers' decisions can and do bring about all the fundamental societal changes we and all but the most politically conservative of our social-science colleagues see as both morally and practically necessary, we do see these decisions as being able to account for a significant degree of such change. Moreover, we maintain that social change effected by alterations of public policy is more feasible and less financially and socially costly than either the more cataclysmic kind of social upheaval our more radical associates promulgate (indeed, the political lethargy everyone working on a college campus today notices among students attests to the "feasibility gap" of the revolutionary activities that were so customary only a few years earlier) or the dogged maintenance of the status quo. We therefore concentrate our research skills and sociological judgment on influencing public policy in a wide variety of areas.

This mission, as we shall see, is considerably less straightforward than it seems at first glance. Some of the problems we were to face became immediately visible during the Center's first year of life in Washington, D.C. From September 1968 through August 1969, Etzioni, Martin Wenglinsky, Murray Milner, Carolyn Atkinson, and I (with Paul Ritterband participating from New York) composed in toto the Center's staff. Since we were brand new and penniless, all of us were working at other jobs simultaneously. Etzioni paid personally for such necessities as a telephone and stationery, while my home address was also the Center's mailing location (once or twice, people who had heard about the Center for Policy Research dropped in unexpectedly and were surprised, to put it mildly, to find the Center's corporate secretary doing the laundry or cooking dinner). With little bookkeeping skill and even less training and inclination, I found myself learning to keep financial records, compute indirect cost rates and fringe benefits, and in general actively participate in a side of research I had taken for granted before. To say that our shop was running on a shoestring is gross understatement.

At the same time, all of us, and particularly Etzioni, were spending lunch hours, evenings, and weekends on three major activities.

2. Amitai Etzioni, "Policy Research," *American Sociologist* 6 (1971 Supplementary Issue): 8.

The first of these activities was writing proposals for policy-research studies. (I will say more about this task later, and about the constraints placed upon us by a research structure of funding specific proposals.) The kind of studies we hoped to do and the differences between the Center's work and that of most research organizations had to be carefully specified. We would do research with *direct* policy implications. For example, a study of black studies programs done by Etzioni and Atkinson for the Office of Education concentrated on comparing the advantages and disadvantages of actual programs rather than, say, the academic and personal characteristics of black as opposed to white students. While a study of the latter type is, of course, policy related (the designing of programs might well see a need to take academic and personality variables into account), it is at least two steps from the programs themselves.

The Center's study, on the other hand, does not depend on the taking of such steps. By specifying the features of actual programs, such policy decisions as the allocation of funds to one program rather than another are immediately relevant. Moreover, while the Center acknowledges that in some areas there are insufficient data on which to base competent policy decisions, in many areas these data have already been collected and need only to be processed and analyzed. We therefore specialize in *secondary analysis* and attempt to avoid major data-collection operations wherever possible.

We also thought it important that our early proposals clarify the difference between our approach and "applied" research more narrowly defined. Rather than merely evaluating a particular program to see if it "worked," we hoped to provide *alternative kinds of programs* to meet the same need. In this way, we go one step back from evaluation research. Thus, traditional proposal format, which tends to encourage either basic or applied research, had to be made sufficiently flexible to deal with the Center's particular focus of attention.

This need of maintaining our own identity within the proposal-writing and fund-allocating structure was especially crucial because of our youth. If we were to develop as an organization, we simply had to acquire funds. The major, if not the only way of amassing funds was through writing proposals, most of which had in the past been precisely of the type that had led us to form the Center—either basic- or applied-research designs. We were caught in a double bind. We could submit the kind of proposal that had been funded in the past and begin to collect research grants but become precisely the kind of research organization from which we were escaping. Or we could be so rigorous in choosing studies that fell within the Center's scope that no funds would be forthcoming and we would never get off the ground. We walked a very thin line, trying both to maintain our integrity and to achieve sufficient support to enable us to grow.

This dilemma seems to me central in policy research. On the one hand, it is easy to displace goals, to judge a Center's success by the number of grants received and the size of their budgets and to jump headlong into the proposal-writing business from the viewpoint of getting as many grants as possible. On the other hand, it is easy to dismiss many potential studies as outside the group's range of interest and to self-select work to the point of dying of attrition.

We at the Center have certainly not found the answer to this problem which confronts us anew each time a new study is planned or a new area of concentration suggested. The problem is hardly of our making; it is, rather, inherent in the granting structure itself. Nevertheless, one major activity in the Center's first year did provide a mechanism for dealing with this situation. We held fairly frequent meetings in which we highly self-consciously and carefully defined and redefined our purposes, interests, goals—what I have called our identity. New project possibilities were discussed not only in terms of their research feasibility but also as they related to our notion of who we were and what we wanted to do. Such meetings were, at the beginning, quite simple to schedule; there were few of us and we worked together anyway. In the larger organization the Center has become, scheduling such meetings is more difficult. But I would argue that a kind of collective superego, with regularized occasions for its expression, is just as necessary for us now as it was in the beginning.

The same can be said of recruiting participants in the Center. At first our absolute shortage of researchers meant that the staffing of particular projects was a major endeavor. In our search for social scientists, it was easy to forget that not only do we want people who are professionally able but also people who share both our theoretical orientation and our notion of policy research. The Center moved to New York in September 1969, and our proximity to many university communities has somewhat mitigated the problem of finding competent staff.

Yet, with over fifty social scientists, most of whom have professional commitments outside the Center as well, other personnel problems have arisen. In Washington, there were so few of us and we had known each other for so long and saw each other so frequently that the interaction among us was easily sustained. With a large number of people, many of whom come and go at odd hours, such interaction is less regularized, and some staff members express feelings of anomie. Attempts to formalize interaction, for example, weekly staff meetings, have had only short-term success; over the summer or during holidays such meetings tend to taper off. On the other hand, although each of us does not talk with every other staff member on any kind of regular basis, we meet quite often with three or four or five people to exchange ideas, read and comment on each other's papers, offer advice, and so on. Although not everyone at the Center would agree, I am not at all sure that it is either possible or desirable for us to become more of a *gemeinschaft* than this.

The fact that almost all the senior researchers at the Center have other, primarily university, affiliations has consequences far beyond limiting intra-Center interaction. On the positive side, it allows a very important freedom of action. To put it baldly, if a study's findings offend the policy agent for whom the study was undertaken, and he terminates the study, the researcher will not starve. While we want to satisfy the policy maker, what we mean by this is providing viable alternatives to a course of action he is contemplating or pursuing; we are certainly not in the business of telling him what he wants to hear. Our lack of total financial dependence upon his largess helps to insulate us from this temptation. Moreover, during the Center's first few years, with its future far from assured, we did not need the added pressure of taking full responsibility for people's livelihoods; too many research organizations have been compelled to take on studies with no scientific or political relevance simply to pay their staff, and we did not want to find ourselves in this position. Part-time people seemed most suitable to our needs.

Less advantageously, however, a social scientist with multiple affiliations may have difficulty finding enough time and energy for policy research. When he has papers to grade or courses to prepare, his Center work may be sloughed off. And policy research, as I have pointed out and will continue to argue, requires both considerable *and* continuous effort and commitment.

The roots of this situation are to be found not within the Center or in the personal work habits and inclinations of the researchers; rather, they lie deep within the structure of the social-science disciplines. Graduate students typically take as their reference group the academic community and plan careers that focus around the university both as a relatively secure living and as an important, if not essential, status attribute.

In the former case, that of the academic life providing a stable if not luxurious livelihood, it can be argued that the situation is changing. When the social sciences were coming into their own, it was a buyers' market insofar as teaching jobs were concerned. Even though the social sciences have not yet felt the pinch that the physical sciences and the humanities have experienced recently, academic positions, at least at major universities, are becoming much more scarce. The need for alternate job sequences is already apparent and is likely to become even more pressing.

The status question is as yet unresolved. The most prestigious and distinguished sociologists are academics, and nonacademic careers are considered of considerably less worth. This further pushes young social scientists in the direction of the ivied halls. We, therefore, did not have a sizable pool of *able* people available for full-time work at the Center; staff of the very high quality we require were able to devote only a part of their time to our work.

From the Center's viewpoint, full-time researchers are now to be encouraged. Not only can we support them in the short run, but our future, at least in terms of available resources, looks quite rosy. We need both more staff in general *and* full-time people who can on their own carry through major projects. Moreover, organizations such as the Center can provide alternate career sequences for social scientists at a time when such options are clearly necessary.

Yet the status structure of the various disciplines must change before many first-rate people will want to work at the Center or other similar organizations on a full-time basis. Research as a career in general, and politically relevant research in particular, must come to be considered equally as desirable as academic positions. Perhaps the structural changes that are narrowing the choice of academic options will help bring about this reevaluation. More likely, however, it must await further recognition of the value of organizations such as the Center.

One final point must be made. People are of course attracted to academic life for reasons other than those of security and status. Teaching and related activities have considerable meaning for many practitioners. Moreover, the relatively unhurried pace of university life is congenial to many people. The long vacations, the time for relaxed conversation and unhurried thought, the relative scarcity of deadlines—all these factors are present to a considerably smaller degree in organizations such as the Center. The pace here is simply faster and more continuous. It therefore should be emphasized that the Center is not the place for everyone. I am saying not that policy research as a career will and should interest all social scientists, but rather that many more of them will find it suitable to both their work interests and their work styles once the security and status constraints on such careers are eliminated. And it is this group—much smaller than the total collection of social scientists, certainly, but much larger than those now willing to make such a career commitment—to whom we appeal.

Thus far, I have discussed two of the Center's early activities—proposal writing and self-definition—which occur at least to some degree in all research organizations. The third major activity is far less common and serves to distinguish the Center from other research outfits most sharply. Since our commitment is to influence public policy, we must *communicate the findings* of our research to the makers of policy. Most research findings are presented in the form of written reports to the client(s) who funded the studies. The Center obviously prepares such reports, but particular care is taken that the language used is relatively jargon-free and familiar to the policy agent and that the study's policy implications are explicitly specified. We see written reports as of only limited usefulness, however. All too often, they are filed away or stacked in a desk drawer never to be referred to again. The Center, therefore, encourages the use of means of communication more suitable to the limited time and attention span of the policy maker. Among such means are articles in the mass media, television interviews, and the presentation of findings orally at conferences and meetings. Not only are such activities encouraged, but we see them as as much a part of a particular policy-research study as are the data collection and analysis or methodology.

The amount of time and effort involved in the communication of findings in the ways suggested here cannot be overemphasized. During the Center's year in Washington, for example, Etzioni spent a good fifteen hours a week on such activities. And this time has to be fit in around more usual research activities, since no research budgets explicitly allow for this aspect. Yet, we suggest, it is this dimension of policy research more than any other that determines its usefulness.

As well as communicating the findings of various studies in ways more suitable to the policy makers than the written report, policy research also involves a closer relationship with the client than other kinds of research. The policy researcher must have interacted with the policy agent enough to become aware of the political, technical, economic, and other constraints under which the decision maker must operate, for unless the research takes such constraints into account, it will have no value from the policy-maker's viewpoint. And this interaction also takes time and effort.

I am not saying that the policy researcher must assume all the policy maker's values and attitudes. Indeed, his lack of personal involvement in what he is studying is part of what allows him to see a situation freshly, to formulate alternatives for those who are so caught up that they cannot see the forest for the trees. Yet without an awareness of the relevant constraints, his research will simply be a utopian exercise in futility.

The Center has grown tremendously since the Washington days, a fact that to some extent vindicates our original assessment of the need for and interest in the kind of work we do both within the sociological community and among policy makers. Our staff now includes more than fifty researchers, including lawyers, engineers, psychologists, and economists as well as sociologists. As solutions to major social problems do not fall neatly within discipline boundaries, so research on such problems cannot be expected to fall within such boundaries, and the Center is organized to facilitate cross-disciplinary studies. Our budget, which in Washington scarcely covered legal incorporation fees, now is more than $500,000, with grants from practically all domestic agencies (the Center does no classified or overseas work), half a score of foundations, and donations.

Other than these quantitative measures of the Center's success, however, what have we done? Have we realized our goals? I will briefly describe two Center projects, which seem to typify how the Center works. The first ran from the Center's beginnings until about a year ago; the second is ongoing.

Etzioni and Atkinson conducted a study for the U.S. Office of Economic Opportunity which assessed various approaches to the problem of poverty. This study took as its starting point the fact that one of the constraints under which any antipoverty program must operate is the attitudes of the public-at-large toward such a program. Since a large outlay of public funds would be involved in any major program, it was hypothesized that congressional approval would be contingent to a considerable degree upon public tolerance, if not support, of the plan. Atkinson and Etzioni, therefore, analyzed public-opinion data on attitudes toward social problems in the United States over the last several decades to specify which features of an antipoverty program would be acceptable and which would not. Particular emphasis was placed on attitudes toward two recent antipoverty plans: negative income tax and family allowance. Contrary to the currently popular "silent majority" notion of a conservative monolith, a wide range of social programs had received broad public support. However, programs that are seen to benefit only or primarily the poor meet with more opposition than programs that have payoffs for the population as a whole. Thus, the policy implications of this study are *direct:* an antipoverty program with benefits for the nonpoor as well as for the poor is much more likely to gain congressional approval than one that limits its activities to those below the poverty line. The researchers did a *secondary analysis* of existing data rather than undertake major data collection responsibilities.

And, finally, they provided a *program alternative* to those which were being considered. This alternative, called antipoverty insurance, would guarantee a fixed income to a person whose income fell below the established poverty line. Two types of insurance policy would be available to everyone and not only to the poor: job insurance for those temporarily unemployed, and subsistence insurance for those unable to work. Since part of the cost would be defrayed by the premiums of those subscribers who could afford them, a lesser expenditure of public funds would be necessary than is the case with most antipoverty plans. With the insurance available to everyone, the stigma of "welfare" would be negated *and* there would be less opposition to the program.

In the course of doing this study, a problem arose that is endemic to policy research. Etzioni reanalyzed the figures on the numbers of poor people in the United States with the conclusion that the "war on poverty" had been less victorious than its generals maintained. Apart from the statistical technicalities of his and OEO's positions, the policy makers took the viewpoint (1) that we were doing things "on their time" which fell outside of the purview of the research they had commissioned, although Etzioni was not working full-time on the study and in no way either publicly or privately related this position to the research; and (2) that his actions were critical not only of the antipoverty program but of them personally—that is, he was being disloyal.

Policy makers have personal as well as ideological commitments to the programs they mount; in fact, their careers are often closely related to the particular actions they advocate. Structurally, they are far less able to be critical of their activities than is the policy researcher who may share their ideological involvement but does not operate under the same structural constraints. This is, of course, one virtue of "out of house" research organizations such as the Center, but there are potential perils. First, a policy maker may become so enraged that he negatively evaluates the policy research study he himself requested; while he may intellectually acknowledge the need for alternative approaches to the one his agency is following, the implied criticism of a mode of action in which he has invested a good deal is difficult to handle. The policy researcher's relationship with this agency is, of course, terminated as quickly as possible under these conditions. Another possible hazard is that the policy researcher, either as a result of overidentification with a sympathetic and attractive policy maker or because he wishes to avoid the above situation, refrains from any activity which can remotely be construed as critical of the agency. His research can assess programs that different policy makers advocated, earlier tries, etc., but stays away from the present client's turf. Such behavior may assure his continued relationship with the policy agency (at least under its present management) but will certainly limit the societal usefulness of the research.

These problems are inherent in the structural positions both of the policy maker and of the policy researcher. The policy maker may be well-meaning and sincere in his commitment to solve the social problem under consideration; the policy researcher may be dedicated and brilliant. Both may be completely unaware of these pressures. Yet a very careful course must be steered between the horns of this dilemma, and the policy researcher must constantly be attuned to the dangers of each side. He must protect both the critical function of his work and his relationship with the policy agent, because if either component is lacking the research will simply not be worth the paper it is reported on.

To get back to the study described above, considerable effort was expended in communicating the policy alternative developed. Etzioni testified about the plan before a congressional committee. The relevant publics were informed through articles in journals (e.g., the *New Leader,* 3 March 1969, and the *Public Administration Review,* November–December 1969) and newspapers throughout the country.

Simultaneously, further research was being conducted on the public acceptability of the insurance plan. Americans in a national sample were asked about their interest in subscribing to such a plan, and more than 50 percent of the respondents expressed positive interest. The *New York Times* (1 November 1970) carried the results of this study. Thus, ongoing research repeatedly feeds into the formulation of policy alternatives; the temporal sequence of research preceding and concluding with the statement of these alternatives is overly simplistic. Rather, the relationship between these two aspects of policy research is optimally continual.

The next question to be raised is, So what? After two years of work, the antipoverty insurance plan has not been adopted. Was all our work wasted? No; I will argue that the time was well spent. While our formulation has not become public policy, neither has any other antipoverty program including the guaranteed-annual-income notion President Nixon has proposed. Our original research in effect predicted this situation; since the Nixon program benefits only the poor, public opposition to its enactment is reflected in congressional reluctance to support it. That is, I am saying that we were "right."

Moreover, we did our part. The research, the insurance plan, and the communication of both to policy makers and the wider society were carried through by the Center. We cannot impose policy; we can only assess alternative courses of action and their consequences. In a society that at least purports to be democratic, we do not have the authority to do more than this, and indeed such authority ought not be ours. Unless we wish to become political actors and give up the advantages as well as the constraints of being primarily researchers, we have taken the antipoverty insurance plan as far as we rightfully can. We have added to the range of antipoverty alternatives a program our research suggested would have certain advantages, and this was our goal from the outset.

The second study I want to discuss is very actively engaging a major team at the Center at this time. Substantively, it hopes to develop viable ways in which modern means of communication—notably cable television (CATV)—can be used to increase citizen knowledge of and involvement with and participation in decisions about community problems. The general theoretical orientation of the study has been summarized as follows:

> The idea that technological developments might be used to reduce the costs and pains entailed in dealing with social problems is appealing. A broad

rationale for this approach is suggested by an analogy between the development of modern techniques of producing consumer goods and the search for new techniques of providing social services. Mass production and considerable reductions in cost per unit of consumer goods were achieved by an increased reliance on machines . . . and a decreased reliance on muscle and brainpower, on persons. However, up to now in social services, in which performance is frequently criticized for falling far below desirable levels, most work has been unmechanized. Since the need for services in these areas is great, available resources low, and trained manpower in short supply, it seems useful to consider replacing the "human touch," at least in part, by new technologies.[3]

To put it more tersely, one very major social problem—the lack of citizen participation in the decisions that affect their lives—might in part be ameliorated through the application of such modern technology as the CATV apparatus.

This study, funded by the National Science Foundation, differs from the OEO study in several important ways. First, there were relatively few directly relevant data; the Center, therefore, is collecting new data to a greater extent than was the case earlier. We are running a laboratory experiment involving eighty small groups of students to see whether or not decisions can be reached and dialogue carried on under conditions other than face-to-face interaction—conference calls on the telephone, in this case. What happens in these groups will be analyzed and compared to what we already know about small-group behavior in face-to-face situations, and differences that are negatively associated with group decision making will be assessed. Ways of improving the technology to take such difficulties into account will then be explored. At the same time, field experiments are being mounted. Communities will be given access to CATV facilities to help them solve similar problems, and various formats will be tried to determine which one(s) will be the most effective.

A second difference between the two studies is the extent to which they are policy relevant. While, as we pointed out, the antipoverty study had direct policy implications, the CATV effort goes one step further and solely considers the consequences of various policy alternatives. In part, the CATV study is able to do this because the area is relatively new. While antipoverty plans had been formulated in many quarters and for many years, the Center could more easily in the CATV instance become actively involved in the process of policy decision making.

And, finally, the Center has been involved in the decision making on the

---

3. Amitai Etzioni and Richard Remp, "Technological 'Shortcuts' to Social Change," *Science* 175 (7 January 1972): 31.

CATV issue at a very early stage of debate. Both Stephen Unger, the electronics engineer on the study, and Etzioni testified before the New York City Council and argued for reserving one third of the new air time for public use of the facilities, and the Center is actively involved in the ongoing discussion about the proper and appropriate allocation of the new resources. We are not entering the scene "after the fact."

One final issue about the Center must be raised here. The studies of public attitudes toward antipoverty programs and of CATV were conducted for government agencies, as indeed has been the case for most of our research efforts. In this sense, therefore, the charge that we are serving the Establishment has some literal truth. Anti-Establishment agencies—for example, welfare recipient organizations, student political movements, feminist groups—do not have the funds to seek our services and, even more important, usually do not find social sciences and their research an ideologically or stylistically suitable means of effecting the kind of social change they (and often we) see as necessary. For one thing, such groups tend to view research as opposed to the kind of "action" orientation to which they subscribe. Research is simply another excuse for inaction, a further "copout." Moreover, our theoretical stance toward using the existing political and decision making structure as the most feasible avenue of change is distasteful to them.

The Center recognizes this problem and would be eager to have clients from among these disaffected parts of the society. Yet it must be said that we do not agree that we have become Establishment tools. The studies we undertake express our commitment to basic societal transformation—for example, the elimination of poverty is a goal we and the anti-Establishment forces would certainly share, as is the greater participation of the citizenry in community decisions. We do not assess alternative weapons systems or preventive detention for alleged criminals. We rather maintain that our method of approaching social problems has a greater chance of righting the wrongs we all see as manifold.

What next? Why ask? Next will come a demand about which you already know all you need to know: that its sole measure is your own strength.

—Dag Hammarskjöld, *Markings*, p. 129.

part eight

SELF-KNOWLEDGE

Too seldom do we make an effort to slow down our efforts, and shift gears instead into a reflective and self-questioning mood. Especially as actionists, we run a dangerous risk of letting the dust we raise cloud our vision, causing us to mistake motion for progress, and movement for accomplishment.

In the 1960s we sought to inject life, motion, and movement into a slothful, sleep-walking sociology; we have a special obligation in the 1970s to reflect more often, more calmly, and more candidly than ever before on our action roles. How have we come to digress from the dominant, non-action pathway in our profession? How do we assess our own progress in our self-defined roles? And, how are we to avoid the error of professional estrangement that tempts us to dismiss our action-disdaining colleagues back on campus? What kind of rapprochement should we seek with those who otherwise relate little with our struggle and beliefs?

Three authors in this section confront these critical matters of self-knowledge. Jon Van Til ruminates in a candid autobiographical fashion on his personal journey into action sociology. Ellwyn Stoddard's typology of action types follows, and Frank J. McVeigh closes the section with some thoughtful reflections on the mediator role ("intellectual") necessary if applied and non-action sociologists are to gain from collaboration. Together the three contributors set us much to ponder, invite an earnest effort at reflection; and hold out promise of ever more clarity, conviction, and craft in our chosen effort.

twenty

ON BECOMING AN APPLIED SOCIOLOGIST: A PERSONAL VIEW
Jon Van Til

How much personal satisfaction can we reasonably expect from our applied sociological efforts? Is the time ripe for clear-cut victories and massive change? How are we to evaluate the seemingly small contributions of those in small niches? These and other equally provocative and fundamental matters are frankly and constructively addressed in this unusual retrospective essay. Especially valuable is the closing advice to those contemplating becoming applied sociologists, and the citation of the part that such a development can play in the securement of a "whole and satisfying life style."

In at least one way, becoming an applied sociologist is not unlike becoming a criminal, if Edward Banfield is to be believed: one requires both the predisposition and the opportunity to pursue the particular line of work.[1] In my own case, the legitimacy of action sociology was never in doubt. My essays for application to graduate school sketched out the four roles I saw myself simultaneously playing as a sociologist: teacher, scholar, writer for a broad audience, and activist seeking to apply sociological knowledge in ongoing social life. Colfax describes this role conception in his article in this volume: "one's research and writing is . . . an integral part of one's political and community activities."[2] None of my graduate school mentors ever sought to dissuade me about the legitimacy of my conception of the roles of the sociologist. I was admitted to graduate school, did reasonably well, and after an indecent interval received my degree. I did not then, and still do not, quarrel with Chairman Philip Selznick's comment to the entering graduate students at Berkeley: "Sociology is a house of many mansions." I do not insist that all sociologists

1. Banfield presents his theory of crime in his *The Unheavenly City* (Boston: Little, Brown, 1970), p. 159.
2. See J. David Colfax, "Sociology and the Politics of Poison," chap. 1 in this volume.

seek to apply what they have learned; my own professional satisfaction, however, would be far less were I discouraged by my college from my predilection toward applied sociology.

Beyond predilection lies opportunity, and the aspiring applied sociologist soon learns that his talents are not in universal and uncritical demand. My own participation in the social politics of welfare began with the invitation to speak before a group of agency professionals and political leaders in the nearby city of Chester in 1968. This presentation, a review of social-science conceptions of the urban crisis, led to the invitation from staffers of the local county Board of Assistance to join the newly formed Public Welfare Advisory Committee of Delaware County. Within a year I had been elected chairman of that group, and had also established close relations with several groups of welfare recipients whose leaders were represented in the advisory committee. Thus, since 1968 I have served as an occasional adviser to the local welfare rights organization and several other client organizations and have also broadened my involvement in the welfare scene to the metropolitan level. I was a founding sponsor of the People's Fund, a community-chest-type organization that seeks to raise money for radical and politically controversial groups typically overlooked by the United Fund; I serve on welfare committees of the Health and Welfare Council; and I was recently appointed to the welfare board of Delaware County, which group I presently serve as acting chairman.

Throughout the course of these involvements, both with governmental agencies and client organizations, I have sought to act both as citizen and sociologist. While serving as chairman of the Public Welfare Advisory Committee, for example, I conducted my dissertation research as a study of organizational problems of three newly forming groups of welfare recipients.[3] My own access to these groups had been provided by the good working relationship I had established with their leaders both as a co-worker for welfare reform and as an adviser to their emergent problems of organization. Throughout the research process, I sought ways to provide immediate feedback from my research to the groups.

Thus, in exploring with the leaders of the welfare organizations the utility they perceived from sociological analysis, the decision was agreed upon to conduct a survey of both members and salient nonmembers of the various groups. The survey was oriented toward discovering why people joined such groups and what kept more people from affiliating themselves. Results from this survey for two of the groups was fed back informally to the groups' leadership structure. The basic message from the survey study

3. The dissertation was titled "Becoming Participants: Dynamics of Access Among the Welfare Poor," and was accepted in 1970 by the University of California (Berkeley).

was "Don't worry about membership size." Most low-income people appear to be prevented from participation in community organizations such as those I studied by the press of time and energy. When an organization demonstrates that it has something to say, and is able visibly to pursue its ends, membership gains tend to accrue. The survey demonstrated that the groups were operating within the context of a basically approving subculture. The proper group response in such a context, it appeared to me, was one of intelligent action, and not the search for membership.

When I completed my research project, I presented as the last chapter of my dissertation a series of guidelines for community organizations who find themselves at the initial stage of group development. These guidelines were phrased in clear and direct language, and were duplicated for distribution under the title "How the Welfare Poor Can Overcome Barriers to Their Organization." This paper has been distributed to agency professionals, community organizers, and community organization members whenever it has seemed to me appropriate to do so. Thus, two years after the chapter of the welfare rights organization that I studied ceased to function as a viable group, a new group emerged assuming the mantle of the local WRO chapter. My paper was distributed to the organizers and leaders of that group. In addition I have tried to make myself available to discuss the substantive implications of my action research with those who have come after the three groups I studied.

Looking back on four years of my own involvement as an applied sociologist in the welfare politics of the Philadelphia metropolis, several aspects of the applied sociologist's role, and my own particular success and failure in playing it, have become rather clear to me, and may be useful to others who see themselves as applied sociologists. The tangible results of my own four-year involvement in welfare politics are small, but perhaps not infinitesimal. It was largely through my own initiative that the Welfare Advisory Committee nominated two welfare recipients for appointment to the county board, and followed this request insistently until Governor Raymond P. Shafer made the appointments, the first to any welfare board within the state. At several other points in the history of the welfare rights organization chapter and the two other client groups, I think I can also point to interventions of my own that contributed to the development of the groups. But these are hardly earth-shattering social changes in a time of social crisis. The welfare rolls in Delaware County have quadrupled over this four-year period; client organization is less evident now than it was four years ago; and the financial crunch has eaten bitterly into the real income of welfare recipients. In many respects, my own attempt to act as an applied sociologist in the welfare field may be seen to involve my own cooptation by "the welfare system."

Has it been worth it? Could I have taken my own commitment toward effecting income equalization and citizen participation in a democratic society on a different and more productive tack? Such questions must trouble all those who seek to smooth the path of social change in a society in crisis, and surely few can conclude that their own work has come to full fruition. For my own part, the frustration of my involvement in welfare politics has often been apparent, but I have seen little opportunity available to myself to work along more productive lines, and hence I have stuck to my initial involvement. The lot of the applied sociologist is not, if my case can be generalized, a happy one if clear-cut successes are demanded. The time is not ripe for clear-cut victories and massive change. In welfare, in particular, the "limits of social policy" often appear to have been reached, at least to the short-run perspective of the participant in welfare reform.[4]

Why then stay within the system, pushing for change by encouraging client militance and public concern? I explain my own continuing involvement in welfare politics on two grounds: first, I learn a great deal from it that is useful to my other sociological roles, particularly teaching; second, however limited the contributions I can make from my particular niche as action sociologist, they seem to be the most productive contribution to social change available to me at this particular point in time. They also serve, I guess I'm saying, who make small contributions to social change from small niches.[5]

I would like to suggest several generalizations from my own experience which other applied sociologists may find useful in reflecting on their own work, and which may be also of use to those who contemplate becoming applied sociologists. The first such generalization is that the sociologist qua sociologist must earn his own position regarding community actors and agencies. The role of "sociologist" itself contains limited legitimacy for one who seeks to participate in the process of social change. Certainly, activists and agency persons are interested to know that one is a college teacher and sociologist; however, it has been my experience that I have had to demonstrate by my own contributions and commitment that I was a person able to help. In other words, much of the applied sociologist's role is achieved within the milieu of social change and not ascribed by a granting of a Ph.D. or the holding of a faculty position. While, to a recently minted Ph.D. it may be distressing to learn that his degree is no automatic guarantor of influence, it has been altogether refreshing to me to learn that

4. The phrase is from Nathan Glazer, "The Limits of Social Policy," *Commentary* (September 1971): p. 51.
5. Reference is made to Robert L. Herrick's insightful article, "Digging Tunnels on the Plains," chap. 14 in this volume.

one must prove his own worth to qualify as a recognized change agent in contemporary social politics. It has been encouraging to learn that the welfare poor and agency professionals alike approach individuals on the basis of contribution, and not imputed authority.

My second generalization involves the nature of the academic sociologist's commitment to the process of social change: it is one that requires constant vigilance as to its integrity. The academic is always tempted to repair to the ivory tower when the going gets rough in the real world. The pressure to write and publish remains; lectures and class preparations are constantly available as an excuse not to go to one more meeting. This is of course the other side of the advantage of the academic's involvement that Colfax has noted. It is easy for the academic to get involved in community affairs; it is also easy for him to return to his campus, while the agency professional must maintain a 9:00-to-5:00 commitment and the welfare recipient a twenty-four-hour commitment to the institutional system in which they participate. The academic is necessarily one whose involvement in social change is partial; this does not mean that the academic must become a hit-and-run expert in social politics. The only way out of this dilemma is to be highly self-critical about the commitments one makes, and to stick with those commitments even when the going gets rough. The applied sociologist who finds the lure of the office too strong, and welches on too many commitments, will soon find himself unwanted by community actors. In the interim, however, he can do a great deal of harm to those with whom he works, for he will basically be assuming a manipulative and dishonest role. Insofar as the applied sociologist leads others on without fulfilling his responsibility, he detracts not only from his own personal integrity but also from the viability of the very role of applied sociologist.

The third generalization from my own work is that the great part of the applied sociologist's role consists of "consulting" and articulating likely consequences of proposed actions rather than directly applying his own research. No matter how directly one ties his research into his involvement as an applied sociologist, he is often called upon for judgments that involve factors beyond those dealt with in his own research. My own view of the role of the applied sociologist is that he should not flinch from such "consulting" but should make it clear that the judgments offered are tentative in whatever degree appropriate. Wherever possible, it seems desirable to seek to apply direct findings from one's own research, by feeding them back into the group process as expeditiously as possible. It is surely utopian, however, to believe that very much research done by action sociologists will have large and immediate payoffs to clients. As a goal, however, we can try to provide much more of this immediate feedback.

The desirability of immediate feedback from research to those upon whom research has been conducted approaches in my mind a responsibility of all sociologists, whether they view themselves as applied or theoretical. If one is studying the poor, for example, and hopes that his research will facilitate the development of a more humane social policy toward the poor, he has still exacted costs in time and energy from his own sample that may require an immediate subsidy. He can of course pay for his interviews, but an alternative strategy for the study of social change in society involves the quick feedback of research findings. Wherever this is feasible and possible, it seems to me a responsibility of all sociologists to seek to make this kind of information available to those whom they study.

Finally, for an academic sociologist, becoming an applied sociologist can form a large part of a whole and satisfying life style. Some years ago Maurice Stein noted that the community sociologist could "enjoy the multiple satisfactions of being an ethnographer, a problem-solver, a theorist, and a social philosopher while pursuing his craft." [6] The same satisfactions are available today to the applied sociologist. In an era in which man finds himself and his work increasingly isolated from each other, it is no minor attraction of a career that it provide the opportunity to see much of what one does, whether in the classroom or the study, on the picket line or in the board room, as part of a single life and a single profession. It is a role that can be played with a large number of scripts and with a great many individual variations. Its frustrations may be ample, but its satisfactions are substantial. The conception of applied sociology, for the academic sociologist, provides an option that may be of great use to his classroom presentation and may even improve some part of the world outside his campus. To me, it is a role worthy of much elaboration and development by those who assume it.

6. Maurice Stein, *The Eclipse of Community* (New York: Harper & Row, 1964), p. 337.

twenty-one

THE CONSULTANT SOCIOLOGIST IN ACTION PROGRAMS
Ellwyn R. Stoddard

Responsive and resilient, the nation's many action sociologists exhibit many different roles and motives. To help us order the diversity among action sociologists so that we may understand the meaningful differences among them, a realistic and productive typology can be employed. In this essay Stoddard is concerned especially with the ways in which the sociologist's self-definition and situational variables combine to organize his ten types into four supratypes of action sociologists. Strengthened by examples drawn from his personal field experience, Stoddard's typology gives a new pointedness to the basic question, Just what is an action sociologist?

A sociologist as a consultant could be an extremely knowledgable professional with a reservoir of sociological dictums. Or he might be a research scientist with considerable empirical-research experience. He could also be a person with personal or class biases who insists on the virtue of certain organizational goals, or he might be an expenditer who lays out alternatives of action with attached consequences of each for the final selection of his project director.[1] The term "consultant" is really a category—a label—encompassing many varied types of consultant-client relationships.

Consultant Types

For increased precision in discussing the functional roles played by

An original essay especially prepared for this volume based upon a paper given at the annual Rural Sociology Society meeting, Denver, 1971, entitled "The Functional Roles of Consultants and 'Con-Artists': Legitimation in Action Programs and Project Policies."
1. Michael Katz, "The unmasking of Dishonest Pretensions: Toward an Interpretation of the Role of Social Science in Constitutional Litigation," *American Sociologist* 6 (June 1971): 54–58.

various types of sociological consultants, I have developed a typology of ten consultant types (as indicated in table 1), six of which were briefly discussed by Sussman[2] and the remainder extracted from my personal field experience with project and consultant personnel. Discussion of each type includes the situational milieu in which the consultant works, his competency or legitimation function, the distinct consultant-client bond, and the basis for consultant fame and notoriety.

The ten functional types of consultants indicated in table 1 might be categorized initially into four major groupings, or supra types. The first includes the *merlin*, the *puppeteer*, and the *shotgun* consultant roles, and it reflects a maximum of professional freedom in which to apply their expertise. The second group, composed of the *self-generating* and the *back-patter* roles, employs human relations and personal acceptance skills in their consultant-client relationships to the exclusion of professional objectivity. The third group, including the *broker*, the *arbitrator*, and the *scapegoat* consultants, is governed largely by situational factors operating prior to the arrival of the consultant on the scene. And the fourth group contains two passive consultant roles, the *archivist* and the *accountant*, who are responsive to client requests only upon demand, and rarely anticipate administrative needs for information or needs for reducing the information gathered to manageable recommendations for administrative use.

These ten consultant types are discussed individually within the four groups outlined herein. Actual accounts of consultants in action programs and institutional reform are cited to further demonstrate their operation within varying structures and existing situations.

The Merlin Consultant. As the name implies (from the legendary sage of King Arthur's court) the merlin deals directly with the highest source of authority. Little effort is therefore needed or expended in gaining access to the high-level decision maker, usually a traumatic and exhaustive experience for other consultant types. For the professional sociologist anxious to make a significant contribution to the betterment of human society, this is the most enviable of all roles inasmuch as it represents a maximum of freedom to employ one's specialized skills without outside interference. Although the analysis and diagnosis of problems must necessarily be cast within the limits prescribed by the client's overall policies, there is little pressure for complete consensus between the merlin and his client. Indeed, there is a built-in requisite that the merlin be completely candid and free to challenge the expected results of proposed policy in order to

2. Marvin B. Sussman, "The Sociologist as a Tool of Social Action," in *Sociology in Action*, ed. Arthur B. Shostak (Homewood, Ill.: Dorsey Press, 1966), pp. 3–12.

TABLE 1

The Functional Basis for Professional-Client Consultant Relations Analyzed by Criteria of Visibility, Responsibility, and Autonomy

SOCIAL-SCIENTIST CONSULTANT TYPE	FUNCTIONAL BASIS FOR OPERATION	VISIBILITY AND PUBLIC EXPOSURE	RESPONSIBILITY TO CLIENT FOR RECOMMENDATIONS	AUTONOMY FROM CLIENT CONTROL
Merlin	intimate access to policy maker	minimum	minimum	maximum
Puppeteer	hidden policy administrator	minimum	minimum	maximum
Shotgun	temporary contact—"brainstormer"	maximum	minimum	maximum
Self-generating	personally dedicated—involved	maximum	medium	varied
Back-patter	"con man" expertise	maximum	med-minimum	minimum
Broker	trust—mediator for negotiations	maximum	medium	minimum
Arbitrator	diplomatic skills—persuasion	maximum	maximum	minimum
Scapegoat	blame absorption	maximum	maximum	minimum
Archivist	data reservoir	minimum	medium	minimum
Accountant	procedural detail	maximum	medium	maximum

enlighten his client as to the possible latent consequences of said policy.

On a national scale, merlins from law, industry, and politics have been commonly observed as presidential and legislative advisers. Sociologists have never achieved this prominence, with the single exception of Daniel Patrick Moynihan with domestic poverty programs during the Nixon administration. Sociologists have been far more numerous as merlins within administrative agencies such as HEW, HUD, and OEO or connected to state and local action programs.

When antisociologist merlins are operative in projects concerning mental health, alcoholism, delinquency, and educational reform, they effectively channel consultancies and program-design responsibilities to *their* colleagues in the legal profession or to academic colleagues in other disciplines. It is often professionally hazardous to operate at lower-action levels as a consultant within a project which has a nonsociologist merlin holding complete veto power over one's consultant duties or implementation of any recommended changes. The merlin has unlimited power for determining the focus, direction and pace of programs as long as his authority "patron," that is, the top administrator, is stabilized in his position.

The Puppeteer Consultant. The puppeteer role is usually developed from another consultant relationship. Once acquainted with a project, he becomes its administrator and decision maker. Soon the puppeteer separates himself from the visible project-administrator role by obtaining local people to assume the titled positions while retaining the power to manipulate policy and program indirectly from behind the scenes. As he determines and implements policy with complete authority, he loses the perspective of an objective external critic of that policy, and sometimes even retains another consultant for that purpose.

For the puppeteer to be successful he must remain anonymous, shun publicity, and deny his real power. He may use social skills, charm, and "con artist" procedures to facilitate the implementation of policy by his "puppets," but his power ultimately to determine project goals is absolute. He cannot legitimate his objectives by publicly revealing his true relationship to the project, and if this occurs his ability to dictate policy which others willingly carry out as if it were their own is drastically diminished.

Because of this requisite of secrecy, the literature is not well documented with successful projects of this type. Usually, the puppeteers who have "blown their cover" are the only ones which have existed as far as the general public is concerned. Such was the ill-fated *Operation Camelot*, a manipulative experiment in the processes of revolutionary reform movements.[3] The overexposure of that project (which was basic research rather than action-oriented according to its sponsors) brought it to an abrupt and unsuccessful end, with overtones of public suspicion of scientists generally being directed toward the entire international scientific community.

One experiment in research-and-development in Peru was a successful puppeteer enterprise.[4] The project goal of the consultants was to produce a greater degree of self-determination through local participation in the decision-making processes among the inhabitants of a public estate-community (*hacienda*). Had the *hacienda* residents been aware of these goals it might have cast a negative reflection upon their present subordinate status (inferring that they *were not* in control of their own destinies and that they *should* be). Thus, these project objectives were disguised under a viable economic façade—the production and economic aspects of the *hacienda* operation. Gradually the project directors faded into the background where, inconspicuously, they were able to deftly manipulate the crucial societal processes leading to the *hacienda*-community residents being capable of controlling a large portion of their own future without external administrative domination. The project was a successful puppeteer venture.

The Shotgun Consultant. This role is performed by "brainstorming" ideas with clients, usually a group of select policy makers, on a one-shot basis. Being an outsider he is impervious to restrictive pressures of local institutions and locally powerful individuals. Being a temporary visitor, the shotgun consultant has a maximum of freedom in making suggestions and recommendations that may be highly critical of existing policies with little fear of reprisal.

Generally he becomes informed of the unique local factors relating to the problem at hand upon his arrival and he applies the general principles of his training to them as they are encountered. Since he will not be present when these suggestions are translated into concrete social action he can safely exaggerate or overemphasize the seriousness of the current difficulties. He may serve as a catalytic agent in exposing vast differences in locally proposed solutions which previously had existed as a superficial coalition but with underlying polar viewpoints. Such an external input would shatter a frail integrative mechanism by forcing it to redefine its relationships in light of the actual problem and to seek realistic points for cooperative support.

The shotgun consultant may adopt an orientation of an objective

3. Irving Louis Horowitz, "The Life and Death of Project Camelot" *Trans-action* 3 (November/December 1965): 3–7, 44–47.

4. Allan R. Holmberg, "The Research-and-Development Approach to Change: Participation Intervention," in *Human Organization Research: Field Relations and Techniques*, ed. R. L. Adams and J. J. Preiss (Homewood, Ill.: Dorsey Press, 1960), pp. 76–89.

scientist or the extreme normative views of either the radical or the Establishment. In any case, when his views are visibly distinct from local norms, this generates varying degrees of hostility from his clients toward his ideas and recommendations. The compressed time of his brief encounter creates a greater reaction formation than occurs in a more permanent consultant arrangement. Oftimes the extent to which clients react with extreme hostility toward the shotgun consultant is used by him as an indicator of the "success" of his visit.

The greater the time lapse or the lower the sense of urgency on the part of a client to resolve his problem, the less impact on policy will result from the shotgun visit. Unless some mechanisms or local organization exists within the community or organization itself which is able to adopt and carry out the suggested program outlined by the shotgun consultant, these ideas deteriorate very rapidly and are again replaced with more traditional solutions sponsored by the representatives of local power interests.

On the other hand, shotgun consultants may be used by more permanent consultants to an action-based program-design project. A case is cited in which external shotgun consultants were called in as resource personnel for research retrieval probing by project consultants and clients as a prelude to immediate community-wide planning for social action by local leadership.[5] This was a successful transfer of shotgun contributions into realistic planning and implementation programs which would have been lost or diluted with the absence of the existing implementation structure.

As a shotgun consultant to Cultural Awareness Seminars being conducted throughout New Mexico, I was given the responsibility to outline for the participants the distinct processes through which scientific and normative evaluations were made. This was highly disconcerting to schoolteachers and administrators but with subsequent days of follow-up with concrete suggestions for implementation, the retention of a more scientific objectivity was possible even though it had been initially presented on a "hit-and-run" basis.

The Self-Generating Consultant. This role carries an emotional base as the motivation for involvement in social-change programs. Rather than remaining detached from the organizational goals of a project, the self-generating consultant becomes a promoter of the project and its policies—a spokesman who tries to change the beliefs of others through emotional pleas and charismatic dynamism. He need have no technical training in the movement which he espouses although he is more useful if

5. Ronald Lippitt, "The Process of Utilization of Social Research to Improve Social Practice," in Shostak, *Sociology in Action*, pp. 276–80.

he has acquired fame and notoriety in some endeavor even in an area unrelated to the present change program.

Self-generating consultants use the "soft sell" (compromise) or the "hard sell" (authoritarian) approaches to gain their objectives. Shostak reports a "soft-sell" situation in which he used his sociological expertise in locating points of sensitivity and irritation among participants in a poverty program in Pennsylvania. Moreover, he was able to offer consultant know-how in developing staff training, in construction of project-measuring instruments, and in minimizing institutional adjustments during abrupt reform periods; all this while alternately generating resource persons and support for the human resource project to which he was personally emotionally committed. His "soft-sell" action role was alternately applied with a highly trained scientific training of bureaucratic management processes. Thus, the self-generating emotional commitment was supplemented by backstage efforts at program evaluation from the perspective of the detached scientist.

An example of the "hard-sell" approach occurred in the Southwest when a sociologist consultant became the spokesman for Mexican-American organizations in that area. Challenging the entrenched power structure of local communities who disregarded the rights and welfare of this ethnic minority in their midst, he combined his professional training as sociologist with the self-generating normative role. As his personal convictions became stronger in defense of the disenfranchised minority, he used the prestige of his professional position to foment change for the benefit of Mexican-American clients. His presence at minority strategy sessions legitimized their goals and supported the militant tactics outlined by the leadership to be deployed. As his position became more and more controversial, the ridicule he received from prominent power figures in the larger society heaped fame upon him from the minority peoples. However, his activity in embracing the emotional goals of the minority peoples dulled his professional acumen. This resulted in short-run gains at the expense of long-term "backlash effects" which proved ultimately more disadvantageous to the minority ethnic population than their recently acquired objectives. The sociologist had achieved fame and notoriety as a self-generating "consultant" based upon his legitimation of the ethnic minority's claims rather than for the accuracy of his professional observations.

The Back-patter Consultant. This consultant is hired for only one purpose—to reinforce and support the present operation of a specific program. His presence *legitimizes* present administrative *practices* and further *legitimates* the *goals of the program* itself. Therefore, consultants whose views are known to support such a program or whose ethics are not so sensitive that they cannot be "bought" are the ones preferred by the program directorate. Some federal agencies have been known to send lists of "friendly" consultants to their action program directors to be retained as needed for legitimation purposes.

The back-patter requires the least amount of technical competency, is the least professional in his selection of clients, and is the most practiced in the friendly art of human relations of all the consultant types discussed here. His "con artist" abilities practiced in the past enables him to achieve instant rapport with directors, to ingratiate himself to project personnel, and to have a highly flattering and complementary attitude toward sponsor and administrative clients.

Not only does his presence produce an unprofessional image of sociologists but it thwarts competent professionals from having access to programs where their training could make a commendable contribution to social reform. Because of the functional service back-patters perform, they achieve even greater notoriety for incompetency and superficiality than do the more knowledgable professional sociologist consultants for their technical expertise.

An experimental juvenile delinquency program in a southwestern border city was having unique successes with one aspect of the program relating to adolescent drug addicts. Hoping to transfer some program funds from contacts with violent gang members to those involved with drug problems, local volunteer sociologist-consultants familiar with the ethnic and international implications of drug supply and addiction made some suggestions regarding future priorities of the project as related to past aspects of greatest success. The Washington officials of the sponsoring agency did not feel that "local consultants" would give them the leverage to justify modifications in the program so they sent a list of "approved consultants" to the project director who immediately engaged one of national reputation. Upon arrival at the border city he spent many hours talking small talk, making superficial inquiries into aspects of the program having nothing to do with the proposed changes, and shopping and entertaining himself across the international border. Following his report to Washington, a long-distance telephone call verified the acceptance of the locally proposed changes. Clearly, the technical expertise had been furnished by local sociologist consultants but the higher echelons of the agency felt the need for "consultant protection" and hired a friendly "name" consultant as a back-patter for a legitimation function.

Back-patters do not fear exposure inasmuch as they are sought out by program directors who want their support or recognize their incompetency and use it to advantage in concealing the inadequacies of a program. In either case the project would suffer if the back-patter were publicly exposed.

The roles of the broker, the arbitrator, and the scapegoat are largely determined by situational variables, although the scapegoat plays a much more passive role than the other two.

The Broker Consultant. This consultant actively seeks to resolve disagreement between two or more parties who would both profit by combining their goods and/or services than remaining aloof or separate from each other. If contact between them leads to unsatisfactory negotiations between the parties, a *broker* provides a face-saving mechanism for resolving their dispute as well as sometimes being privy to resources which would assist in resolving differences.

A school administration and their teaching staff in a small southwest Texas community were so hostile toward each other that no mechanisms for continuing negotiations of contract and grievances were available. Mistrust had eroded any professional liaison between the two groups. A broker consultant (from a respected university faculty nearby) produced the necessary element of trust to begin serious communications which contained favorable offers and counteroffers to accommodate the existing impasse. The consultant confided to me that the problem was resolved *with his presence* prior to his discovering the factors which had caused the bitterness and resentment. They "capitulated" to him, the external expert, without "losing face" to the other side.

A directed-change project in a large bureaucratic school system employed multiple consultant-directors who dealt strictly with separate levels of school operation.[6] One worked with teachers and the other with principals and the superintendent. This two-man team served the function of broker by providing a short-cut communication system for transmitting suggestions and information through the consultants directly rather than through the formal channels with the accompanying threats of reprisal and counter accusations.

Great notoriety accompanies the resolution of a conflict by a broker consultant although it is the presence of the broker, independent of his professional training and performance, which is the key to resolving the dispute.

The Arbitrator Consultant. Though superficially similar to the broker role, the arbitrator is the most demanding of all consultant roles for the combination of professional skills and personal diplomacy. The situation that requires an *arbitrator* presumes contending parties with unyielding polar positions on an issue refuse to compromise their demands. The consultant must hold them at bay while creating a new set of agreement points which he must then "sell" to the parties. His plan must be visibly

6. Mario D. Fantini and Gerald Weinstein, "Strategies for Initiating Educational Change in Large Bureaucratic School Systems," in Shostak, *Sociology in Action,* pp. 22–32.

different from those of each adversary so as not to be viewed as partial to one or the other party. He must make the solution appear that neither party has given in to the other while in reality causing each to relinquish a portion of their demands.

His formula for mediation is created as he proceeds and must adjust with situational factors which arise both internally and externally. Although he may emerge a hero, he might well be the object of ridicule from each opposing party if his compromise efforts fail and they use him as a scapegoat for the breakdown in bargaining.

A nonunion company engaged in producing and distributing tile and brick products was suffering a decline in production figures and an increasing amount of worker discontent. This erupted into an overt informal strike among the Mexican-American and commuting Mexican laborers who were demanding better working conditions, higher wages, and no makeup time for late arrival to work or prearranged absenteeism. Company owners demanded a given production quota be met before any thought of hour reductions or wage rate increases could be considered. An arbitrator consultant was called in to mediate the dispute and come up with a formula for increasing production *and* satisfying the workers. His solution consisted of transferring to another position an Anglo-American supervisor who was overtly hostile toward the Mexican-American workers, discontinuing the IBM punch-card system of arrival and leaving work with docked time reducing wages, and allowing workers time off for funerals and weddings of close relatives (time to be made up on successive days). Although management was reluctant to concede to this formula except on a one-month "trial" basis, the production jump during this month after the changes were made was so evident that it soon became permanent policy . For the rest of that year, production showed higher profits than at any time during the previous decade.

The Scapegoat Consultant. This consultant has the function of transferring any responsibility for failure from program administrators and sponsors to himself. As a professional, he is relatively insulated from legal sanctions for errors in judgment. Thus, the voluntary assumption of being the project scapegoat vicariously assumes the negative sanctions for the vulnerable project directors in return for which the consultant receives financial, political, or other consultation. Sometimes a consultant becomes an involuntary scapegoat when a questionable program looks for a "patsy" or "fall guy" and hires him for the eventual purpose of blaming him for the project's failures. In either case, when too many consultants from a single discipline—such as sociology—assume this negative role, inadvertently they cast their entire profession into the role of incompetents or charlatans.

As a novice college teacher and researcher at a high-status private university in the Midwest, I had agreed to assist a student committee in researching the problem of housing discrimination against black students. My final data showed discrimination both in "approved off-campus housing" and in "on-campus housing" (i.e., fraternities and sororities). The student committee chairman made my findings public before the administrative representatives of the committee had been able to "study" (lose) the report. The reactions were swift and thorough.

Irate fraternity alumni and local financial interests, currently supporting an immense endowment fund for the university, plainly indicated to the top administrators that they would withdraw their support for university funding unless "corrective action" were taken against the "smear on the good name of the university." The university administration reported that this had been a procedural "accident" by a new faculty member and corrective action would be taken to prevent recurrences of a similar action. No overt retaliation was taken against me although an absolute-minimum salary increase was my annual prize for two years following the incident. (University officials privately confided their gratitude for having made the report public, although external pressures made it impossible for them to publicly acknowledge this.) They had punished the wayward professor and had simultaneously brought into public view an increasingly sticky social problem which was resolved subsequently without further incident. Only the scapegoat suffered.

The last two consultant types to be considered are less directly involved with using technical skills to influence policy decisions than consultant types formerly discussed. The archivist and the accountant consultants are somewhat removed from active roles in the local action programs although they have an important potential for altering policy decisions.

The Archivist Consultant. The archivist is a passive consultant role, serving as a repository of data and resource materials available to program directors upon request. National projections of welfare needs, educational resources and usage, and various aspects of budgetary planning are made upon expert advice of archivist economists, engineers, sociologists and others. Sociologist consultants are hired by industry to research market receptivity for new products or attitudes toward those already on the market. In medical- and mental-health fields, sociologist consultants with cross-cultural training are critical in programs dealing with lower-class or minority-group values which differ from the middle-class institutions administering the services. Manpower utilization and occupational profiles for minority groups furnished by sociologist archivists are needed to provide a base study from which social action programs can make priority goals and launch change programs in occupational retraining and rehabilitation.

The *archivist* is one who *has* knowledge and the implementation or application of knowledge is not a major consideration for this consultant role. He is usually not visible to the general public and normally remains in the background except to the top action policy makers who rely on his current data for program updating.

A local school board debated as to whether to recommend additional school construction. They hired a local demographer from a nearby sociology department to present them with an estimated school population profile for the next decade. The results showed a temporary increase in grammar-school students (a student "population bulge") that would rise slowly up through high school, but following this would taper off to normal student enrollments. They voted to use temporary buildings and temporary bussing to less-crowded schools to handle the temporary student influx and did not build new schools for the three years of current expanded enrollment. The archivist (in this case, the demographer) furnished the basic information leading to an intelligent and money-saving decision.

It can readily be seen that an archivist is only effective when the ability of the client is developed to ask important questions toward which archivists can produce meaningful data. Their limitations are that this consultant type offers little or no assistance which is not specifically requested by project supervisors.

The Accountant Consultant. In a day of federally sponsored programs, this type of consultant attached to project upper echelons of centralized administration and financial accounting is one of the most prominent consultant types found in expanding social-action programs. Social and financial accounting of action programs is a crucial part of any effort toward directed change. It is the accountant consultant who descends to the grass-roots or client-contact level of the change program to investigate and to determine whether policy guidelines and procedures set by the original program designers are being properly instituted and followed.

An accountant consultant is usually less concerned with the actual operation of a program than in its bureaucratic paperwork. Vast amounts of time are spent going through forms and reports—"nit-picking" activities—which are assembled in vast pages of accumulated information, none of which is summarized, and less of which is ever referred to again or digested as usable recommendations for either higher-echelon administrators or local program directors.

A consultant hired by a national relief organization spent a few days at the disaster headquarters of an ongoing disaster operation. He surveyed the completed forms requesting emergency aid, the forms authorizing food and medical expenditures, the system of enumerating meals served, miles traveled, hours volunteered, building rental, purchase of supplies locally etc. and pronounced the operation one of the most efficient he had ever witnessed. Yet this high level of procedural dispatch had created an extremely negative reaction among the disaster victims.[7] The consultant had only incidentally visited the relief operation and had not conversed with the disaster victims and did not see the low volunteer morale which had been paid for by the priority given to correct procedural operation. This accountant had evaluated the efficiency of the paperwork operation and had avoided an assessment of the actual disaster relief operation in progress.

Summary

It has been demonstrated that the term sociologist consultant is nothing more than a loose category containing many varied types of consultant-client relationships based upon different functional goals and operating structures within which consultants are required to operate. Though these ten consultant types are not exhaustive of the functional relationships that exist between sponsors and consultants, consultants and clients, or between one consultant and another, they cover most of the existing roles assumed by professional sociologists in carrying out their professional contributions to ongoing action programs.

7. Ellwyn R. Stoddard, "Some Latent Consequences of Bureaucratic Efficiency in Disaster Relief," *Human Organization*, 28 (Fall 1969): 177–89.

twenty-two

CHANGING ROLE EXPECTATIONS IN THE SOCIOLOGY OF A MASS SOCIETY
Frank J. McVeigh

How can one be an action sociologist and a campus-based intellectual at the same time—and with equal success? The role strains are undeniably taxing. The two roles are vitally complementary; even so, members of both camps cannot resist the temptation to disdain haughtily the members of the other. This essay suggests that action sociologists may not use every available constructive lesson in the role model of the intellectual. It sets out several of these lessons to ensure that the intellectual legacy that joins activist with nonactivist in a common cause will not be overlooked.

With his characteristic incisiveness the late C. Wright Mills observed some years ago that "many people have some sociological knowledge and understanding of some aspects of social life but they lack the sociological imagination to see their own places in society." [1] I want to try with this paper to apply some imagination and analysis to help us in sociology to better see our own special place in our mass society, especially our place as campus-based intellectuals ("a group for whom the analysis of ideas in their own right [i.e., for no pragmatic end] is a central occupation" [2]). Essentially, then, I contend that the truly vital essence of the sociological role in modern times can be found in certain key features of the related role of the intellectual; these especially include disinterested intelligence, generalizing power, free speculation, fresh observation, creative novelty, and radical criticism. [3]

Paper presented at the Annual Meeting of the Pennsylvania Sociological Society, October 30, 1971.

1. C. Wright Mills, *The Sociological Imagination* (New York: Oxford University Press, 1959), p. 19.
2. Melvin Seeman, "The Intellectual and the Language of Minorities," *American Journal of Sociology* 65 (July 1958): 25–35.
3. Richard Hofstadter, *Anti-intellectualism in American Life* (New York: Alfred Knopf, 1963), p. 27.

How is this germane to the modern dilemmas of action sociology? An analogy of mine might help here: If the pure or theoretical role can be viewed as analogous to the superego of sociologists (calling for repressing and restraining one's actions), and if the applied or action role can be viewed as the id (calling for immediate satisfaction of impulses and desires), then the intellectual role of sociologists should progressively serve as our ego, or mediator. In the future of our profession that I want to help shape, our fundamental role as intellectuals should serve as a critical balancing wheel between the narrow armchair role possible as theorist or basic researcher, and the comparably unbalanced role available as a hot-shot action sociologist.[4]

Mass Society and the Role of the Intellectual

A question to begin with asks, How does our mass society affect the strategic balancing-wheel aspect of the intellectual role itself? Critical here are certain negative consequences of mass education and of specialization, the two most obvious social developments that have, and will, long affect the intellectual component of the role of all sociologists.

Mass education appears to have already tipped the balancing wheel unnaturally in favor of the applied-action possibilities in sociology. Some of this uneven development is traceable to the pronounced desire by various campus intellectuals to court, capture, or recapture a sense of primary relations with their large numbers of otherwise anonymous students. And, according to Kenniston, a large number of students desire and encourage just such "personalism."[5] In an intimately related way, many mass-educated students also seem to insist on a relevant, partisan kind of sociology rather than on the far more traditional brand of value-free and detached variety.

In this connection, Martin Trow has noted the difference between the "autonomous" and the "popular" functions American colleges and universities have pursued in the drive toward universal education in our mass society.[6] The autonomous functions the university defines for itself; and

4. There is a long sociological tradition in perceiving an intellectual as a social role starting with Florian Znaniecki's *The Social Role of the Man of Knowledge*. Two other notable works in this tradition were Robert Merton's "Role of the Intellectual in Public Bureaucracy" and Harold Wilensky's *Intellectuals in Labor Unions*. As far as definitions of an intellectual are concerned, there are about as many definitions of that term as there are articles or books on the subject.

5. Kenneth Kenniston, "Youth, Change and Violence," *American Scholar* 37 (Spring 1968): 227–45.

6. Martin Trow, "Reflections on the Transition from Mass to Universal Higher Education," 99 *Daedalus* (Winter 1970): 1–42.

they are intrinsic to itself. Conversely the "popular" functions are extrinsic commitments to provide useful knowledge and service to nearly every group and institution that wants it. As these demands for service are increasing all the time and will escalate in the future, the intellectual role of the sociologist may slowly but surely be converted to the applied-action-oriented role.

Perhaps the most far-reaching impact, however, of the mass society on the intellectual role has been its development toward greater specialization and functional differentiation. This insistence on functional differentiation may transform would-be intellectuals into bureaucratic technicians. In this way the future role of the professional sociologist might become far more technical or bureaucratic—that of a "sociocrat"—an old term attributed to Comte and Ward.[7] Should this role of "sociocrat" come to dominate the profession, the detached intellectual role could seriously recede in primacy, potency, and power. Only if the action sociologist keeps clearly in mind the interrelated nature of the social problems that preoccupy him will be able, in a world of increasing specialization, to stay in touch with his "higher" role obligations as an intellectual—and neutralize the blandishments of the alternative "lower" role of bureaucratic technician.

Changes in Traditional Role Expectations—Two Special Topics

In addition to, and in many ways because of, mass education and specialization, our mass society appears to be sharply changing the traditional role expectations of its intellectuals. More specifically, the old role expectation that one would be primarily theoretical is increasingly directed now toward the more practical aspects of things. From the old expectation of open-minded inclusion of all views we have gone over to expecting a commitment to one view or another from each other. From modification and improvement of ideas the stress has moved toward the selling and marketing of ideas. And, from a rational hearing from fellow intellectuals in one's profession the shift is now toward securing approval from the masses on the basis of often simplistic and frequently emotionally laden writing. To help make clear the serious and mixed implications of all this for action sociology I should like to briefly comment on the first two of these developments.

As our society has moved from an elite intellectual base to a more dramatic mass society, ideas had to be made to "pay off." It is now

7. Samuel Seiffer, "Sociology, Bureaucracy, and Training: The Rise of the Sociocrat" (Paper presented at the Annual Meeting of the Eastern Sociological Society, New York, April 1971), p. 1.

expected that they be immediate, relevant, practical, useful, and applied. For example, evaluating and judging the success or failure of a poverty program or a training class (or school class) on a "cost-benefit" approach is symptomatic of this "payoff" of ideas. But to imagine that people's lives can be changed to accommodate a fiscal year or budget period is to do violence to any really substantial understanding of man and environmental influences. A more rational and intellectual orientation would discern that the impact of a program on a person's behavior or attitudes may take years to evaluate properly. The traditional role expectation of being theoretical and abstract was based in the understanding that application of theories and ideas takes time—maybe years or centuries. Today our mass society (and its social institutions) insists that intellectuals perform in accordance with a breakneck rate of change, so evident in the technological realm, between an idea and its practical application.[8] This commonly leaves the intellectual grossly inadequate time to think in peace and quiet.[9]

The unqualified insistence by the mass society on the stark utility of ideas (which will become more insistent in the future) has driven many intellectuals into a dependent institutional role. Some have become incorporated or encapsulated into the organization's way of thinking, and as such no longer operate as independent or "unattached" intellectuals who perform the critical and evaluative function about the goals, values, and ends of society.[10] As for the sociologist of this stripe, he "has surrendered his autonomy, his freedom to act as an independent man of ideas." [11]

A second change in role expectations of intellectuals has been mounting pressure from society for them to make an ideological commitment. In spite of all the talk and writing about "the end of ideology" elements of mass society pressure intellectuals, and sociologists in particular, to make a commitment. Lipset's warning is still timely:

> The participation of intellectuals in politics even in a democratic society, even if it marks a victory—the acceptance of the contribution of the

8. Roger Christian, "Manufacturing Today: A Surge of Changes That Challenge You," *Factory* (June 1964): 25.

9. It is quite apparent how difficult our mass society has made it for anyone to contemplate, reflect, and think. One is constantly bombarded by noise pollution in our urban environment—from screaming jets to screeching brakes, from the ubiquitous motorcycle to the chorus of barking dogs in our neighborhoods. Even the traditional "sanctuary of silence," the library, has become a modern meeting hall for group projects, students, friends, and neighbors who engage in loud verbal interaction which at times borders on a class reunion. There is in our mass society a constant "conspiracy of chatter" against the contemplative, thinking man.

10. Edward Shils, "Intellectuals and the Powers," in *On Intellectuals*, ed. Philip Rieff (Garden City, N.Y.: Anchor Books, 1970), pp. 27–51.

11. Seiffer, "Sociology, Bureaucracy, and Training," p. 4.

intellectual as valuable, or the growing influence of certain groups of intellectuals and their ideas—also marks the increasing commitment of intellectuals to institutions of the status quo and their potential transformation into apologists.[12]

Similarly, within the profession of sociology this insistence on commitment has been institutionalized in the form of the Sociology Liberation Movement. If any sociologist read the handbills of that movement at recent conventions of the Eastern Sociological Society, he or she can understand just how persistent and insistent this demand is for the intellectual-sociologist to commit himself to a particular point of view. Even though I may personally agree with some views of the Sociology Liberation Movement, it is more important to defend and retain the intellectual freedom of our colleagues and profession than to insist that they must agree with us.

Pulling It All Together

What are some implications for the future of the sociology profession evident in the foregoing analysis?

First, it is vital that the profession soon become more cognizant of, and sensitive to, the social milieu and environment within which it operates. The profession in the future should come to appreciate the precarious and marginal position its intellectual role is in when it is operating in a mass society. More specifically, sociologists must redirect their efforts, in and out of the profession, to protect and preserve their intellectual role. Should they surrender it, they surrender also their credibility in society. And all that will be left will be to become just another bureaucratic technician or political activist.

Second, the profession must come to see that the polemic between the theoretical-empirical sociologist and the action-sociologist is misdirected. The future sociologist should better appreciate the distinctive functional role which each kind of sociologist performs in advancing the frontiers of knowledge. Instead of a sterile in-the-family conflict, the focus in the future should be on the intellectual role which both breeds of sociologist fundamentally hold in common, a common blood and bond.

Third, the profession must come to see that times change and if a profession is to remain viable and valuable to society (and itself), it must change. But in changing, the profession should not be so adaptive to

12. Seymour M. Lipset, *Political Man: The Social Bases of Politics* (New York: Anchor Books, 1960), p. 334.

outside forces and pressures as to throw out the intellectual baby with the archaic bath water. The profession in the future must recapture some of its already lost intellectual legacy. If it is to retain its truly professional character, it must recognize that unless it preserves its critical intellectual role it runs a critical risk of becoming a kept profession—either by the Establishment, or by incipient social movements in our mass society. As Howard Zinn has written:

> . . . it is the responsibility of intellectuals not only to tell the truth to questions asked of us, but to ask our own questions. In the early sixteenth century Machiavelli and More, in a long-range moral duel, laid out the alternatives for intellectuals of the whole modern era: to serve the Prince with unquestioning efficiency; or to ask Why and for what purpose, and who will live and who will die as a result of my efficiency.[13]

13. Howard Zinn, "The First Major Rebel," *American Report* 1 (2 July 1971): 1.

Action
Job Corps and
HeadStart
Coming Soon!
Register this
Wednesday
Thursday
From
3 p.m.
5 p.m.

We are what we pretend to be
so we must be careful about
what we pretend to be.

—Kurt Vonnegut, Jr.

part nine

SELF-
IMPROVEMENT

This concluding section focuses sharply on the action sociologist himself. Sometimes he is perplexed by the ethical issues that his field

work raises. The first essay in this section pinpoints a major locus of improvement for him in an exceedingly hazardous situation.

Sometimes the action sociologist is troubled by the seeming contradiction between the demands of action and the demands of intellectual deliberation. The second essay here addresses this issue and gives advice founded on the intellectual moorings of the profession itself.

Sometimes the action sociologist is not skeptical enough of his own motives, as the gratifications of the active role cloud his insight into his personal motives. The third essay here artfully explores this delicate issue and sensitively gives it back to each of us for solution. Plainly, action sociology in the 1970s requires that we see ourselves clearly if we are to succeed in helping others to help themselves.

twenty-three

THE CONSULTANT SOCIOLOGIST, CONSULTANT ABUSE, AND PROFESSIONALISM
Ellwyn R. Stoddard

The concept of accountability will strengthen applied sociology in the 1970s. Until recently we have not been accountable to anyone or anything in particular: clients were easily misled or even defamed, and there were no common standards of performance. Now the sociological sophistication of the public is growing, expectations are becoming more precise, and clients are evaluating program results more carefully. Action sociologists thus are becoming more accountable. This essay challenges the profession to set its house in order. It outlines a number of practical approaches to self-imposed ethical standards that seek to eliminate abuses in action sociology. How to accomplish throughout the profession the internalized code of ethics that it advocates remains an unanswered question.

Sociology has a rather short history of large-scale demand as consultants. Thus few ethical principles dealing with this activity have been advanced within the profession. I want to explore the significance of the fact that it has been left to the individual sociologist to determine his ethical limits on how his name, title, the discipline of sociology, and his final evaluation report will be utilized.

Sociologist Consultants: "Con Artist" or Technical Expert?

The function of a consultant is directly related to the organizational structure of the project or operation into which he is thrust. Modifying factors such as the latitude of power or restraints allowed, the specific or diffuse nature of his role within the project, as well as the program objectives and service nature of the program toward their clientele, will create very different situations within which the consultant must act out his role.[1]

---

1. William R. Rosengren, "Sociologists in Medicine: Contexts and Careers," in *The*

In a milieu of exploding social reform-programs, many of which reflect new and innovative techniques and strategies, few criteria are developed to indicate whether novel approaches to salient social-problem solutions are totally ineffective or just ineffective in the short run. Every social scientist knows that rigid beliefs regarding race, religion, ethnicity, criminality, and poverty that have been developed over many generations are not immediately assuaged in a matter of weeks by sincere pleas for tolerance and understanding. Thus, there is often a felt need to support an embryonic program of change whose program design would yield results over an extended period but which initially functions contrary to "common sense" practices extant in society.

This functional role of short-run *project legitimation* for both the totally inept action projects and the programs whose long-range successes are temporarily nondemonstrable might best be performed by a sociologist who is insensitive to professional and ethical restraints. In the absence of sociological competency he would be less sensitive and less critical of apparent deficiencies of its present operation.

For example, the explosive number of short-term experimental and innovative programs emerging during the 1960 era of unrest and protest created a functional need for back-patter consultants. These high-risk programs were often "trial balloons"—expendable when public sentiment against them appeared to be negative. They were funded initially for one or two years, and program personnel were offered no guarantee of occupational security nor opportunity for advancement after the project termination.

The most stable professional who was either currently committed to a tenured position or who possessed the potential for upward mobility upon demonstrating some personal competency was not recruited for these novel programs. Moreover, the experimental nature of many of these programs required that their directors and staff function in unconventional organizations using highly unusual procedures to gain unusual project objectives. This attracted both marginal-type individuals incapable of creating a favorable Establishment image and the perennially mobile person whose past performance did not warrant an offer of permanent employment elsewhere. Such factors did not lead to a high level of professionalism within the program operation nor in the recruitment of consultants to assist them.

In addition, a single year of program operation is often inadequate to show long-range effects of social-change schemas designed to change

Professional in the Organization, ed. Mark Abrahamson (New York: Rand McNally, 1967), pp. 143–55.

entrenched attitudes and traditional behavior patterns. The superficial attention paid by back-patter consultants to the project itself would not expose the program's weaknesses, but their "con artist" skills would counter growing negative opinions and legitimate the project. Clearly, they would be functionally of greater use to the project in the short run than a more competent and critical professional consultant. In time the lack of project efficiency and its unconventional orientation would eventually spell failure for such operations.[2] With public disclosure of the fiasco its stigma is cast on the back-patter sociologist *and his discipline* even though the reasons for project failure may have been partially a result of being evaluated by conventional standards of achievement as the sole criterion for measuring effectiveness.

This situation points up both the functional demand for back-patters and the public disenchantment with the sociology profession because of those prostituting their professional role for gain. The problem becomes one of what to do about it and how to proceed to prevent this from recurring. Theoretically, there could be a majority of present sociologist consultants who presently employ "con artist" skills rather than technical proficiency and whose standards of excellence would favor those with "con artist" abilities. Even if the profession could be assured that only the most highly professional sociologist were identifiable, and that they would accept the task to set standards for sociologist consultants, would this be so restrictive that consultants with novel or experimental insights would not be able to be effective? Which of the ten basic consultant types (See chap. twenty-one in this volume) are "legitimate" to the profession? Which of them should be allowed to be practiced when and if professional standards are set for consultant activities? It is a highly complex problem that rejects an oversimplified answer.

If sociology, as all other professions, declares itself beyond external public evaluation and criticism, it must come to grips with this problem of unprofessional conduct by itself.

Professionalism and the Curtailment of Consultant Abuse

For any analysis of consultant control it is necessary to know both what a profession is and those distinct operating mechanisms that distinguish it

---

2. In making this point it is recognized that excessive efficiency and overly bureaucratized procedures (normally associated with efficiency) might well produce the opposite reaction among the clients. To illustrate from a disaster relief operation, one relief organization which operated according to standardized procedures of efficiency was rated very low by the victims it aided. Another relief organization, whose procedures for food and service distribution was very inadequate, was rated high by the disaster victims because of the personalized and emotionally satisfying concern of their volunteers. See Ellwyn R. Stoddard, "Some Latent Consequences of Bureaucratic Efficiency in Disaster Relief," *Human Organization* 28 (Fall 1969): 177–89.

from other occupational categories. This will help determine what action can be taken, if any, to limit consultant charlatanism among sociologists.

Goode characterizes a profession as a community of colleagues who exist within another community, the larger society.[3] This professional community maintains a monopoly on recruitment and socialization of their future colleagues in order to perpetuate standards of knowledge competency and internal adherence to professional norms. Thus, a sociologist consultant must first be recognized as having been trained as a sociologist; as such he is now operational in the functional role of consultant—applying the training and expertise of his discipline.

Sociology prides itself on being a profession. To distinguish professionals from other occupational enterprises, the criteria of personal and professional autonomy are the most salient, though not the exclusive determinants of professionalism. Greenwood indicates five attributes which designates a profession from other work activity.[4] These include

—a systematic body of theory and extensive training program
—professional authority and monopoly of judgment
—the sanction of the larger community
—a regulative code of ethics
—a professional culture and lay stereotypes of the profession

These attributes, in turn, can be condensed into two major aspects: first, the professional content, knowledge, and process of professionalism associated with a subject area, as reflected in the first and last items above; second, the various types of freedom from restraints or the dimensions of autonomy enjoyed, as reflected in the three middle items.

Goode, in speaking of items basic to a professional relationship, emphasized the body of esoteric knowledge accumulated through a scientific ethic (as opposed to on-the-job technical skills) and the internalization of a service orientation toward clients.[5] Cheek substitutes the professional's duty of using his acquired knowledge to create a state of client well-being in place of the specifics indicated above.[6] Employing either description, our sociologist consultants could create a false euphoria

3. William J. Goode, "Community within a Community: The Professions" *American Sociological Review* 22 (April 1957): 194–200.
4. E. Greenwood, "Attributes of a Profession," in *Man, Work and Society: A Reader in the Sociology of Occupations*, ed. Sigmund Nosow and William H. Form (New York: Basic Books, 1962), pp. 207–18.
5. William J. Goode, "Encroachment, Charlatanism and the Emerging Profession: Psychology, Sociology and Medicine," *American Sociological Review* 25 (December 1960): 902–14.
6. Neil H. Cheek, Jr., "The Social Role of the Professional," in *The Professional in the Organization*, ed. Mark Abrahamson (New York: Rand McNally, 1967), pp. 9–16.

in a client arising from a temporary feeling of well-being, or become oversolicitous toward a client as a service to him. These could be achieved equally well as a "con artist" or as a technically competent professional. Thus, this aspect of professionalism—changing the degree of commitment to service for mankind or to specific clients—has little promise for containing consultant violations of professional ethics.

Traditionally professionals were recognized by their high degree of technical skill, unmatched by other occupations. Today, in our complex industrial society an extremely sophisticated technology has produced technicians with training and performance skills equally the level of most professionals.[7] Accordingly, the manifestation of technical skills is no longer a meaningful distinguishing characteristic of a professional as compared to nonprofessional workers.

Ultimately, then, the internalization of professional standards as a code of ethics during the professionalization process becomes critical: it is the only point at which curtailment of consultant abuses can be instituted without destroying the degree of autonomy which enables the profession to expand its knowledge and, through experimentation, to discover new and better means of solving social problems. Since the term "autonomy" encompasses various dimensions, the ensuing discussion deals separately with autonomy from the larger community, autonomy from one's professional organizations and colleagues, and autonomy from one's clients as distinct phenomena (although in reality they are inseparably interconnected.)

The larger society has clearly relinquished some control over sociology. As a profession it accepts a mandate from governmental officials to establish programs leading to formal university degrees. Sociologists are allowed to recommend core curricula, screen applicants for advanced degrees, and make final recommendations regarding the conferring of degrees to successful candidates. To this degree sociology is not restrained by the larger society nor are those sociologists who have become consultant practitioners restrained in accepting consultancies. However, the consultant role (outside the teaching field) is the most prominent public-display case for the sociology profession. Images that emerge from current efforts at applied sociology will undoubtedly be critical among those which will affect the degree of autonomy granted by the larger community.

Personal autonomy from professional organizations or from other professionals is a very delicate matter. Too-extensive regulation of

7. Ronald M. Pavolko, *Sociology of Occupations and Professions* (Itasca: F. E. Peacock, 1971), p. 29.

professional behavior by associations or colleagues destroys the very freedom that underlies scientific inquiry and the unrestrained pursuit of truth for truth's sake. Yet minimum standards of professional conduct must be maintained for the profession to survive. Too loose a coordination of professional norms among sociologists (and therefore sociologist consultants) allows such wide diversity in ethical standards as to undermine the public trust in the profession itself. This may lead to external regulation for those who refuse to maintain internal controls through their professional associations. However, the power of censure is jealously guarded by all professionals, and the act of criticizing a fellow professional for behavior other than most henious and disgusting acts is a step toward having others of his peers sit in judgment *on him*. It is a process that no one individual wishes to initiate and thus it becomes delegated to the amorphous "professional association" to initiate when deemed necessary for the good of the profession as a whole.

Once a professional has completed the formal procedures for the "union card" and been accepted as a fellow sociologist by his peers, there is little direct control which can be applied over him other than the common ground rules incorporated in the code of ethics pertaining to his profession. When a sociologist deviates too far from these public declarations of ethical behavior, he relinquishes the respect and support supplied by his professional colleagues.

If sociology is considered a *learned society of scientists* its overall code of ethics is determined by the entire scientific community. As a more specific guideline, the American Sociological Association recently implemented a code of ethics primarily directed toward the field research activities of its membership which became effective in September 1971.[8] However, code phrases such as "suppressing information" or the "misuse of knowledge" are so vague as to require some test cases and actual interpretations through adjudication to be more than mere verbal guidelines. Thus, it appears that in our own sociology profession, as in older behavioral science associations such as the French Psychological Society, our codes might be more accurately described as ultimate ideals rather than as realistic guides to current professional behavior.[9]

An alternative to the code of ethics approach characteristic of a *learned society* is the *guild-related* licensure and certification system for subspecialties within a professional community. This has been discussed as a

8. American Sociological Association, *Code of Ethics* (Washington, D.C.: American Sociological Association, Standing Committee on Professional Ethics, 1971).

9. Bernard L. Bloom, "The Code of Ethics of the French Psychological Society," *American Psychologist* 19 (March 1964): 183–85.

viable plan for sociology,[10] but as Goode declares, if sociologists are scientists, their professional associations

> are not guilds, imposing rigid controls over members in their client-professional relations, or protecting the guild member against lay evaluations. Rather, these associations are learned societies. The allegiance of the members is primarily to the substantive field, not to the guild. Their professional behavior is guided far more by the ethic of science than by an ethic of the client-professional relationship.[11]

Goode cites the illustration of the clinical psychologists who have established their own certification program: This select group "uses" the parent American Psychological Association as an overall umbrella to shield their public operations from lay criticism while simultaneously directing all of their own resources and efforts to advance the cause of only their small specialty subgroup. Such a licensure or certification approach would destroy the strength of sociology as a learned society of scholars. It would create a cluster of vocational specialties directed toward various fields of applied practice, as in the medical profession. It appears in short, that most of the gains presently enjoyed by the sociology profession would be diminished through an extensive adaptation to *guildlike* licensing procedures.

Historically, "free professionals" were not only free from the organizational restraints of their colleagues but were free also from client-control through adopting special types of occupational norms developed among themselves.[12] Professional authority reflecting autonomy from client-control is maintained only after the entire profession's autonomy from external constraints of the society at large has been achieved. While academic sociology has maintained a great deal of freedom from client (student or administration) control, most of the consultant roles previously discussed in my earlier essay (with the exception of the back-patter or scapegoat consultant types) are almost completely free from client manipulation. The personal ethics of the individual consultant, not the client, dictates whether his consultant obligations are an ethical violation or not. So even though functional situations arise demanding a client-dominated consultant, such as a back-patter, the individual sociologist consultant is ultimately the one who decides whether to play the role or refuse the appointment.

10. Anonymous, "Toward a Code of Ethics for Sociologists" *American Sociologist* 3 (November 1968): 316–18; Edgar A. Schuler, "Toward a Code of Professional Ethics for Sociologists: A Historical Note, *American Sociologist* 4 (May 1969): 144–46.

11. Goode, "Encroachment, Charlatanism," p. 6.

12. Mark Abrahamson, ed., *The Professional in the Organization* (New York: Rand McNally, 1967), p. 7.

It becomes clear that to preserve the various dimensions of professional autonomy and to curtail consultant abuse of professional standards, the point at which this can most effectively be pursued is during the professionalization process itself. Professionalism must be considered as a continuing process[13] rather than a point at which a formal degree entitles the bearer to indiscriminate behavior without any restraints whatsoever. This process must cause a person to shift his orientation from a "common sense" approach to a more objective and professional viewpoint.[14] There is a great deal of evidence that this process of internalizing the scientific ethic as an occupational guideline is not being practiced even in beginning sociology courses. It is verbally espoused by many teachers who, while training future sociologists themselves, could not qualify as professionals.[15] Moreover, the recent movement to make sociology more sensitive to societal problems through a more humanistic approach has created a dimension of added complexity; sociology now struggles to agree upon its very goals and the basic means by which these should be achieved.[16]

Various factions within the discipline of sociology are always in turmoil as to what a sociologist *is*, and what one "should" be doing *to, with*, or *for society*. Since sociologist consultants are merely professional sociologists in applied roles, this lack of consensus within the entire parent profession directly affects those few who chose to fill various consultant roles. Therefore, it is evident that no greater ethical perfection can be expected in applied sociology than in other professional roles operating within the sociology discipline itself.

In summary, then, sociologist consultants, like professionals in law enforcement, medicine, the legal professional and others, suffer from a common malady: they are required to adhere to an ethical code verbally extolled by the profession at the same time that fame and monetary rewards are being dispensed to colleagues who openly violate ethical practices with the implied sanction of the profession itself.[17]

13. Rue Bucher and Joan Stelling, "Characteristics of Professional Organizations," *Journal of Health and Social Behavior* 10 (March 1969): 3–15.
14. Alan F. Blum and Larry Rosenberg, "Some Problems Involved in Professionalizing Social Interaction: The Case of Psychotherapeutic Training," *Journal of Health and Social Behavior* 9 (March 1968): 72–85.
15. Ellwyn R. Stoddard, "A 'Loophole' in the Sociologist's Claim to Professionalism: The Junior College Sociology Instructor," *American Sociologist* 3 (May 1968): 132–35; idem, "The Normative Presentation of Scientific Sociology: A Professional Anathema," *Summation* 3 (August 1971): 1–16.
16. This is reflected in the thrust of the "new sociology" movements, the various ethnic and female caucuses, and ASA reform committees. Not only has the direct effects of this "involvement" orientation been visible in specific sociologists but the themes of the various national professional meetings increasingly deal with the role of sociology in public development and social-action programs.
17. Abraham S. Blumberg, "The Practice of Law as Confidence Game: Organizational Cooptation of a Profession," *Law and Society Review* 1 (June 1967): 15–39; Julian B.

Only a strong internalized code of ethics trained into each sociologist during his professionalization period will curtail ethical abuse among consultants or any other occupational position in sociology. Until this is done, sociologist consultants will continue to respond both to "con artist" *legitimation* functions as well as to the legitimate *technical expert* role according to their professional abilities, their accessibility, and the current market demand for these services.

Roebuck and R. Bruce Hunter, "Medical Quackery as Deviant Behavior," *Criminalogia* 8 (January 1970): 46–62; Ellwyn R. Stoddard, "The Informal 'Code' of Police Deviancy: A Group Approach to 'Blue-Coat Crime,' " *Journal of Criminal Law, Criminology and Policy Science* 59 (June 1968): 201–13; James Leo Walsh and Ray H. Ellin, "Professionalism and the Poor—Structural Effects and Professional Behavior," *Journal of Health and Social Behavior* 9 (March 1968): 16–18.

twenty-four

THE FLAWED CONSULTANT—A FANTASY
Meyer M. Cahn

Offering the poor choice of wiser-than-thou consultation to clients, rather than collaboration with them, we are confronted thereby with various temptations and pitfalls which we sometimes only barely perceive. This essay exposes the intimate psychological risks we incur when we attempt to apply social-science skills and perspectives to real-world problems. It explores how our own consultative role can tempt us into exaggerated feelings of personal power and self-importance. It also explains how our role threatens to separate us from other men and lure us into foibles we can share with our ill-served clients. As we prepare, then, for tours of duty as action sociologists, we are obliged earnestly to search our souls to know our private dreams and goals.

> Excerpt from: American Assembly of Applied Behavioral Science (AAABS)
> Articles of Organization
> Section 3: The Triannual Review
>
> Members of AAABS will appear before a board of their peers every three years in order to prove qualification. Such proof will consist of their ability to disclose the overwhelming nature of their own personal deficiencies and professional inadequacies. Qualification will be determined by the examined members themselves with the help of their examiners.

In a moment it would begin. Edding sauntered to a heavily-cushioned seat in the hotel room. The other three were about to seat themselves, too. It was going to be friendly; no doctor's oral or any of that sort of thing. These triannual reviews were decent little gatherings of colleagues who simply wanted to help their fellow consultants hold onto their perspectives. On another day Edding would be a board member himself, with one of these same fellows appearing before him. Nevertheless, he wiped the moisture from his forehead and tried to settle back comfortably. The chair was not comfortable. The hotel room was still warm from the sunny afternoon. The others were seated now, each of them smiling in some protective way. Now they would begin.

If he could forget what was at stake, the whole thing might be like a game. But acceptance as a journeyman practitioner in the applied behavioral sciences was central to Edding and to his examiners. Most of their living was made in the executive suites of large organizations, in corporations, and out in the community. Edding's work was heavy in community organizations. So viewing this experience as a mere game was not really possible for him. Still, Edding tried to ease up on himself.

As a candidate for renewal, he would be obliged to state his *lack* of qualifications to continue pursuit of his profession, to show that he really understood how deeply unqualified he was to work in the solution of people's problems. He must not fake this disclosure of incompetence; it had to be for real.

Edding started by recalling his almost pathological history of sibling rivalry, and the many ramifications in his subsequent relationships. Then came his childhood nightmares, a particular prevailing dream, and his nearly dropping out of high school. One of the examiners, lifting a sheet before him, interrupted. "I think we went over this material last time." He added, reading from the list, "Was called crybaby as a preadolescent, sore loser at athletic events, sensitive to losing some of his hair at age sixteen, somewhat afraid of girls until twenty-one."

Edding took it up from there. He had been thinking lately, he said, that aside from these historical matters, there were new things cropping up to make him doubt his consultant qualifications. He was wondering, now, about *power*. "I never had much power as a kid, or even later. But now, in working with groups and organizations, I get lots of it."

The examiners were comfortable with his silence. It was one of their trade tools. But then one of them said slowly, "Yes?"

"I'm beginning to like it," Edding said. "I even think I'm beginning to need it." He explained that his current sense of self-worth required frequent reinforcements of power experiences. "If not, I sometimes get petulant."

"That's a good one," said the youngest examiner, also slightly balding, but with a small goatee. "I like that."

Encouraged, Edding went on. "It's not all clear to me. But if I'm not in one of my consulting group activities or setting things straight somewhere, I get to wondering, sometimes, who I am. Then I find myself washing dishes, vacuuming, running errands for my kids and . . ." An embarrassed smile crossed his lips as he thought of a recent setback at the hands of his bossy teen-agers. Then his mind jumped to a picture of himself confidently facing tough executives in the midst of a theory session at his command. He held onto this scene doggedly.

Edding had been a committed human-factors consultant ever since that whirlwind fortnight seven years ago, when he saw executives change in front of his own eyes, change from being stiff, sharp, efficient, ramrod straight, almost robotlike, to just plain human beings. It was a big decision, Edding knew, to leave the university, but the social turmoil on the outside, and his newly emerging skills offered more for his idealism than teaching graduate students in social psychology. But often, during those seven years, the decision came up for reconsideration. On many occasions, particularly when programs were stifled from men above with the power, or when he got to thinking about the exceedingly complex realities of behavior, he would wonder if he hadn't forced open a can of worms that was just too wriggly. He was beginning to feel this way again right now.

The head of the examining committee leaned forward toward Edding. "Well, besides this power thing, what have we got?"

Edding inhaled thoughtfully. At one time he had thought of a speech he might give the examiners to get something off his chest. Perhaps this was the time. But now, with these people who place high credence on impulsivity (and low on planned statements), the idea of a speech seemed ridiculous. So he did the impulsive thing. He talked about speeches. "I like to make speeches to the world," he said. "I do this in the morning, in the shower. Sometimes to the whole world—to everyone in it, especially to world leaders."

The youngest of the examiners seemed to enjoy this. He nodded with amusement. The other two had more inquiring looks.

"Morning world feedback, I call it. I let off steam that way. The things I can't do anything about anyway. You know, the world situation, and all that."

He paused, tilted his head, and thought of what he was saying. "Is that crazy?" he asked.

The examiners weren't sure whether Edding wanted the question answered or not.

"Is it?" Edding repeated.

"Why . . . no," one examiner came in. "Not at all."

"You don't sound convincing," said Edding. "Maybe you do think it's crazy. Do you?"

The examiner wasn't prepared for this confrontation. He straightened up. "No, as I think of it, there are some matters you can't do a damned thing about, anyway . . . so you may as well."

"Well, I think it's crazy," said Edding. "In fact, sometimes I think I'm crazy. Yes. I have serious doubts about my sanity."

It seemed to the examiners that Edding was about to make some kind of dramatic admission. They leaned forward. But Edding was not too anxious to talk now. He seemed more involved in his own thoughts.

As Edding debated to himself the pros and cons of whether he was crazy or not, he knew that the thought had occurred to him at other times, particularly when he was in serious disagreement with his colleagues about something he considered central to people's behavior. Or when sudden and deep differences came up between himself and his wife. On a few dire occasions he had even thought of doing away with himself. There, that would do it swiftly, and he wouldn't have to decide whether he was insane or not.

He told all this to the examiners—but it did not stir them. Edding questioned this, too. Isn't this whole procedure here a symptom of our mutual craziness? Look how understanding they are about everything, about my quirks, or my thoughts of doing away with myself. *They understand!*

He decided to be more mundane. "Oh, there are other things," he said. "I like to have my own way, but I like to make it seem that the other people, the clients, are making their own choice. You know?"

The examiners' heads nodded with knowing looks. This seemed like more comfortable material for them to deal with. "In our business, who doesn't?" said the younger one, who was now amused with his own agreement with Edding.

There was a fairly long pause at this point and Edding realized that he would have to dig deeper, seek fresher evidence of his flaws. Then he thought of something, and he started to grin to himself.

"How's this?" he said. "I get very easily distracted by attractive women in my groups."

The examiners laughed heartily. It helped clear the distance between them. One of them laughed especially long at this slight reference to the erotic element of group life which so seldom gets talked about.

Edding found himself feeling oppositional toward the examiners, so that when they now laughed, he felt anger rising within him. He remembered his own lifelong difficulty in verbalizing anger, in confronting others with his hostile feelings.

"There's less conflict in my groups, compared to others. Maybe I'm responsible for that, stifling it, maybe." As he said this, he could think of three or four consultants who seemed to have a compulsive need to start fights in the immediate world around them, including their groups. They made a big virtue of "dealing with aggression," "bringing hostile feelings out into the open," "letting it all hang out." Edding believed in these things, too. There just weren't as many fights in his groups.

The chairman made a note on his paper while Edding continued. "I tell myself that I'm in a quest for creative experience. I say to my groups, 'Can't we minimize the ugly side of life?' Let me tell you about one day at Carmel: Some of the group were sitting on the white sand; others were watching the otters at play in the ocean. I was feeling especially exuberant that day. I told the group, 'Who needs the ugly side of life? If we can push it aside, we can fly to the moon on our joy. We can dream. We can make a new world that nobody is bothering to make.' "

One of the examiners cut in, "Aren't you getting a little too preachy?"

"Yes, that's certainly a shortcoming of mine," Edding admitted, cravenly shifting to his glib professional humility. "My preachiness—sometimes I hide it. But if you look closely it's there. I keep thinking I can save this world. That I'm going to save it. Or that I *am* saving it."

The young goateed examiner reminded Edding that the world was in one hell of a mess. Edding agreed vigorously.

"Add that to your list," said the young examiner to the other two.

"What?"

"Thinks the world is his to save. Or something like that."

Edding laughed. "I hadn't thought about that," he said. As he did think about it, he knew that he was sometimes confused about this—how much to try, how much to take responsibility for. How perfect a world does a guy leave behind him anyhow? Before he could speak of this, the chairman interrupted. He reminded Edding that he had the impression that Edding was getting onto "tangential issues" and that much of the data presented thus far was quite confused.

Edding felt a new streak of anger. How professorial did that examiner mean to be? How distant? His voice was impatient, his manner hardly bearable. Edding wondered now how much more he wanted to say to the examining group. He just sat still for awhile, his motionless eyes in thought.

"I'm sorry," said the chairman in a voice now penitent. "We're here to listen, aren't we?" He turned to his colleagues on this.

Edding sat quiet, conscious of his choices. He could pout, he could act like a martyr, he could methodically announce more of his hangup behaviors from childhood, or he could win some imaginary points by proving how petulant he could really be by raising a hell of an argument about something, just anything. But now he truly was displeased. He didn't know how to put it. One examiner leaned forward in his chair as though to help him.

"It's . . . this whole nonsense of what it's all about," Edding said. He looked out the window toward the park outside. His voice dropped to a monotone. "It's not only about clients. It's economics. Ambition. Power. Yes, power. And the status. And, oh yes, the cliques in AAABS. No matter what you say, they're there, aren't they?" He wasn't really expecting an answer, but the chairman cut in.

"Are you speaking for yourself, Edding?"

"Of course," said Edding. "What we do to people."

The examiners seemed especially interested in this new point. Edding told them about the prim little high school principal in one of his groups who could jiggle reality into ready-made excuses that just fit her fine. He had thought much of her lately. Did her spirit break? She had held her fragile world together in one way or another, tight as it all was, with fake fronts, and nervous knots in her stomach.

"Opening her up to the truth of her own feelings and the reactions of others—as though it helps," Edding mumbled.

"It helps," said the chairman defensively.

"Not for her," said Edding. "That look in her eyes was more than the anxiety of growing." He pondered. He had been wondering about her. What else might he have done, besides the referral to Dr. Knotts?

They were all pensive now. It was quite unlike Edding to be so much in command, but Edding realized this was the case. It was obviously up to him now. So they waited. In the long silence, lights silently popped on in the park across the street. Then, with a strong sigh, Edding was ready to speak.

"I'm just wondering about the whole damned thing. Who in the hell are we to show people new ways to feel and behave? Who in the hell are we to help them? I mean . . ." The words seemed to get cluttered up in his anger, petulance and disbelief. He went on to explain that even the best of theories, the most efficacious of experiences, the skill sessions, the unstructured stuff, the leveling, the processing of the experiences—the whole bit—no matter how good we could make it, it might just be a giant hoax on ourselves.

"Aren't you talking like a John Bircher?" said the chairman.

"Heavens no!" snapped Edding. "They're like me, but worse. They're sure *they* can do it, tell people how to live, what's best for them."

"We don't do anything of the sort," said the second examiner.

The younger one answered him. "Oh, yes we do. Only we're clever about it."

The chairman reminded them that it was Edding who was on the docket, not they. "Your turn will come up soon enough," he reminded them.

"You see," Edding said, "our problem is that we work so much in groups. Mind you, we've got other problems, too. The psychoanalysts don't have this problem, do they? They don't impose as much—you know how powerfully a group can impose. The one-to-one therapists can do a thorough job. But look at us. We get a room full of people with enough history that would take a century to unravel. We say to them—we don't really say it. Or do we? We say, life will be better. But what they don't know is that it just might and it just might not. And nobody will ever know. Don't talk to me about research. Scientology, therapy, group process, they're all efficacious. Just take your pick. . . ."

The chairman looked impatient, but Edding did not see him. He continued. "Sometimes I think we're a bunch of silly omnipotents who think we can do for others what the world could never do till now—you know, change a way of life, and do it in a society that is flying apart, flying off into space. . . ."

Edding didn't really know if he believed these things or not. He just wanted to say them. They came in a burst of association and they felt right to say. What he had meant to say was that he felt at times that it was tough—"I can't go on leading these groups as though I know what life is all about. Even when I try to share my doubts and ignorance with clients, they insist on holding me aloft and expecting me to know special things that would require a seer or a sage. I can help them increase candor and feedback and concern for their feelings. I can improve their decision making and leadership effectiveness. But that is not *life*. Even when I'm functioning at my best in an intensive group, there is something dreadfully missing. We can hug and hold hands, kiss, look deeply into the dark wells of our eyes, but when it is over, there is always this other thing—ourselves alone, and the enigmatic reminders of memories and bad dreams, old habits and old fears, and the rest of the people in the world who have not learned to hold hands in this kind of a moment. Worse yet, hardly bearable, is the fact that we, too, will soon behave like the others. Too much of our other life is still with us. The picture of group euphoria is just that—just a picture. Snap. Here is the picture of our group. See how we hug. For *now*. But later? Maybe. Maybe not . . ."

Edding wasn't sure now whether he was saying these things or just thinking them. The dismal thoughts of group life were driving along. The disappointments that had come through the years. The long-time friend, an AAABS member, who had faded out of his life, who could confront him with their differences all right, but when it came to doing something about them, they were both like fumbling amateurs. How many times had they urged their clients to confront, to get third parties to help them, and then to resolve their differences? So warm and friendly one year, like strangers the next. "It is enough to make you wonder," he said. "We don't hold a gun in our hands or rob anybody, exactly. We offer brains and love—the edge of tomorrow. We are cool and quite solid. And we have the benefits of feedback from our colleagues. We just can't go wrong. Can we?"

His attempt at irony was getting through at least to himself. He asked the question again, this time to himself. It seemed to confuse him. He was like an aging man. His face seemed disproportioned, as though a warped mirror had changed it. His expression held onto that strangeness.

"Or can we?" he asked. He did not face the examiners. He seemed to be projecting beyond them, outside and above, out into the city and upward toward the circling planes.

"I-do-not-know" he said intoningly. And again more slowly, "I-do-not-know."

In the silence that followed, the examiners looked at each other with straight faces. They were no longer comfortable.

One of them spoke. "So you are saying . . ."

Edding hit the table with his fist. "Stop helping me! Stop being a therapist. Stop being a . . . professional, a helper. *Oh heavens! Am I one of these?* . . ."

Yes, he said to himself. You are. You are one of these. You always are. You have learned the language, the ploys. You "know the literature." You have been "trained." You have even advanced among them politically so that they swear to your capabilities. And you are "helpful."

He rose to his feet and swayed on the cushioned carpet. Should he say good-bye to these well-meaning examiners? He paused at the door, tempted to try one last self-justification. Then he rushed into the hall and slammed the door behind him.

In time the examiners recovered. The room seemed stale with Edding gone. They had been silent a long while. Then the chairman began to speak. "A remarkable examination performance—I will send in a report."

The others nodded their heads, then rose to leave. As they walked out, they whispered to each other. They spoke with praise of the triannual reviews, of the rewards of being a professional examiner, and of the impressive stature of their colleague Edding.

epilogue

Action sociology dates back to the nineteenth-century origins of American sociology and, in a profound and prophetic way, to the social engineering predispositions of Comte and Saint-Simon, the eighteenth-century founders of modern sociology. In this country the earliest professional sociologists were keenly involved in social reform efforts, and one of the first national sociological journals was entitled *The Journal of Applied Sociology* (now revealingly retitled *Sociology and Social Research*).

In intervening years the fortunes of applied sociology have shifted dramatically, with the foreseeable future remaining fully as uncertain now as past oscillations would suggest. Neglected in the 1920s and 1950s in apparent deference to general societal quietism and specific professional scientism (theoretical and methodological sophistry), the specialty knew much greater popularity in the 1930s and 1960s, thanks in no small part to the general societal crisis and the relevant prominence of "conflict school" theorists among the "Young Turks."

Today, contradictory signs cloud any prognostication. On the one hand, there is a backlash of sorts evident in the profession itself where off-campus applications of sociological insights are concerned. Provoked by alleged excesses of the sort that Stoddard and others properly criticize in preceding pages, the anti-action reaction puts new pressure on graduate students and young academics to stay closer to home and to the campus and the Academy's concerns. On the other hand, there is life yet in the Sociology Liberation Movement and in the dynamism of a new breed of change-oriented "enlistee" in the graduate student ranks. To this one must add the rapidly growing need for more and more applied sociological help in government (including the action sociology components of the proposed New Towns, the National Service Corps, and the Leisure-centric Life Style) along with prescriptions from inside the profession for new interpretations of the sociological mission (such as Alvin Gouldner's substantial writings, with their "reflexive" sociological incorporation of self-conscious action endeavors). Which will dominate, the action-deprecating backlash or the action-encouraging forces, is far from clear.

All that is certain is that the kind of contribution to the profession and to society represented by the twenty-six essays in this volume merits the most exacting possible assessment from *you*—before you are drawn irreversibly into partisanship in this controversy. I have tried with this volume to present a full and fair portrait of action sociology, even to its ambivalences, its considerable "dues," and its various disappointments. Believing with my collaborators that sociological theory building is anemic without action-based inputs, and that sociological methodology is puerile without action-oriented refinement, I have sought a hearing for the critical argument that sociology without a full-scale action component is both ill advised and possibly fatally misguided as well. The burden of my thesis is carried by the preceding case studies—if they help convince you of the integrity and modernity of our old-as-the-profession-itself thesis, all the better. If they help recruit you for action sociology itself, better still. In any case, we appreciate the attention you have paid to this subject, invite your constructive criticisms of our efforts, and especially welcome an action report of your own for possible inclusion in a future edition of this volume.

ANNOTATED BIBLIOGRAPHY

Although we have some exceptional literature at our disposal, the items cited below constitute a very small, though hopefully representative sample of what I judge to be outstanding.

Agel, Jerome. *The Radical Therapist.* New York: Ballantine, 1971.
Celebrates in anthology form the recent emergence of RTC ("therapy means political change . . . not peanut butter"). Argues that "a 'struggle for mental health' is bullshit unless it involves changing this society which turns us into machines. . . . Current therapy offers 'solutions' only to people who buy the system and want to maintain their place in it. . . . That's why we need to develop alternatives."

American Psychological Association. *Environment and the Social Sciences: Perspectives and Applications.* Washington, D.C.: APA, 1972.
Sociologists and others explore studies of general environmental conditions, special environmental settings, and environmental decision making: "Not only does this book discuss the successes and applications of social science research but also the deficiencies and problems in the areas involved. . . ."

Asbell, Bernard, ed. *Careers in Urban Affairs: Six Young People Talk about Their Professions in the Inner City.* New York: Peter H. Wyden, 1970.
A school social worker, a community organizer, a public-housing expert, a city planner for a large city, a city planner for a consulting firm, and an assistant to a big-city mayor offer their thoughts and feelings about their work. The editor contends that "never have career opportunities been better for those who would 'do well by doing good.'"

Benveniste, Guy. *The Politics of Experience.* Berkeley, Calif.: Glendessary Press, 1972.
Advertised as "a penetrating foray into the wilderness of systems analysis, planning, and policy making. Who are the planners? Whose interests do they serve? How does the new breed of advisors influence policy in the corridors of power? Joins theory with practical experience to challenge the images of expertise, especially those created by experts themselves."

Bernard, Jessie. "Where the Action Is." *Probe* 1, no. 2 (December 1971): 2–10.

An informal account of a "vague, shadowy kind of power" that can accompany participation as a sociologist on public boards and committees. Touches on issues in radical sociology, welfare policies, black life-style research, no-fault divorce law reforms, and premarriage educational changes.

Brokensha, David, and Hodge, Peter. *Community Development: An Interpretation.* San Francisco: Chandler, 1969.

Aim is to present "a summary of the history and course of community development, examining various origins and influences, and considering what it has set out to do, how these goals have been achieved, and with what success."

Bugental, James F. T. "The Humanistic Ethic—The Individual in Psychotherapy as a Societal Change Agent." *Journal of Humanistic Psychology* 11, no. 1 (Spring 1971): 11–25.

The author suggests that many who have had a growthful therapeutic course emerge from that experience as societal agents themselves. They may come to have a heightened concern about society and an increased potential to express that concern in effective ways. He goes on to espouse the cause of a therapeutic humanistic ethic, and warns: ". . . make no mistake about it, we who share this emerging ethic are a threat to the establishment. It is only that the size and pervasiveness of that threat is as yet unrealized."

Caldwell, William A., ed. *How to Save Urban America: Regional Plan Association, Choices for '76.* New York: Signet 1973.

Based on a series of twentieth-century town meetings that posed an opportunity to choose among alternative policies dealing with the major urban problems of housing, transportation, poverty, environment, cities, and government. Employing a TV series and viewer vote responses, the RPA aims to promote citizen participation in planning.

Clifton, James A., ed. *Applied Athropology: Readings in the Uses of the Science of Man.* Boston: Houghton Mifflin, 1970.

Anthropologists "who have willingly and knowingly assumed roles as active participants in developmental change point up, discuss, and evaluate . . . matters such as the ethics of intervention, the influence of the existential setting of anthropological inquiry, the problems of less than detached sponsorship, the limits of the trained spectator's role, and questions of relationships with clients and subjects."

Cochrane, Glynn. *Development Anthropology.* New York: Oxford University Press, 1971.

Attempts to explain why applied anthropology suffers from a lack of academic respectability and policy successes. Goes on to prescribe a cure for both its theoretical and its practical weaknesses. Urges training of "general practitioner" anthropologists with action orientations.

Cohen, Harold L. and Filipczak, James. *A New Learning Environment: A Case for Learning.* San Francisco: Jossey-Bass, 1971.

Report on a new money-for-learning hope for reaching dropouts and unemployables via a learning approach that can be applied in public schools and reformatories anywhere. Based at the National Training School for Boys in Washington, D.C., the approach uses operantly formulated contingency systems and the design of a special environment to produce remarkable behavioral and attitudinal changes.

Cosby, Arthur G. "An Experimental Approach to the Study of Poverty." *Sociology and Social Research* (January 1969): 163–69.
Urges the action sociologist to take advantage of opportunities to use rigorous experimental research designs in his field work, for such designs may offer more than reliance on campus-based laboratory experiments. Illustrates several research techniques against backdrop of "war on poverty" research possibilities.

Dalkey, Norman C. *Studies in the Quality of Life: Delphi and Decision-making.* Lexington, Mass.: Lexington Books, 1972.
An examination of the use of the Delphi method of the Rand Corporation for the generation of organization and individual values and objectives. This book provides a detailed study of how science is being applied in the field of social-reform decision making.

Dickey, John W.; Glancy, David M.; and Jennelle, Ernest M. *Technology Assessment.* Lexington, Mass.: Lexington Books, 1973.
A pilot study of technology assessment in local decision making, this study involves itself with the nitty-gritty of how we can judge the advantages and impact of technology in specific applications. The volume concludes with an examination of the application of this methodology to the Solid Waste Management Programs of Fairfax, Virginia.

Douglas, Jack D., ed. *The Impact of Sociology: Readings in the Social Sciences.* New York: Appleton-Century-Crofts, 1970.
Sixteen essays that explore the significance of the social sciences becoming the "primary means by which we seek to determine social policies which will rationally order our everyday lives." Contributors include Tawney, Cassirer, Kahler, Berger, Bierstedt, Lynd, Friedrichs, Garfinkel, Tumin, Baritz, Dahrendorf, Krasner, Bauer, Bennis, Bottomore, and the editor.

Douglas, Jack D., ed. *The Relevance of Sociology.* New York: Appleton-Century-Crofts, 1970.
Eleven essays concerning personal involvement, objectivity, and the importance of sociology in understanding and solving America's current social problems. Contributors include Mills, Galbraith, Moore, Weber, Gouldner, Seeley, Becker, Tumin, Waitzkin, and the editor.

Etzioni, Amitai. *The Active Society: A Theory of Societal and Political Processes.* New York: Free Press, 1970.
Develops the idea of a flexible, responsive, stable society, and shows why such a society is desirable. Constructs a working model for social action in terms of which any society or social process, or pathology thereof, may be analyzed. Hails the efforts of the Activists, in whom "lies the hope for an initiation of the transformation of the unauthentic society."

274 / ANNOTATED BIBLIOGRAPHY

Friedrichs, Robert W. *A Sociology of Sociology*. New York: Free Press, 1971.
Traces the coalescing of sociology into a mature social scientific discipline around the paradigmatic notion of "system" in the 1940s, the confrontation of the anomaly of "change" in the 1950s, and the challenge by the "conflict" image of the 1960s. Predictions are made as to the direction the community of sociology is likely to take in the 1970s.

Gastil, R. D. " 'Selling Out' and the Sociology of Knowledge." *Policy Sciences* (Summer 1971): 271–77.
Unusual call for a discipline-based, hard-headed realism in advice giving, rather than in the more customary "soft liberal approaches." Urges intellectuals to recognize and operationalize a responsibility to themselves to search for the truth independent of the assumptions of their own subculture, e.g., the soft liberal model of the world. The applied sociologist must attempt to rise above his social position, his cultural milieu, the role he plays in society, and the personal role that he has established for himself: ". . . in the fuzzy areas of social analysis and international strategies thinking about real problems as far as possible from methodology and abstract theorizing is most likely to allow one to escape from the tyranny of the assumptions of his peer group."

Gerlach, Luther P., and Hine, Virginia H. *Lifeway Leap: The Dynamics of Change in America*. Minneapolis: University of Minnesota Press, 1973.
The authors provide the conceptual tools to help the reader understand and participate creatively in social change. "Gerlach and Hine not only grasp the essentials of our transformation but give us a real sense of its direction and sources."—Harrison Salisbury.

Goodman, Robert. *After the Planners*. New York: Simon & Shuster, 1971.
Argues that fundamental political, social, and economic change must take place before planners and architects can make any significant contribution to the whole community process. Advocates a system of "community socialism" in which people in actual communities "determine their own objectives, select their own environmental criteria (and social and economic, as well), and, in general, arrange their lives together."

Gottlieb, David. "VISTA, Pepsi, and Poverty." *Society* (February 1972): 6, 8.
Among other reforms the essay advocates providing the young with "the resources and license to create their own programs and strategies of social change, and the creation of a social climate where the young can establish and test alternative ways of resolving problems."

Halleck, Seymour L. *The Politics of Therapy*. New York: Science House, 1971.
Challenges the notion that psychiatrists are, by nature, apolitical. Instead, contends there are radicals, moderates, and reactionaries as in other professions concerned with present and emerging social problems. See especially the chapters on "The Need for Vision" and "The Human Condition."

Harberger, Arnold C., ed. *Project Evaluation: Collected Papers*. Chicago: Markham, 1972.

Focuses on the theory of project evaluation and its applications, with emphasis on public-sector investments designed to promote economic development. Offers measures of key parameters needed for the social evaluation of projects in transportation, electric power, and irrigation.

Hartinger, Walter; Eldefonso, Edward; and Coffey, Alan. *Corrections: A Component of the Criminal Justice System*. Pacific Palisades, Calif.: Goodyear, 1973.
A clearly written basic introduction to the correctional system which relates the correctional components to the administration of the criminal justice process. The authors stress programs for rehabilitation, placing particular emphasis on those based in the community.

Haug, Marie R., and Sussman, Marvin B. "Professional Autonomy and the Revolt of the Client." *Social Problems* (Fall 1969): 153–61.
Explores the implications of the refusal by students, the poor, and the black community to uncritically accept the service offerings of the establishment. May prove less a curse than a blessing in disguise as it could enable the professional to give up the "whole man" approach to service and treatment, and revert to a more specialized expert role.

Horn, Robert E., and Zuckerman, David W. *The Guide to Simulation Games for Education and Training*. Lexington, Mass.: Information Resources Inc., 1970.
A list of over 400 games and simulations for education in schools and colleges, and training in graduate schools and businesses; "the most complete and authoritative source of information on currently available educational games and simulations."

Hornstein, Harvey A., et al., eds. *Social Intervention: A Behavioral Science Approach*. New York: Free Press, 1971.
Ranging from studies of Alinsky to assessments of nonviolent action, the anthology identifies and systematizes some of the psychological and sociological assumptions underlying strategies of social change. Special attention is paid to lessons for change in different social situations.

Hoult, Thomas Ford. ". . . Who Shall Prepare Himself to the Battle?" *American Sociologist* (February 1968): 3–7.
"Underlying the discussion at every point is the writer's conviction that the future welfare of society and of sociology are interlocked—that the special knowledge and empirical methods of modern sociologists are two of the most crucial tools needed for development of the 'good society,' and that sociology's very existence is dependent upon preservation of those aspects of the good society that we symbolize by the term 'liberalism.'"

Kegeles, S. Stephan. "A Field Experimental Attempt to Change Beliefs and Behavior of Women in an Urban Ghetto." *Journal of Health and Social Behavior* 10, no. 2 (June 1969): 115–24.
Recounts an exploratory effort to successfully change beliefs of women regarding cervical cancer in order to induce them to make clinic visits for cervical cytology. Lends support to the social action strategy which leans on survey

findings, rather than that which either ignores or rejects the importance of attitudes and beliefs for programming.

Lakey, George. *Strategy for a Living Revolution.* New York: Grossman, 1973.
A former director of the Friends Peace Committee in Philadelphia has written a sensible and humane rejection of violent tactics.

Lekachman, Robert. "Between Apostles and Technicians: Mind-Blowing and Problem-Solving." *Dissent* (April 1971): 128–40.
A searching assessment of contradictory styles of problem solving favored by the Consciousness III adherents or by technocrats. Indicts both for having taken flight from real politics. Outlines briefly a criterion of judgment and a political tactic thought better suited to the "good socialist dream of redistribution of privilege, power, property, and income."

Lurie, Ellen. *How to Change the Schools: A Parent's Action Handbook on How to Fight the System.* New York: Random House, 1971.
A practical guidebook to winning, complete with a series of Action Checklists on how to use state and federal funds to force educational reform, how to use a public hearing for your own purposes, and other bases one must cover when setting out to achieve a specific change.

Lyons, Gene M., ed. "Social Science and the Federal Government." *The Annals*, 394, March 1971.
Eleven essays explore the "uneasy partnership" of democratic government and the social sciences. Stresses the challenge posed by "the limits of social science research, the often unfulfilled expectations of policy-makers for firm solutions from research findings, and the threat that knowledge poses for preconceived notions of social and economic phenomena."

Marx, Gary T., ed. *Muckraking Sociology.* New Brunswick N.J.: Transaction Books, 1972.
Focused empirical studies with profound implications for social policy, the reprinted essays (originally published in *Trans-Action*) deal with justice, decision makers, social class, education, and health. Each documents conditions that clash with basic values, fix responsibility, and show why they are capable of generating moral outrage.

Milkman, Raymond; Walton, Howard; Lyford, Beverly; and Bladen, Christopher. *Alleviating Economic Distress: Evaluating a Federal Effort.* Lexington Mass.: Lexington Books, 1972.
A comprehensive examination and evaluation of a domestic federal economic development program. Actual projects at the state, county, and local levels are analyzed using a new methodology developed by the authors.

Moffet, Toby. *The Participation Put-On.* New York: Delacorte Press, 1971.
The twenty-five-year-old ex-head of the Office of Education's Office of Students and Youths recounts the sources of his disenchantment with social action efforts in HEW. Promoted as a "gallows humor account of bureaucracy in inaction, and a forceful narrative of a young man's disintegrating hopes for doing 'constructive work' within the government."

Moynihan, Daniel P. *The Politics of a Guaranteed Income: The Nixon Administration and the Family Assistance Plan.* New York: Random House, 1973.
An account of the operation of American government at its highest levels, and why a major social reform failed to achieve approval. Moynihan writes dramatically of the "most important piece of social legislation in the country's history."

Murton, Tom. "One Year of Prison Reform." *The Nation,* 12 January 1970, pp. 12–17.
An unsparing account by a criminologist-turned-prison administrator in Arkansas of his short-lived effort to reform one of the nation's most evil penal systems. Warns that "power structures can tolerate only a limited amount of integrity."

National Academy of Sciences and Social Science. *The Behavioral and Social Sciences—Outlook and Needs.* Englewood Cliffs, N.J.: Prentice-Hall, 1969.
The report represents "the first large-scale effort of the behavioral and social science disciplines to assemble an overall picture . . . and a set of recommendations for public policy that will encourage their rapid and healthy progress over the years ahead." Urges expanded university training, across existing disciplinary boundaries in applied social science.

National Science Board. *Knowledge Into Action: Improving the Nation's Use of the Social Sciences.* Washington, D.C.: Government Printing Office, 1969.
Report of a special Commission on the Social Sciences charged with making recommendations for increasing the useful application of the social sciences in the solution of contemporary social problems.

O. M. Collective. *The Organizer's Manual.* New York: Bantam, 1971.
"We, the O. M. Collective, wrote this book so that you, the reader, might go on writing it in practice. In a real sense it is addressed to its own authors, members of the larger collective of all people who want fundamental social change. Where it falls short, your experience may make up for our lack of it. Where it proves useful, use it to write the next chapters of a book about peace and freedom."

O'Toole, Richard, ed. *The Organization, Management and Tactics of Social Research.* Cambridge, Mass.: Schenkman, 1971.
Fifteen original essays based on the assumption that "as many research efforts fail to meet their full potential because of . . . managerial problems as fail because of more traditional methodological problems, such as faulty designs, or measurement techniques." The closing essay asks researchers "to get involved in the total problems of men. . . ."

Pettigrew, Thomas F. "Sociological Consulting in Race Relations." *American Sociologist* (June 1971): 44–47.
Out of a vast personal experience the author comments on the conditions for effective consulting, political pressures, and needed remedies. Contending that social science *is* relevant, the author identifies the central issue instead as one of translating its relevance into effective influence on social policy. He calls for new

structures here such as a National Social Science Foundation, "advocacy sociology," and others.

Policy Sciences: An International Journal for the Policy Sciences (Elsevier Publ. Co., P. O. Box 211, Amsterdam, The Netherlands).

An attempt to "provide a forum for the developing interest in the application of structured rationality, systematic analysis, and interdisciplinary knowledge to problems of policy. . . . It hopes to pay close attention to the application of policy science to real decisions, aiming to improve the outcome as well as the state-of-the-art and to attract the participation and respect of practioners."

Reynolds, Larry T. and Henslin, James M., eds. *American Society: A Critical Analysis.* New York: David McKay Co. 1973.

A collection of radical antiestablishment essays emphasizing sociology as a study of man's relationships with his fellows. "Establishment sociologists" consider whoever deviates from society's norms in their idealized forms to be a social problem. "So . . . sociology has fallen into the realm of polite amusement or dead science (while) this pious cloister of priestly technocrats remains as one additional barrier to the creation of a visible study of man."

Reynolds, Larry T., and Reynolds, Janice M., eds. *The Sociology of Sociology.* New York: David McKay Co., 1970.

A collection of 22 essays offered not only as partial proof of a renewed interest in the discipline's theories and practices, but "more importantly in the hope that the reading of this book will move our colleagues and students to more self-conscious thought and research." Contributors include Dusky Lee Smith, Martin Nicolaus, C. Wright Mills, Irving Louis Horowitz, and others.

Rist, Ray C., ed. *Restructuring American Education: Innovation and Alternatives.* New York: E. P. Dutton, 1972.

Argues that America's dual educational goals—free inquiry and social mobility— are not being met. Various contributors argue that alternatives must be investigated outside the present educational structure, such as ungraded schools and private schools for black children. The alternatives to schooling itself are also touched upon.

Rivlin, Alice M. *Systematic Thinking for Social Action.* Washington, D.C.: Brookings Institution, 1971.

An attempt to give a "midterm report card" on the progress of the analysts in improving the basis for public decisions on social action programs. Urges systematic experiments with different ways of delivering social services and analyzing the results.

Scheff, Thomas J. "Reevaluation Counseling: Social Implications." *Journal of Humanistic Psychology* 12, no. 1 (Spring 1972): 58–71.

The essay explores the cultural and social aspects of a new form of peer self-help psychotherapy, one which "may offer a humanistic solution to the economic and psychological problems that arise out of dependence on professional experts for psychotherapy, since it trains laymen to become psychotherapists for each other." The author, himself an innovator with this approach, is chairman of the Department of Sociology at Santa Barbara, California.

Shaftel, Fanny. *Role Playing for Social Values.* Englewood Cliffs, N.J.: Prentice-Hall, 1967.
Valuable pioneering exploration of practical applications of games to social value education. Unique in its focus on elementary school employ of gaming and simulation techniques.

Sharp, Gene. *Exploring Nonviolent Approaches.* Boston: Porter Sargent, 1971.
A basic introduction to the technique of nonviolence and noncooperation, its previous uses, and its need for further study. Includes an argument for national defense without armaments, a course program in civilian defense, and an extensive bibliography.

Solomon, Lawrence N. "Humanism and the Training of Applied Behavioral Scientists." *Journal of Applied Behavioral Science* 7, no. 5 (1971): 531–47.
Outlines a model for humanistic training that could help us get beyond such current abuses as a generalized fear of control, a movement toward anarchy, and a narrowing antiintellectualism. Notes in conclusion that "it is imperative for the disciplined development of applied behavioral science that practitioners be rigorously humanistic, precisely phenomenological, and incisively existential. This process should require neither the sacrifice of academic excellence nor the loss of poetic sensitivity."

Spiegel, John. *Transactions: The Interplay between Individual, Family, and Society.* New York: Science House, 1971.
Hailed by a reviewer as "really quite staggering; something between research and action but partaking of both; more thoughtful than 'action research' and more conscientious than social science." Among other points the author demonstrates that as long as the underlying structure of social conflict is not modified, increments of social change which allow for marginal allocations of power do nothing but delay inevitable recurrences of even more devastating conflict.

Targ, Harry R. "Social Science and a New Social Order." *Journal of Peace Research,* no. 8 (1971).
Urges the social scientist to study various alternative designs for new social orders. Offers a model of his own based on concept of *community* that functions to provide for the socioeconomic and psychic needs of its members. A critical goal of his new social order is ultimately to secure the dominance of social over technological organization: The society proposed builds on semiautonomous communities, participatory democracy, socialism, and sophisticated technologies. Valuable for the yardstick it offers against which to measure our programmatic goals as action sociologists vulnerable to cultural myopia.

Twelker, Paul, et al., eds. *Simulation/Gaming/News.* Published five times a year, Box 8899, Stanford University, Stanford, Calif. 94305.
"SGN departs from tradition in two ways: (1) It attempts to provide readers with

practical, 'applicable' information, in addition to more theoretical considerations, and (2) it attempts to treat the application of simulation and gaming to most areas of experience, in and out of formal institutions."

Vollmer, Howard M. "Toward a Sociology of Applied Science." *American Sociologist* (August 1969): 244–48.
Explores the typical pattern of organization of applied science and policy implications related thereto. Suggests that "mankind as a whole could benefit greatly from *more* sociologists performing professional consulting and applied research roles." Urges reconciliation of scholars and professionals: "It makes no sense for the eye to say to the hand, 'I have no need of you!.' "

Walzer, Michael. *Political Action: A Practical Guide to Movement Politics.* Chicago: Quadrangle, 1971.
Twenty-five chapters that deal in careful detail with how to solicit for funds, how to organize democratically, how to provide effective leadership, and so on, including the psychological satisfaction to be gained from active participation in a movement.

Watts, William, and Tree, Lloyd A., eds. *State of the Nation.* New York: Universal Books, 1973.
The first systematic attempt to measure "the other GNP"—the Gross National Psychology—by combining exhaustive national polling specially conducted for this book with a series of expert analysis of current national issues. This work identifies levels of public concern, willingness to spend tax dollars, and desire for government action on a wide range of problems. Among the areas reviewed are health care, justice, crime and law, defense, and aid.

Williams, Walter. *Social Policy Research and Analysis: The Experience in the Federal Social Agencies.* New York: American Elsevier Publishing, 1971.
Drawing on his OEO experience the author analyzes flaws in both the social science research community and in the federal social agencies that help explain why social science research is seldom relevant to major policy decisions. His reforms include a call for "some mechanism (a staff office) . . . that can work in a peer relationship with the social science researchers and the federal bureaucracy."

Yezierska, Anzia. "One Thousand Pages of Research." *Commentary* (July 1963): 60–63.
A rare and moving account of the frustration that research subjects feel when they conclude that sociological research involving them may lead to little or no desired change in their immediate lives.

Zimbardo, Philip, and Ebbesen, Ebbe B. *Influencing Attitudes and Changing Behavior: A Basic Introduction to Relevant Methodology, Theory, and Applications.* Reading, Mass.: Addison-Wesley, 1970.
Considers such questions as "What findings do social psychologists offer which may be useful in building a technology of attitude change? Where do such findings come from?" Goes on to explore psychological warfare, prejudice, police interrogation, consumer motivation, and supersalesmanship.

CONTRIBUTORS

Leonard Blumberg
Professor of sociology, Temple University. Co-director of research of the Diagnostic and Rehabilitation Center/Philadelphia. Co-director of the NIMH-sponsored study, "A Study of the Prevention of Skid Row." Co-author with T. E. Shipley, Jr., and I. W. Shandler of *Skid Row and Its Alternatives* (Philadelphia: Temple University Press, 1973).

Robert Busby
Associate professor, Department of Mathematics, Drexel University.

Edward E. Cahill
Research associate, Institute for Behavioral Research, University of Georgia. Co-author with Yvonne S. Perry, *The Community Leadership Seminar: A Joint Venture in University-Community Relations* (Philadelphia: Human Resources Center, University of Pennsylvania, 1971).

Meyer M. Cahn
Professor, School of Education, San Francisco State College, San Francisco, California.

J. David Colfax
Co-editor with Jack L. Roach, *Radical Sociology* (New York: Basic Books, 1971).

Thomas J. Cottle
Author of *Time's Children: Impressions of Youth* (Boston: Little, Brown, 1972): Co-author with Craig R. Eisendrath, *Out of Discontent: Visions of the Contemporary University* (New York: Schenkman, 1972); *The Prospect of Youth: Contexts for Sociological Inquiry* (Boston: Little, Brown, 1972).

C. M. Deasy
Partner in the architectural firm of Deasy and Bolling, Los Angeles, California.

Henry Etzkowitz
Assistant professor, Department of Sociology, State University of New York, Purchase, New York. Co-author with Gerald Schaflander, *Ghetto Crisis: Progress vs. Bureaucracy in Bedford Stuyvesant* (Boston: Little, Brown paperback, 1972).

281

Irving Goldaber
Adjunct assistant professor of sociology at Brooklyn College of the City University of New York. A founding partner of Community Confrontation and Communication Associates.

Cathy S. Greenblat
Associate professor of sociology at Douglass College; associate member of the Graduate Sociology Department of Rutgers University; co-author with P. Stein and N. Washburne of *The Marriage Game: A Simulation of Marital Decision-Making* (New York: Random House, 1973); member, Executive Committee, National Gaming Council.

A. Paul Hare
Professor of sociology, Haverford College. Author of *Handbook of Small Group Research* (New York: Free Press, 1962).

Sarajane Heidt
Research associate, Center for Policy Research, Inc., New York City.

Robert L. Herrick
Chairman, Department of Sociology, Westmar College, Le Mars, Iowa.

Michael J. Hindelang
Assistant professor of criminal justice, School of Criminal Justice, State University of New York at Albany.

Otto G. Hoiberg
Head of the Community Development Staff in the University of Nebraska Extension Division, Lincoln, Nebraska; professor of sociology: author of *Exploring the Small Community* (Lincoln: University of Nebraska Press, 1955.)

Robert Johansen
Research associate, Institute for the Future, Menlo Park, California. Co-author of the Computerized Conferencing System, ORACLE.

Thomas E. Lasswell
Professor of sociology at the University of Southern California, Los Angeles, California. Co-editor with John H. Burme and Sidney Aronson, *Life in Society* (2nd ed.; Chicago: Scott, Foresman, 1971).

Andrew Levinson
Research associate of the Martin Luther King, Jr., Center for Non-violent Social Change, Atlanta, Georgia.

Frank J. McVeigh
Assistant professor, Department of Sociology and Anthropology, Muhlenberg College, Allentown, Pennsylvania.

Holly G. Porter
A founding partner with Professor Irving Goldaber of Community Confrontation and Communication Associates.

Thomas E. Shipley, Jr.
Associate professor of psychology, Temple University. Co-director of research of the Diagnostic and Rehabilitation Center/Philadelphia. Co-director of the NIMH-sponsored study, "A Study of the Prevention of Skid Row." Co-author with L. Blumberg and I. W. Shandler, *Skid Row and Its Alternatives* (Philadelphia: Temple University Press, 1973).

Ellwyn R. Stoddard
Professor, Department of Sociology, The University of Texas at El Paso, Texas. Author of *Mexican Americans* (New York: Random House, 1972).

Rafael Valdivieso
Teaches at the School of Social Work, Columbia University.

Jon Van Til
Chairman, Department of Urban Studies and Community Development, Rutgers University, Camden, New Jersey.

Sally Bould Van Til
Assistant professor, Department of Sociology, University of Delaware.